The Architecture of British Transport in the Twentieth Century

Studies in British Art 13

The Architecture of British Transport in the Twentieth Century

Edited by

Julian Holder and Steven Parissien

Published for
The Paul Mellon Centre for Studies in British Art
The Yale Center for British Art

Yale University Press, New Haven & London

Typeset in Adobe Garamond
Printed in Great Britain by BAS Printers Limited, Salisbury, Wiltshire

Library of Congress Control Number 2004111695
ISBN 0-300-10624-6

A catalogue record for this book is available from the British Library.

Contents

Preface

In his need to distinguish architecture from building Nikolaus Pevsner wrote the now infamous sentence: 'A bicycle shed is a building, Lincoln cathedral is a piece of architecture.'[1] This volume of essays, however, is more concerned with bicycle sheds than cathedrals. Although Pevsner's definition has been seized upon by his detractors to attack him ever since we have no such desire. Indeed, no such distinction is necessary; our purpose in this collection of essays is to look at transport buildings of the twentieth century in their considerable variety — from utilitarian buildings, to magnificent examples of architecture. They are all buildings which travellers hope to have only brief encounters with. Yet as epitomised by the film *Brief Encounter*[2] — transport buildings are not only functional, but can also act as sites for dramatic and emotive events.

Scholarly attention on these building types to date has understandably concentrated on Britain's rich heritage of nineteenth-century railway stations. Although still functioning today, during the twentieth century they were viewed with admiration and disgust in equal measure. Nevertheless, the railway station supplied the principal architectural typology for an age of mass transport. Elsewhere, existing building types were adapted, as stables became garages and the village blacksmith, as in the case of George Sturt, became the local mechanic.[3] Yet some new modes of transport demanded entirely new building types as passengers took to the roads, and especially the skies.

In the historiography of twentieth-century architecture, new forms of transport were expected to produce timely paradigms for the development of a new architecture. With the formulation of the modernist 'machine aesthetic', the machine most readily admired was the motor-car; yet lessons were learned from all forms of transport — as the work of Le Corbusier famously demonstrates. Uniquely, this collection of essays looks more at the temporary buildings designed for these machines and their passengers.

Few British architects specialised in designing transport buildings, though several — notably Charles Holden, Wallace Gilbert and Partners, and Norman Foster — have become synonymous with transport architecture at its best. Other architects, such as W. H. Hamlyn of the LMS and J. R. Scott of the LSWR, left their mark more anonymously as official company architects.

Interestingly, this book of essays strongly refutes the argument that there was an automatic alliance between modernist architecture and modern forms of transport. The diversity of transport during the twentieth century was instead mirrored in the diversity and richness of styles employed.

It is clear that Pevsner was not against transport buildings *per se*. Nor did he want to exclude them from the pantheon of architecture as evidenced by the praise he gave to many of the buildings contained in this volume — particularly Charles Holden's London Underground stations. However it could be argued that while Stansted airport is architecture and a bicycle shed is a building both make important contributions to the evolution of transport architecture as we embark on longer, faster, and more environmentally friendly journeys. More research still needs to be done in the less self-evidently important corners of the subject: the bicycle shed together with its slightly more glamorous cousins, the tramshed, airship hanger, ferry terminal, domestic garage and bus shelter, do not feature in this collection. All, though, represent fruitful areas for further research as part of the increasingly blurred edges of architectural history and cultural studies that these essays explore.

Apart from encouraging further scholarship, we hope that by highlighting this area of architectural practice in its entirety we may facilitate a more thoughtful and informed response to the conservation of the best and most interesting examples of transport architecture. Many of the buildings illustrated in this collection have been demolished; many are under threat of demolition. It is time we took these crucial indicators of our technological aspirations and our social evolution seriously.

Recent years have witnessed something of a second transport revolution in Britain. Former state monopolies have been privatised, existing facilities expanded, and new ones built. Arguments over road building continue, and the country's first national toll road has been established. This series of essays begins to explore the diversity of twentieth-century transport buildings which, to echo the words of Sigfried Giedion, have given us 'space, time, and architecture.'[4]

JULIAN HOLDER
STEVEN PARISSIEN

1   Nikolaus Pevsner, *An Outline of European Architecure* (Harmondsworth, 1943).
2   Carnforth Station, where much of David Lean's 1946 film was filmed, was largely demolished two decades later. However, during the 1990s pressure grew to rebuild at least part of the structure in order to create a *Brief Encounter*-themed experience, a vivid instance of the heritage industry seeking to shut the stable door long after the architectural horse has bolted.
3   George Sturt, *The Wheelwright's Shop* (Cambridge, 1923).
4   Sigfried Giedion, *Space, Time and Architecture: The Growth of a New Tradition* (Cambridge, 1941).

Introduction

Brian Edwards

TRAVEL IS A MEASURE of civilization and the buildings that serve transport are icons of modernism itself. Transport buildings reflect current concerns in architecture with their interest in light, space and technology. In many ways transport architecture in Britain in the twentieth century mirrors the formal and functionalist agenda of the age. Whether at the airport terminal, railway or bus station, ferry terminal, suburban car showroom or motorway service station, the adoption of modern architecture became the dominant image for the building type. Although national character was reflected in some early transport buildings, by the mid-century innovation in the technology of transport buildings and in the engineering of the wide-span structures led to an exciting new architecture.

In many ways modern transport architecture in Britain not only reflected the priorities of the twentieth century but led to a climate of wider acceptance of the benefits of contemporary design. It is the story of modernity acted out in ever more daring manifestations of interior space, light, technology and speed. Within the

1 Lancaster South Motorway Service Station, 1963, by T. P. Bennett and Partners. Photograph: Brian Edwards.

2   Station roof, Kings Cross Station, London. Photograph: Brian Edwards.

2   *Edwards*

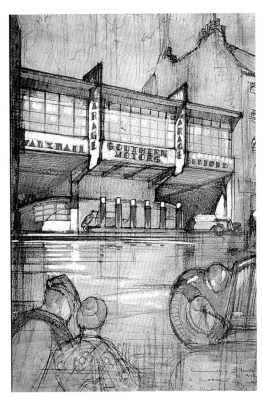

3 Southern Motors Garage, Causewayside, Edinburgh. Perspective drawing in ink, pencil and colour chalk by Basil Spence, 1935. Courtesy of RIAS.

major railway stations, bus stations, ferry and airport terminals there are the fundamental elements of modern city form: urbanism based upon rapid movement, large fluid spaces for social and commercial exchange, and building construction pushed to its technical limits. Architectural design throughout the twentieth century sought to give form and imagery to these dramatic buildings. All the major architects of the century from Charles Holden to Basil Spence and later Norman Foster engaged in the search for a new language of expression for these dynamic buildings.

Transport buildings are both a gateway to travel and, in the opposite direction, a portal through which to experience cities and continents. This was not only the metaphor behind the Euston Arch, one of the greatest losses to transport architecture in the century, but also the design of Robert Matthew's Turnhouse Airport in Edinburgh and more recently Nicholas Grimshaw's EuroStar terminal at Waterloo. Metaphor is a recurring theme in transport buildings, giving the building type its charm, character and meaning. The metaphors employed often mirror the mode of transport served: early service stations have the functional and streamlined appearance of sports cars (as in Basil Spence's Causewayside Garage in Edinburgh, 1935, fig. 3) and airport terminals draw upon the imagery of the aircraft themselves (as Southampton Airport by Manser Associates, 1995, see fig. 88, inspired perhaps by Eero Saarinen's TWA Terminal at Kennedy Airport, New York, see fig. 7).

Transport buildings come in many types. There are railway stations (mainline, terminal and branch line), airport terminals (international, domestic and hub), bus stations (intercity and local), ferry terminals (freight, drive-on and cruise) and facilities for the motorist (service stations, motels, garages). Added to this, a hybrid began to emerge as the twentieth century closed: the 'interchange' where passengers move between rail, bus, air, car, and sometimes sea, in a single multi-leveled building. Although new in name, the interchange had existed in many nineteenth-century railway termini such as Kings Cross and Victoria Stations in London but was revived as the twentieth century closed partly in response to the demands of sustainable development. All of these types, however, share common characteristics of function and spatial configuration. The figure in plan includes a large interior gathering space, external connection via roads, bridges and pedestrian malls, linear spaces where travel is obtained (platforms or gate piers), and an array of movement structures (lifts, escalators, staircases). Added to these there are customer facilities of various kinds (shops, cafes, etc.) which colonize the space as well as ticketing and travel information which tends to occupy the edges. This agglomeration of functions exists usually within a single all-embracing roof whose span requires a bold structural solution. As a consequence structural elements such as the column, truss and beam provide a major part of the architectural experience of British transport buildings of the twentieth century. The technical demands of ever bigger volumes as the century unfolded led to the exploration of new materials or new uses of old ones. Also, the need to provide orientation for often fatigued and disorientated passengers, resulted in natural light being harnessed as a way-marking guide. Sunlight taken through windows above roof-trusses spills down (as at Canary Wharf Docklands Light Railway Station, fig. 4) onto concourses, creating diagonal shadows which are often experienced at speed and used to articulate the interior volumes. To travel through such spaces is to capture the very essence of twentieth-century architecture. And to travel through at speed, viewing the building from say a train window or car windscreen, is to enjoy the thrill and anticipation of modernity itself.

Although transport buildings are primarily concerned with the efficient movement of people and goods, the best examples seek to provide dignity and hospitality for travellers. Dignity is reflected in the large volumes which constitute the booking halls and reception points; hospitality in the many shops and

4   Canary Wharf Station on the Docklands Light Railway, 1987, designed by I. M. Pei.
Photograph: Brian Edwards.

cafes which are constructed within transport buildings. In fact, as the twentieth
century unfolded, retail facilities expanded to the point where the railway station
and the filling station became a corner shop for local residents. Architecturally the
invasion of commerce and retail into stations, airports and motorway service
areas has been at considerable aesthetic cost. The visual chaos that followed
tended to undermine the ordered architectural arrangement sought by the original designers. This is most marked in locations (such as Stansted Airport designed
by Norman Foster) where the initial conception embraced the coordinated
design of the structure, building finishes, furniture and light fittings. As the twentieth century closed transport buildings, from railway stations to airport terminals and bus stations, began to resemble the market halls of Victorian cities.

Different transport architects have orchestrated the interaction of architectural volumes in different ways. Charles Holden at various London Underground
railway stations set prisms of glass against brick cubes and cylinders in a fashion
which landmarked his stations in the nondescript suburbs of north and west
London. More recently Yorke Rosenburg and Mardell (YRM) at Gatwick Airport, Scott Brownrigg and Turner at Manchester Airport and Michael Hopkins

at Westminster Jubilee Line Station have animated travel through a combination of large geometric volumes and structural boldness. These more recent developments suggest the celebration of travel rather than the mere serving of passenger needs at a utilitarian level. They continue a theme of design ambition whose roots lie in the nineteenth century (as in Rowand Anderson's design of Central Station, Glasgow) but seem to have been overlooked in much of the twentieth.

In spite of the different manifestations of the architecture of transport in Britain in the twentieth century, the fundamentals of the building type have changed little since nineteenth-century precedents. In *A History of Building Types* (1976) Nikolaus Pevsner devotes one of his seventeen chapters to the evolution of railway and bus stations and (as a footnote) to that of airport terminals. He starts by stating the obvious that the building of new types of transport facility presupposes the existence of new modes of travel. Hence airports only came into existence after the introduction of movement by aircraft, bus stations by buses, garages by cars. The significant point is that new means of travel lead to the modification and evolution of earlier transport building types. As a consequence typological evolution is not usually driven by the migration of ideas from outside the type. Transport architecture depends, therefore, upon the development of a tradition (fig. 5) as later chapters demonstrate.

5 Refurbished Manchester Piccadilly Station by BDP. A nineteenth-century building type brought up to date in the late twentieth century. Photograph: Brian Edwards .

The sense of lineage in transport buildings is important in understanding the changing functional demands and the adoption of different approaches to design by the architects and engineers involved. Railway stations were a particularly difficult design problem because no obvious precedent existed in the nineteenth century for the type. Their architects evolved a form which airport and bus station designers later adopted. The key elements of the type, common to all transport buildings, is a gathering space where tickets and information are obtained, and a separate space where boarding occurs. The first space is enclosed, lofty, often round and architecturally contained; the second is open and linear. The geometry of space mirrors the pattern of activity involved in moving from a public to a semi-public realm, and in negotiating a change in speed facilitated by joining a train, plane or bus. Since these conditions are constant for all transportation building types, Pevsner is right in grouping them around a central genealogical core.

The twentieth century witnessed the expansion of transportation to the point where in terms of passenger throughput a single facility such as Heathrow Airport handled in a single year more that the whole population of England. Even the railway station, after a period of stagnation at mid-century, was re-vitalised by innovations in high speed traction (such as the French TGV system and its offshoot EuroStar). Whereas Heathrow handled 64 million passengers a year in 2003, Kings Cross Station in London has nearly 32 million passing beneath its elegant arched roof each year and Waverley Station in Edinburgh over 8 million. From relatively humble beginnings early in the nineteenth century, the architecture of transportation emerged in the twentieth as a significant force not only in the evolution of building types but in the shaping of cities themselves.

Growth in transport infrastructure in the twentieth century provided British architects and engineers with the opportunity to test and develop new forms of construction technology. Reinforced concrete stations with cantilevered platform canopies were introduced in the 1930s (Leeds Station, 1937), laminated timber platform roofs (Manchester Oxford Road Station, 1960) and light-weight wide-span steel roofs at airports in the 1960s (Heathrow Terminal 1, 1961). Not only were large column free spaces required but roofs were often cranked to allow for light penetration and cross ventilation. Many of the initiatives in concrete wide-span station construction stemmed from continental Europe where architect engineers such as Pier Luigi Nervi led the way. The tradition in Europe of the joint training of architects and engineers provided opportunities for design collaboration rarely seen in Britain. The post-war reconstruction of European cities

6 Rome Terminal, 1951, designed by Euginion Montouri and Leo Calini.
Photograph: Brian Edwards.

led to innovation in station design (Rome Terminal 1951, fig. 6, and Naples Central 1955) which influenced the design of both bus and railway stations in Britain. Similarly the expansion of US airports in the 1950s under pressure from the US Government and airline companies such as TWA led to the introduction of multi-storey airport terminals which then became commonplace throughout the world. Waves of innovation are a feature of transport architecture whether in facility planning, design or engineering.

Size too is a characteristic of the type. Few structures are as large as transport buildings and bigness is not just a feature of the twentieth century but carries in its wake opportunities for fresh modes of architectural expression. Architects such as Eero Saarinen at Dulles International Airport (1958, fig. 7) and E. A. Riphafen at the Airfreight Centre at Schipol Airport (1960) were notable exponents of exciting roof shapes. Bigness too led to prefabricated construction, particularly the use of modular structural systems. Eventually even on quite small stations such as at Croydon Station or Milton Keynes Station, unit construction in steel, timber or concrete became commonplace. One advantage of system building of stations was the adoption of a language of materials and details which tended to unify the various stations along a line.

7   Dulles Airport by Eero Saarinen. Photograph © SOM.

Technological innovation has been a significant force in giving shape and
identity to transport buildings in the twentieth century. The need for large internal volumes led to the adoption of wide-span roofs, sometimes suspended from
pylons. As a consequence, the railway station, bus station and airport terminal is
invariably an essay in steel, glass and concrete. Walls where they occur tend not
to reach to the ceiling. The result is the creation of rooms within bigger spaces,
often given rounded shapes so as not to impede pedestrian flows. The presence
of bold architectural structure is a recurring theme of this building type.
Columns define routes and mark the edge of platforms. In their turn the
columns which support the roof trusses help orientate the passenger inside and
give identity to the building within the external cityscape. Such structures
became a useful means of landmarking early motorway service stations.

Space in transport buildings comes in two main forms — a gathering space
represented at the railway station by the booking hall and at the airport terminal
by the arrivals lounge — and a transfer space characterised by the platform (station) and gate lounge (airport). A similar distinction occurs in the motorway
service station with the linear stand of petrol pumps and the square enclosure of
the pay-station. As scale increases so too does the complexity but the distinction

remains: two types of passenger space, one round or contained, the other open, linear and in direct contact with the mode of transport. In addition, there is other accommodation such as offices, security areas and control points. The latter consists of prominent structures overlooking the track in the case of the signal box and the air traffic control tower at the end of the runway in the case of the airport. How these various elements are expressed or forged into a whole provides considerable opportunity for the architect. As a consequence the railway station, like the airport and motorway service area, becomes a small city of structures instantly recognisable.

Ferry terminals are another manifestation of the globalisation of transport architecture in the twentieth century. Whether in the utilitarian form of the Dover car ferry terminal (1952) designed by J.M.Wilson and H.C. Mason or the more sophisticated Ocean Terminal at Southampton (1950), ferry terminals sit between railway stations and airports in their aspiration towards a truly contemporary architecture. Like airport buildings, ferry buildings often contain large customs halls some of which were decidedly nautical in character.

The image of a typical transport building in Britain is one of a large muscular structure set invariably in an area of open and decidedly functional external space. The space is needed for multi-modal circulation, security and for visibility. As a result the railway station is perceived as a gateway to the train just as the airport terminal is to the plane. This sense of gateway has influenced the architectural image of the building type, inspiring often bizarre exercises in plastic form. But in the opposite direction the station and airport are also gateways to cities and to continents. To arrive in this type of building is often to experience a whole new world. As the twentieth century unfolded 'place' gradually invaded the culture and anonymity of modernity. Towards the end of the century stations and airports became fashioned by the social, climatic and geographical nuances of the locality, for example, the rebuilding of Charing Cross Station, London to designs by Terry Farrell, 1990 (fig. 8). In this sense twentieth-century transport architecture in Britain became more caught in the cross-currents of history and of geography than any other building type.

Compared to railway and bus stations in Britain, those in Europe and the USA tended to have a more planned relationship with their surrounding areas. Stations and civic spaces were considered as one with squares placed at transportation entrances. For example, Union Station, Washington, designed by Daniel Burnham in 1903 had a large external forecourt linked to the main booking hall which led axially to the underground passenger concourse. Penn Station

8 Air rights development, Charing Cross Station, London, 1988,
designed by Sir Terry Farrell and Partners.

in New York by McKim, Mead and White, 1910, follows a similar pattern. Here
the station fills a whole city block with offices above and a bus station to one
side. In both cases there was integration between transport and the city. Similar
planned relationships are found in Paris (Gare St Lazare, 1912), Frankfurt
(Frankfurt on Main, 1915), Buenos Aires (Retiro Terminal, 1915) and Sydney
(Central Station, 1910). Of the London termini it was only Waterloo, following
the Memorial Entrance extension of 1922, which approached the planned
grandeur of Continental or American examples. Where bus or rail stations are
grand (Victoria Coach Station) the relationship to the wider urban area is often
poorly considered.

By the early 1960s Britain had begun to realise that railways were both an asset
and a problem. The over-provision of train services had led to inefficiency which
the Beeching Plan of 1962 sought to rectify. However, in parallel there was a growing awareness in British Rail of the potential benefit of good design to the effective running of a modern railway. The image conscious sixties led to a review of
station design including signage and the uniforms of staff. New rules were introduced to co-ordinate the design and layout of platforms, of ticketing, booking

halls, seats and staff apparel. The legacy of the Festival of Britain style can be seen in the redesign of Chichester Station (architect N G T Wikely, 1961) and of new Coventry Station (W R Headly, 1962). Design and image were regarded by British Rail as important under the growing influence of the Design Council (established in 1964) and as a spin-off of marketing initiatives in the airline industry.

Stations, and to a lesser degree airport terminals, have become corridors of corporate identity. The values of a railway company were historically extended from one end of the country to another, and of airline companies across continents. The corporate image was expressed in new forms of architecture, interior design, costume and station graphics. Both railway and airline companies as well as petroleum suppliers in their ubiquitous filling stations were in effect promoters of new designs and new technologies. The linear avenues of development affected the way of life of ordinary people, and in this transport buildings were increasingly the emblem of modernity. However, not all transport companies embraced the symbolism of modern design — many harboured more picturesque ambition even up to the Second World War. But beneath the veneer of historicism there existed a ruthless ability to parcel life into measurable time units, to manage affairs for maximum profit, and to exploit innovations in traction technology. In the process the twentieth century saw the death of distance and of many regional cultures.

In the nineteenth century an ambiguity often existed between the inner world of transport buildings and their exterior facade. Behind the station front rich in decorative stonework or polychrome brickwork there often existed a spectacular iron framed interior. The dialogue between the competing agendas of architecture and engineering gave considerable charm to early stations and found its way into the modern age. Victorian architects such as John Dobson in Newcastle sought a station façade which acknowledged the values of the city and a platform enclosure which addressed the train. Whereas the former had classical overtones, the latter was an exercise in wide span construction, daring use of wafer-thin glass and slender iron and later steel columns. Airports in the twentieth century, however, did not suffer the same sense of divided priority, mostly because airports existed in a world devoid of traditional urban values. The placeless airport responded to the romance of flying rather that to the external physical landscape. So early airports took their imagery either from the Bauhaus model of modernity or from the smooth curved lines of the aircraft themselves. Early filling stations did the same, though the references were to the gracious limousines of the day.

Though the exterior architecture of airports, rail and bus stations provided less of an opportunity for the construction of artificial image than in the interiors, branding through design became a useful form of advertising as the century shifted from public to private providers of transport services. Airline companies like British Caledonian and Virgin, branded their services with the same tartans, colours and graphics in an attempt to create customer loyalty. Just as with the earlier generation of railway, bus and underground train companies, the imposition of identity extended from the means of transport (planes), to the gate lounge, concourse area, staff uniforms and ticket graphics. Style became useful in the search for identity for businesses where place, time and distance were increasingly eroded. Technology in such a world held the key to architectural expression resulting eventually in an almost universal 'high tech' language for the twentieth-century transport building which contrasted with the 'low tech' one for the franchisers inside. In this sense British transport buildings are a useful barometer of the changing visual taste of the nation.

The fashion for circular airport terminals was a feature of the 1930s. One of the first of the type was at Gatwick, built in 1935, followed by Helsinki, 1938. Both contained radiating piers extending like fingers from a central round concourse. A ring of offices and bars separated the central public space from the customs hall which formed an outer ring overlooking the runway. Although the plan evolved on the basis of an appropriate 'airport image' it proved incapable of incremental growth and was subsequently abandoned in favour of rectangular terminals. Both Gatwick and Helsinki integrated airport and railway facilities — an idea in the UK only revived in 1989 with Norman Foster's design of Stansted (fig. 9). The circular shape allowed passengers to move smoothly down to the train using gentle curved ramps and staircases. But the rotunda shape also served as a useful icon for the emerging building type confirming the importance of image and meaning in reinforcing an architectural typology. It quickly became adopted for garages and private car showrooms.

The ambition of a typical railway company often extended beyond the edges of the stations. Land development was undertaken to exploit the opportunities which railways brought for commercial expansion. The first phase of railway construction saw land around stations increasingly used for sidings and warehouses. By the beginning of the twentieth century this land was redeveloped for hotels, offices and retail development. Major cities such as Leeds and Glasgow had impressive hotels which towered above the mainline rail and bus stations, reaping profits for the companies involved. The standardisation of

9 Interior of check-in lounge,
Stansted Airport, 1989.
Sir Norman Foster and Partners.
Photograph Brian Edwards.

architectural style, often Art Deco, reflected the need to appear progressive in spirit. In this airport authorities in the latter half of the twentieth century followed obvious precedent.

Design was a convenient tool to identify the products of a company whom the travelling public increasingly saw as providing a service beyond than of mere transportation. Airport authorities played their part by providing land whereby an airline company could build a terminal, hotel and car park as an integrated package commercially and architecturally. Under this influence airports had matured by the 1990s into a new kind of transport-based city. Airports like Heathrow contained the competing agendas of different airlines, each with their design philosophy, as well as a multitude of retailers (W.H. Smith, Sockshop, Starbucks, Macdonald's, etc.). The nineteenth-century station was a measured and controlled environment of commerce compared to the modern-day airport, but the seeds of exploitation of the travelling public were sown in the great railway terminals of London, Paris and New York.

10 Design for Terminal 5 at Heathrow Airport , 1995, by Richard Rogers and Partners RRP.

Railway and bus stations, airports and ferry terminals exist where the needs of people to travel and the means of transportation concur. Transport buildings serve people and commerce but do so where the train, bus, boat or plane decides. Stations require access to tracks, and tracks to trains, and trains require to stop and pick up passengers and to refuel. Ultimately, it is the train, bus, plane, boat and car which decides the spatial geometry of the transport system not the existence of people or urban areas. Trains are taken into cities and where the station is built growth and prosperity occurs. Where planes are required to stop to pick up crew or to refuel, sometimes in the middle of nowhere, here too airports grow and so eventually do towns.

Just as road transportation grew on the back of mechanical skills and entrepreneurship generated by the First World War, so airports owed their initial conception to military expansion between the wars. Wartime flying led to the development of civil aircraft in the 1920s and to commercial passenger planes in the 1930s. Many early airports were shared between military and civil authorities (for example, Croydon, Surrey 1930). The arrangement was not without difficulty, especially when passport and customs controls were involved. Neither were the airside relationships smooth since military flights naturally took priority over civil ones. Congested airways, inadequate access to road and rail systems, and security concerns led to the separation of airports into separate civil and military establishments after the Second World War. Thus Heathrow and Gatwick were born (fig. 10).

The crossing of the paths of trains and of planes was once thought an irrelevance but today the concept of inter-modality brings the transport systems together. Only recently, however, have the benefits of an integrated transport system been acknowledged in spite of countless Victorian precedents. To arrive at an airport by train having previously caught a local bus to the station, provides benefits for the public though less tangible ones for the companies involved. Profit requires a degree of 'dwell time' at the station or the airport which efficient integration often denies. Over the past hundred years competition between transport providers led to considerable inefficiency and redundancy of infrastructure. Though the Beeching Report made obsolete about 40% of Britain's railway network, it did little to promote an integrated rail system which effectively interfaced trains, buses and planes. Recently, however, buildings for transportation have learnt to acknowledge the benefits of bringing all transport modes together under one roof. So instead of the railway station, bus station and airport, the twenty-first century has 'interchanges' — places where the lines and corridors of movement coincide. The formal consequence of the hybridisation is the emergence of a new type of transport building. The modern interchange (Waterloo is a good example, fig. 11) is part station, part departure lounge, part bus concourse. The internal imagery draws upon the different design influences, yet in spite of the complexity, these are still recognisably transport buildings.

What many modern interchanges lack is a sense of location. Their position is the result of an abstract play of lines drawn upon the face of a city or its surrounding countryside. But there is a placeless beauty in these megastructures — a sublime scale and sense of engineering whose roots take us back to the heroic origins of nineteenth-century railway stations. The denial of place, of season and of geography allows the modern interchange to explore space, light and construction as a largely abstract architectural order. No longer is style a metaphor for an externalised image — these new stations-cum-airports are the very essence of transport architecture using a deep and enduring language of technology and form. The authenticity of shared public space rather than commercial space, of structure which honestly expresses the laws of physics, and well-lit volumes which sparkle in the sunlight, provide an image which takes transport architecture into the twenty-first century. One has only to walk through the new Canary Wharf Station in London to experience the re-birth of a type.

Transport architecture in the twentieth century was torn between the utilitarian

11 Passenger concourse, Waterloo
International Station,
Sir Nicholas Grimshaw & Partners.
Photograph: Peter Cook.

and the romantic. For many the station or terminal is a functional building which provides the connection to train, bus or plane. For others it is a place to welcome friends and lovers, the backcloth to more emotional moments. The volume of the building acts as a container for memories as well as providing the functional means of access to cities or trains. This is perhaps why the building type has evolved into an interior of height, volume and light. The station and airport lounge is the arena of memories, of encounters and goodbyes captured memorably in film. As such it is a spacious container whose dimensions go beyond that which can be justified by function and utility alone.

In many transport buildings the simplicity of the initial design gives way over time to richness and plurality. Order beloved of system planners and engineers erodes under the pressure of use into romantic complexity. It is the dichotomy between human life acted out on the concourses and the feats of engineering above which helps define the character of transport buildings. The ambiguity of meaning is most prevalent in the booking halls and public concourses of transport buildings. It is less evident in the platform and gate lounge areas where smaller and more linear volumes prevail. The interaction between contained, yet spacious, volumes and the linearity of platforms forms the basic chemistry of the building type. Added to this there are often bridges or tunnels to cross the railway tracks, roads and runways. The three station elements of hall, platform and bridge are repeated in the airport in the form of concourse, lounge and gate.

Early stations in the nineteenth century were merely sheds which protected passengers at the point where they purchased tickets. Platform canopies occurred later. As the type matured in the twentieth century the platform dominated the concourse except at larger stations and terminals. The glass roofs and iron-framing of the platform was repeated at the airport and in the bus station. Within the platform area two theatres were acted out — that of the train and that of the passengers. Often, but not always, the two would meet but for through-trains the platforms were a landscape of flashing columns, name boards and bands of light, darkness and faces.

So whereas the concourse and booking hall is the theatre of romantic encounter, the platform became a place of more mechanical drama. The same is true of bus stations, ferry terminals and aircraft terminals. Some architects such as John McAslin at Redhill Station have exploited these ambiguous qualities. Normally it is people who instil meaning into often neutral transport volumes. It is the passengers who give meaning, identity and ultimately authenticity to transport buildings by their interaction with the world of speed, technology and architectural space.

By way of contrast to the architecture of public transport, the twentieth century saw an unprecedented growth in private transportation. The car was the very symbol of freedom and private pleasure. Near universal car ownership led to the evolution of a range of new building types — filling stations, motorway service areas, motels, multi-storey car parks and garages. With them went a new sense of independence, adventure and style. Some of the new building types for the private motorist were based on older models but most were entirely new. The multi-storey car park for instance, had no parallels in the nineteenth century and the motel has little in common typologically with the hotel.

The new buildings constructed to serve the needs of cars and their owners were 'modern' in an aesthetic sense. They drew their inspiration from Hollywood and the cinema rather than the functionalist or Bauhaus modernist tradition. As such the new roadhouses, motels and garages were often Art Deco in flavour or streamlined moderne as at Catford Filling Station, 1932, in South London. The new coach stations of the period were similarly dressed, although, as with garages and roadhouses, behind the white and pale blue painted stucco facades, the rational planning of facilities was of a high order. Victoria Coach Station in London by architects Wallis, Gilbert and Partners (1931) drew upon American practice with a central information point, angled wings and clean lines. Also in London, Stockwell Bus Garage by Adie, Button and Partners and Newbury Bus Station by Oliver Hill, both built in the 1940s, suggest the influence of the Italian engineer Pier Luigi Nervi. In these and other garages of the period reinforced concrete was to reach new levels of refinement and sometimes bravura.

By the 1950s new towns in Britain were designed around the needs of the motorist. Hemel Hemstead is an early car-oriented new settlement north of London and Milton Keynes a later example. Both new towns have elaborate road systems linked to car parks, shopping centres and the national motorway system. As was common practice at the time pedestrian and motorist needs were kept separate: each was a system which figured road layout with cars dominating in commercial areas and pedestrians in residential ones. Unlike Letchworth New Town, based upon a central train station, the later new towns were built around roads and neighbourhood units — not streets and squares as in the nineteenth-century city. Roads implied service stations, motels, flyovers and segregation. In this sense the 'open road' led to the 'open city' with an inevitable loss in urban design and what we now call sustainability. It is the challenge of the twenty-first century to reconcile the realm of the private car with public modes of transportation.

TRAINS

Early Twentieth-Century Stations

Gavin Stamp

'YOU WILL RECALL that English architects and engineers were the pioneers of railway architecture in the early nineteenth century.' So began Albert Richardson's lecture to the Royal Institute of British Architects in 1939 on that topical subject, 'Railway Stations'. 'What finer testimony to their genius can be found than the structural excellence of their conjoint labours: the roads, the viaducts, embankments, cuttings and tunnels.' And, if the achievements of their twentieth-century successors seemed less impressive to his audience, 'You must remember, too, that it is not the fault of architects of to-day that they have not been more generally consulted for rebuilding obsolete stations.'[1]

This essay is concerned with Britain's railways—excluding the London underground system—during the first half of the last century; that is, from the opening of the last main line to London—the Great Central—in 1899 to the nationalisation of the British railway system in 1948. From the point of view of railway architecture, this was not an inspiring period. Compared with the preceding half century in Britain, or with contemporary networks abroad—let alone with the achievement of Frank Pick and the London Passenger Transport Board—Britain's railway companies in the first half of the twentieth century generally failed to commission really good or memorable examples of new architecture. Most new or rebuilt stations were, on the whole, mediocre and often very conservative buildings: the initiative had passed to the designers of buildings and structures connected with roads.

The period from 1890 until the outbreak of war in 1914 is often described as the 'Golden Age' on Britain's railways. It may have been a Golden Age in terms of efficiency, comfort and rolling stock and locomotive design, but it was, in fact, a time when the established railway companies were becoming complacent, even though they were beginning to suffer from the problems created by financial restraints imposed by Parliament—problems which would become serious after the First World War. Nor was it a particularly good time in terms of labour relations; as Adrian Vaughan has recently written, the only railway 'age' which did last from 1890 until 1914 was 'the Age of Industrial Unrest, as the railway workers set out in earnest to achieve proper pay and working conditions.'[2]

It was certainly not a Golden Age in terms of railway architecture. Britain suffered from being the pioneer in the development of railways and the heroic period of railway architecture was the mid-nineteenth century, from the 1840s until the 1870s. The design of the urban terminus was worked out during these decades when King's Cross, Paddington, Charing Cross, Cannon Street, St Pancras, Manchester Central, Liverpool Lime Street and Glasgow St Enoch were created — all with innovative and magnificent train sheds. Once built, such hugely expensive structures had to suffice. Perhaps the last expression of this dynamic phase was the great steel bridge across the Firth of Forth opened in 1890, a wonder of the world which has rightly been praised as so much more advanced, and useful, than the contemporary Eiffel Tower.

After the Forth Bridge, Britain's railways produced nothing to compare with the massive railway structures raised in Western Europe and North America in the first two decades of the twentieth century. Fuelled by nationalism as well as by civic pride, expanding metropolises created huge new urban stations in which buildings of Roman grandeur were combined with vast train sheds of steel and glass. This was the period which saw the rebuilding of the central stations in Leipzig, Frankfort, Hamburg, Helsinki and Milan and, across the Atlantic, the Pennsylvania Station and Grand Central in New York, the Union Stations in Chicago, Washington and elsewhere (not to mention those in South America).

To turn to Britain after contemplating McKim, Mead & White's new Baths of Caracalla in Seventh Avenue, or the six arched spans at Leipzig, each 147 feet wide, is, to say the least, a considerable disappointment. Such buildings were certainly known here. H. Charlton Bradshaw won the Soane Medallion in 1912 for his design for a grand Classical terminus made at the Liverpool School of Architecture while at the Glasgow School J.M. Whitelaw's prize-winning design of 1913 was clearly inspired by American stations.[3] And in 1918 William Haywood published his ideal scheme for improving Birmingham New Street by building a noble hall above the existing subterranean platforms.[4] But while students and ambitious architects might dream of raising such vaults in British cities — nothing worthy was ever actually achieved. Most new stations were conservative in style and scarcely innovative in their functional arrangements or planning.

Opportunities for grand conceptions there certainly were, however. In 1899, the Great Central Railway, the renamed Manchester, Sheffield and Lincolnshire Railway, realised part of the dream of that rebarbative megalomaniac, Sir Edward Watkin, and opened the last main line to reach London. Superbly engineered to a Continental loading gauge to accommodate the Channel Tunnel

12 Marylebone Station by H. W. Braddock for the Great Central Railway, 1899. Photograph: André Goulancourt, 1978.

traffic that Watkin confidently anticipated, it ended up just north of the Marylebone Road behind Colonel Edis's incoherent Great Central Hotel. The result is rather an anti-climax (fig. 12). As John Betjeman put it,

> The Great Central had run out of cash by the time in reached the metropolis. The little terminus, three storied and of red brick, was not the work of a well known architect but the company's civil engineer. On the street side it looks like a branch public library in a Manchester suburb.[5]

(In fact, the architectural detail was supplied by H.W. Braddock). As for the train shed behind, it is nothing special at all and is not even complete as three more platforms were over-optimistically envisaged in the future.

Many stations were certainly being modernised in Britain, but the results were mediocre, if perfectly acceptable. In London, that twin station at Victoria was partly rebuilt at the turn of the century. Between 1899 and 1906, the

Brighton line—to use Lady Bracknell's careful distinction—erected a new train shed with rows of tall, iron Ionic columns fronted by an irrational Wrenaissance block, of which the railway historian Hamilton Ellis observed that 'No railway station front in Europe looks so like a gigantic mid-nineteenth century over-mantel, with its acropolitan clock in the middle.'[6] The South Eastern & Chatham Railway soon followed by refronting its half of the terminus with an Edwardian Baroque facade designed by Alfred W. Blomfield in 1907-08. Unfor-tunately, at Charing Cross after John Fowler's arched shed partially collapsed in 1905 the same company replaced it with a banal and depressing structure with a horizontal roof of lattice girders—itself now gone.

Elsewhere, Sheffield was rebuilt after 1904 with endless arcades by the Mid-land Railway's old-established architect, Charles Trubshaw. At Nottingham at the same time—no doubt in response to the competition of the Great Central's Victoria Station—the Midland rebuilt its station in jolly Edwardian Baroque in (by now) rather old-fashioned terra-cotta, to the designs of A.E. Lambert. In 1909, the Lancashire & Yorkshire Railway gave Manchester Victoria a long but fussy new Edwardian Baroque facade, designed by William Davies. Compare this with the awesome monumentality of Leipzig, say, or even Victor Laloux's Gare d'Orsai in Paris, and Britain's railway architecture of the Golden Age seems at once pretentious and provincial. The baton had passed across the Channel.

The only good Edwardian stations, in architectural terms, were the smaller ones. The London & North Western Railway employed Gerald Horsley, that talented if rather conservative pupil of Norman Shaw and a founder of the Art-Workers' Guild, to rebuild stations on the main line to Watford when the suburban tracks were electrified in 1911. The results, at Harrow & Wealdstone, Hatch End and Bushey, are charming buildings of brick and stone in a free Wrenaissance manner, 'a style halfway between that of a bank and a medium-sized country house,' as Betjeman put it.[7] Equally good are the stations rebuilt by the Caledonian Railway to the designs of James Miller working with the railway engineer, Donald Mathieson. Perth and Stirling were given well-planned, spacious halls and overbridges, but best of all is Wemyss Bay, of 1903, where architecture and engineering are happily fused and arched girders radiate from a circular ticket office.

The great lost opportunity was Waterloo, the terminus of the London & South Western Railway, which was enlarged and rebuilt over two decades after 1900. The product of piecemeal expansion on a confined site, Waterloo acquired a curving concourse, 770 feet long, which is efficient and impressive. But instead of covering this and the twenty-one platforms with a fine new arched steel shed, the L&SWR

13 War Memorial Arch, Waterloo Station, by John Robb Scott for the London & South Western Railway, 1922. Photograph: Gavin Stamp, 2000.

merely added to the existing sheds of 1885 with a repetitive structure of horizontal lattice girders above a forest of utilitarian stanchions designed by J.W. Jacombe Hood, chief engineer. Although, in 1910, the *Railway Gazette* could describe the tiled 'gentlemen's court' as 'perhaps the finest in England,' the only grand architectural gesture is the entrance arch at the north-west corner (fig. 13).

Redesigned as a war memorial by the company's architect, John Robb Scott, to honour 585 employees killed, this monumental feature was opened by Queen Mary in 1922 just before the L&SWR was absorbed into the new Southern Railway. To quote Betjeman again, 'clearly Mr Scott when he designed this great entrance to the new Waterloo after the 1914 War was determined to outdo Sir [*sic*] Ralph Knott's enormous County Hall on the Thames only a few yards away. He had had a look at Piranesi, the etchings of Brangwyn and Muirhead Bone and the rich Edwardian baroque of provincial Town Halls.'[8] All in vain. Hemmed in by the South Eastern Railway's ugly viaduct into Charing Cross, this pompous gesture could not redeem the lack of urban vision and civic amenity represented by the muddle of Waterloo—a lack which was the despair of architects and town planners between the World Wars.

Britain's railways achieved much, and suffered much, during the First World War. Almost the entire system was placed under the orders of the Railway Executive Committee, that is, the government, in 1914 and the system coped with the war effort despite so many railwaymen having left for the Front. At the end of the war, the railways were run down and in need of capital investment, yet they did not receive all the compensation promised by government, nor were they handed back to their owners intact. Instead, the wartime methods of co-ordination and planning were to be imposed on the railways in peacetime. Under the Railways Act of 1921 which took effect two years later, the several independent companies were 'grouped' into four new companies. In what was, in fact, 'a disguised nationalisation,' Britain's railways were now divided between the London, Midland & Scottish Railway, the London & North Eastern Railway, the Southern Railway and the Great Western Railway—the only company to survive with its name as well as its traditions intact.

These four concerns faced huge and growing problems. The need for new stations was not a high priority, even though the architectural legacy of the Victorians was now much despised. Much more important was the ominous fact that the war had given a huge boost to the motor industry and both the private car and the motor lorry were now beginning to undermine the monopoly of the railways. Yet, at first, the railways were not allowed directly to compete with the growing number of unlicensed road hauliers while the rates for rail freight were controlled by Parliament. As many complained, the railways were having to fight the competition from the roads with 'one hand tied behind our back.' From 1924, the general trend was decline. With the exception of the Southern Railway, the big companies earned over half their revenue from freight and so were badly affected by the Depression after 1929. Increasing economic difficulties exacerbated a sense of grievance which resulted in the 'Railways Demand a Square Deal' campaign launched in 1938.[9]

The railways responded to the changed climate by making the first closures and cuts—in 1928 the Great Western axed seven expresses, including the Cheltenham Flyer—although they were reinstated following public outrage. Positive steps were also taken. Faster and better expresses were introduced, culminating in the competition between the streamlined express trains of the LMS and the LNER—the *Coronation Scot* and the *Flying Scotsman*—in the late 1930s. In 1938 the LNER's *Mallard* designed by Nigel Gresley achieved the fastest ever speed for a steam locomotive: 126 m.p.h. The companies also invested in feeder buses and road haulage to bring traffic back to the railways — the GWR even (briefly) operated aeroplanes while the LMS came up with the 'Ro-Railer', a bus that could travel on road or rail. However, what was really needed was a comprehensive programme of electrification.

All this represented a necessary and increasingly desperate attempt to change the image of the railways, which were widely perceived as run-down, dirty and complacent. 'Cost, in face of falling revenues, is an important point,' as the *Architect & Building News* recognised in 1930, 'but the moral to be drawn is that the railways must make increased efforts to win back the traffic, and that can only be done by greater attention to the comfort and convenience of the passenger.'[10] It was here that Architecture could play a part, but, even if the chief architect in each of the Big Four could heed Frank Pick's plea to contribute 'a justness of proportion, a simplicity of outline, a severity of treatment' within the limits set by the chief engineer, there was simply not the capital available to invest in large, modern urban stations such as Mussolini was building in Florence, Rome and elsewhere.[11] The ambitious scheme, so often mooted and widely desired, to abolish Charing Cross altogether and build a new bridge together with a new, combined terminus for the Southern Railway's lines on the South Bank at Waterloo, remained a town planner's dream (fig. 14).[12]

14 Unexecuted design for rebuilding Charing Cross Station by William Walcot, 1926.
The late Roderick Gradidge.

Nevertheless, in his famous study of the history of *The Railway Station* published in 1957, Carroll Meek could write that 'After World War I Britain had a minor renaissance of station building. In modest stations on limited budgets she showed that she was still capable of distinguished designs. These reflected the functional approach as well as her great 19th-century terminals reflected the picturesque approach.'[13] Other than the London Transport stations commissioned by Pick, however, the only examples he could cite were all illustrated in Christian Barman's 1950 book, *An Introduction to Railway Architecture*: Queen's Park, Surbiton, Leeds City and (not correctly identified) Malden Manor. As far as Hamilton Ellis was concerned, while Pick's 'new, and most meritorious style' was the most impressive achievement in inter-war railway architecture,

> The same cannot be said for the new suburban stations of the Southern Railway; white and chastely bleak. Their main merit is a negative one; they are never vulgar. Indeed no railway company stooped to the sort of thing one sees along the Great Western Road and on similar highways all about the country.[14]

'Why is it that British railway stations are so uniformly hideous?' wondered the *Architect & Building News* in 1930. 'Built with all the engineer's love of firmness and possessing commodity in varying degrees, they are almost all completely devoid of delight.'[15] Even so, there was still something to be said for Britain's railways — at least to judge by the impact they made on the young modern architect Ernö Goldfinger on his first visit to London in 1926: 'Terrific — much better than now.' He had crossed over from Dunkirk to Tilbury, presumably then proceeding from Sir Edwin Cooper's new Baggage Hall to St Pancras on the old London, Tilbury & Southend Railway, by now part of the LMS. 'Left Paris at nine at night and arrived in London at nine in the morning. The trains were wonderful. I had breakfast on the train from Tilbury to London: fantastic! unbelievable! At one time I travelled very posh on the Continent. In my early days I travelled Paris–Budapest on the Orient Express — very nice; but the LMS was better than the Continental trains.'[16] As Adrian Vaughan has written,

> In spite of their difficulties between 1921 and 1939, the companies had managed to restore their track, stations and rolling stock and achieve a high standard of maintenance — although nearly 40 per cent of locomotives were over thirty years old. They certainly took pride in the work: even though ill-paid, the trackmen kept the road pristine — as any contemporary photograph will show.[17]

Of the 'Big Four', the Southern Railway would seem to have built most new stations between the wars and became willing to use a modernistic style to convey a progressive image. As only a quarter of its revenue came from freight, the Southern was particularly keen to build up commuter traffic. Sir Herbert Walker, the general manager of the Southern, did this by both embarking on an extensive campaign of electrification — using the third rail system — on its existing network and by constructing new lines in outer London to both encourage and exploit suburban growth. 'Southern Electric' was a great success which also encouraged passenger growth on its main lines, with the *Brighton Belle* adding glamour to the faster journey to the South Coast after 1933. The company also invested heavily in Southampton Docks since first the White Star Line and then Cunard shifted their operations from the Mersey to the Solent.

The Southern inherited a dense network south of the Thames with many cheap and inadequate stations as well as a multiplicity of lines resulting from decades of suicidal competition between the former smaller companies. Rationalisation was required and this occasionally demanded entirely new stations on new sites, as on the Isle of Thanet where the railways were rearranged in 1924–26. The new Ramsgate Station was distinguished by a noble booking hall lit by three arched windows clearly inspired by Continental and American examples (figs. 15 and 16). The architect would seem to have been the young Edwin Maxwell Fry (1899–1987), the future designer of the Sun House in Hampstead and the partner of Walter Gropius, who, in 1923, for a while became the chief assistant in the company's architect's department.[18] Ramsgate, and the contemporary and associated new station at nearby Margate, reflects Fry's Classical training under Charles Reilly at the Liverpool School rather than his subsequent embrace of Continental modernism.

In his amnesiac and misleading autobiography, Fry described how 'the offices above the glass roofing of Waterloo Station shamed me by their rambling banality' and how

> the Chief Architect, a lumbering Scotsman only waiting for the salmon rivers to rise, fell into my hands like a ripe plum as by one of those sudden spurts of decisive action I took over the hotel design that was beyond him, and was installed by the Chief Engineer as his deputy and working factotum. This took days only. My salary was doubled. The little office manager called me 'Sir Maxwell' by mistake and I immediately set about reinforcing the time-serving staff of old bodies with all the friends and acquaintances I could

15, 16 Ramsgate Sation, Kent, probably by E. Maxwell Fry for the Southern Railway, 1926, exterior (above) and interior of booking hall (below). Photographs: Gavin Stamp, 2000.

lay hold of. There was plenty of work and one by one I signed on an assortment of young men who transformed the place of lingering fears and deceptions so that old crocks who formerly spent hours in the lavatory because they dared not creep out to the pub or the bookmaker stayed to enjoy the careless chatter of the young.[19]

17   Exeter Central Station, Devon, rebuilt by the Southern Railway, 1933.
Photograph: Gavin Stamp, 2000.

Who were these young men? Did they stay on to design the modernistic
Southern Railway stations of the following decade? Presumably the 'lumbering
Scotsman' was John Robb Scott, who had designed the Waterloo Memorial
arch; the son of the co-architect of the (dreadful) North British Hotel in Edinburgh, he had joined the old London & South-Western in 1907 and it is certainly hard to believe that he could also have been responsible for, say, slick, Art
Deco Surbiton station.[20]

In the 1920s, the Southern favoured that polite, reticent Neo-Georgian
which was popular for official buildings like Post Offices at the time. Bromley
North, of 1925, is a good example and this style was still being used in 1933 for the
rebuilding of Exeter Central with its attendant terraces of shops (fig. 17). Hastings, of 1931, with its octagonal 'booking concourse', is in the more monumental
Classical manner established by Fry at Ramsgate. But, at the same time, the
Southern Railway was beginning to go Modern or, rather, *moderne*. Because of
the peculiar topography of London, combined with the vagaries of railway history, the Underground system scarcely extended south of the Thames, leaving
the Southern Railway as its overground counterpart as the dominant operator.
The SR therefore not only built up an electrified commuter network in South

18 Surbiton Station, Surrey, rebuilt
by the Southern Railway, 1937.
Photograph: Gavin Stamp, 2001.

London but seems to have adopted a modern image in emulation of, or to vie
with, that achieved by Frank Pick with his new buildings by Charles Holden on
the other side of the river. The rebuilt Wimbledon station, faced in Portland
stone and completed by 1930, which 'states itself in plain language without cir-
cumlocution', was surely a direct response to the new white, rectilinear stations
on the Northern Line's extension to Morden, that bold incursion into the
Southern's territory.[21]

The Southern's stations, however, usually lacked the austere rationality of
Holden's later brick and concrete buildings. Instead, they often adopted a flashy,
horizontal style strongly influenced by cinema architecture. At Surbiton, where
the booking hall of 1937 sports Art Deco fins between the tall windows, there is
also a tower reminiscent of the Odeon, Leicester Square (fig. 18). Sometimes the
rebuilt stations were combined with shops to increase their importance as an
urban focus, as at Wimbledon and Richmond (1938). On the new suburban line
to Chessington South (opened in 1938–39) and elsewhere, a modernistic,

streamlined manner was achieved in brick as well as in cement render. Malden Manor, on that line, has curved reinforced concrete platform canopies; St Mary Cray, in brick, is streamlined with rounded corners while Horsham is a good example of the application of the wireless-set aesthetic.[22]

Despite being alone in inheriting a tradition and a resonant name and being often regarded as 'God's Wonderful Railway', the Great Western also felt obliged to change its image to go with its enterprising ventures like operating aeroplanes. Unfortunately, like the Southern, it went modernistic rather than Modern. For Betjeman, writing in the 1950s, 'there was an unfortunate period in the nineteen-thirties when the Great Western went 'Modern' in the Great West Road sense of that word, with its new office buildings at Paddington. It adopted at this time too that hideous monogram on its engines.'[23] Earlier, he had categorised that monogram and the buildings designed by Percy Emerson Culverhouse (1872–1953) at Paddington in 1933 as 'jazz-modern' which was, as he put it in 1937, 'the product of insensitive minds. It is the decoration of art-school students. You all know it. The "modernistic suites" to be seen in hire purchase catalogues, the dashing milk-bars which have dispensed with the need for capital letters. ...'[24]

Some GWR stations were given a 'jazz-modern' face-lift in the 1930s with the application of buff tiles to the walls of platforms and underpasses, as at Bristol Temple Meads. As for new buildings, it cannot really be claimed that the company's limited architectural patronage was very distinguished. Cardiff was rebuilt by Culverhouse in mediocre Classical as late as 1932–34; Leamington Spa in timid modernistic in 1938, while Bourton-on-the-Water and Stow-on-the-Wold on a less prominent branch line were rebuilt in 'Cotswold style architecture' in local stone the same year—which was probably a mercy.[25] The most beautiful aspect of the Great Western—apart from the legacy of Brunel—was its engines and its livery.

The London & North Eastern Railway and the London, Midland & Scottish suffered most from the economic depression. Both railways depended heavily on freight traffic and both served the areas in Northern England and Scotland dominated by the old heavy industries which were now in decline. Both railways needed investment in modernisation and to make economies; both were perceived as operating a run-down and decrepit Victorian network. Hence the emphasis on glamorous express trains and good publicity—although these did little for the users of branch lines in depressed industrial areas.

The record of the London & North Eastern in terms of architecture in not very extensive or very distinguished. Welwyn was enlarged in 1927 with a Neo-Georgian station building to harmonise with the dominant style of the new

19 Doncaster Station, Yorkshire, exterior of booking hall rebuilt by the London & North Eastern Railway. Photograph: Gavin Stamp, 1980s.

Garden City while Doncaster Station on its main East Coast line was given a new frontage and booking hall in the 1930s designed in a simple, modernistic manner and faced in red brick (fig. 19). In Leeds, the LNER combined with the LMS to rebuilt the old and confusing joint station. W.H. Hamlyn, architect to the LMS, designed a new long concourse in reinforced concrete (possibly in emulation of Holden's angular arched concrete shed at Cockfosters) and, in front, the Queen's Hotel was rebuilt by the LMS with the distinguished London architect W. Curtis Green as consultant, but little more was done to that large and awkward station at the time (fig. 20).

Rather more impressive is the architecture planned on the line from Woodford to Ongar as part of the New Works Programme carried out at the end of the decade in conjunction with the London Passenger Transport Board. In the event, only Loughton Station on the LNER's commuter lines in north-east London was rebuilt in 1937–40 to the designs of Murray Easton (1889–1975), the partner of Howard Robertson. Now part of the Underground network, it has a plain, cubic booking hall faced in brick and lit by a single arched window while the elevated concrete platform canopies are rounded and streamlined (fig. 21). Loughton is altogether an interesting variation on the theme set by Holden. The new Stratford

20   Queen's Hotel, Leeds, rebuilt by W. H. Hamlyn with W. Curtis Green, consultant, for the London Midland & Scottish Railway, 1936–37. Photograph: Gavin Stamp, 1986.

21   Loughton Station, Essex, by Easton & Robertson for the London & North Eastern Railway, 1937–40. Photograph: Gavin Stamp, 1987.

station, on the other hand, rebuilt during the Second World War and faced in clinical off-white tiles, was rather less impressive.[26]

The record of the London, Midland & Scottish Railway in terms of architectural patronage was the most distinguished, and intelligent. The LMS had the largest network of the 'Big Four' and faced the most severe economic problems. In the 1920s, its services were slower than before the war, and new locomotives were not introduced until the 1930s. Trains such as the *Coronation Scot* may have captivated schoolboys, but there was rather less glamour to most of the system. To quote Adrian Vaughan, 'the locomotivemen did wonders with pre-war locomotives, using their great skill and physical endurance to run the heavier, post-war trains at pre-war speeds. The efforts of the footplatemen and especially the sooty firemen, shovelling an average of 50 lb of coal a minute on 60 mph express journeys lasting from 2½ to 5 hours (and even as much as 7½ hours on the LMS expresses Euston–Glasgow or Birmingham–Perth) make the much-lauded efforts of Olympic athletes running round in a circle look rather ridiculous.'[27]

The LMS inherited more large urban stations than any other company, and many desperately needed rebuilding, or at least a facelift. With W.H. Hamlyn as its chief architect, it also rebuilt a considerable number of small stations, sometimes building new ones on newly electrified lines as in the Wirral or on its anomalous eastern province, the old London, Tilbury & Southend Railway. For many of these, a sort of chunky, modernistic Classic was adopted, as at Squires Gate, near Blackpool. (The LMS offices in Eversholt Street next to Euston was a rather larger essay of 1931–33 in the same style by Hamlyn with A. Victor Heal, which Nikolaus Pevsner thought 'modernistic and quite uncommonly bad').[28] New sans-serif lettering and a company logo — the 'Hawkseye Sign' — were also introduced in 1935 and standardised in 1938, in clear emulation of the house style of London Transport.[29] Later, towards the end of the 1930s, Hamlyn produced stations in a more convincing modern manner, simple and streamlined, which showed the influence of Holden. Upminster West and Elm Park in Essex are good examples, while Hoylake, in the Wirral, is remarkable for its curved frontage and projecting canopy and circular booking hall (fig. 22). One of the larger stations to be redesigned was Luton, rebuilt in brick and concrete in 1939.

Unlike the shadowy J.R. Scott of the Southern or Culverhouse of the GWR, William Henry Hamlyn (1888–1968) was an accomplished and experienced architect in his own right and he seems to have exercised greater responsibility than they did. A pupil of R. Wynn Owen of Liverpool, he had been a prizewinning student at the Royal Academy Schools while working for the London &

22   Hoylake Station. Photograph: Elain Harwood, 2000.

North Western Railway.[30] His LMS School of Transport at Derby, designed in modernistic Georgian, won an RIBA bronze medal in 1939. Under Hamlyn's direction, the Architects' Department of the LMS was also remarkable for having a research department, established in 1930. In 1939 J.L. Martin (1908–2000), the future co-designer of the Royal Festival Hall, joined the LMS Architects' Department as Principal Assistant Architect: he delighted in having a mobile drawing office which could be attached to ordinary trains.

Martin worked on schemes for standardised and prefabricated small station buildings, developing ideas which had already been tried out by Hamlyn in steel in 1933–35 at South Kenton and in reinforced concrete at Apsley in 1938.[31] Because of the outbreak of war, the first experimental unit—steel-framed and clad in steel panels, and with a distinctive two-step canopy—was not erected until 1945 at Queen's Park; later it was moved to West Hampstead. This little structure is important as it predated the celebrated Hertfordshire Schools building system. In all, this system was used for buildings at seventeen stations, but this story really belongs to that of British Railways rather than the LMS. (Also worth mentioning are the stark, cubic reinforced concrete lineside mechanical coaling plants and bunkers supplied and erected by Henry Lees & Co. Ltd after

1933 which were admired and photographed by James Gowan and James Stirling in the 1950s.)[32]

The LMS also invested in holiday resorts, perhaps recognising in them more scope for improving the company's image through modern architecture and so encouraging holiday traffic. The 'New Architecture' would seem to have been more acceptable to the public by the sea than inland, and so the railway invested in the Pleasure Beach at Blackpool, designed by Joseph Emberton, and in creating Prestatyn Holiday Camp, 'The Chalet Village by the Sea', in Wales. This was designed by the company's own architect, Hamlyn, who claimed it was the first such development to be treated as a total architectural conception. 'There is abundant evidence that people of all classes in this country react to artistic surroundings, and therefore as much consideration and care have been devoted to the design of the Prestatyn Holiday Camp as have been applied to the most costly and important buildings erected by the Railway Company for its own purposes.'[33]

The earliest and best example of the LMS's flirtation with modernity was the new, replacement Midland Hotel at Morecambe designed by the celebrated and fashionable architect Oliver Hill (1887–1968). The result, opened in 1933 and much illustrated, became one of the most striking and popular modern buildings of the 1930s. With its aerodynamic plan, and its streamlined elevations with curved corners, the Midland gave an entirely new image to the railway hotel. Hill got the job as he was a friend of one of the directors, and the architect's biographer, Alan Powers, notes that Arthur Towle, the LMS Controller of Hotels, 'was repeatedly alarmed by Hill's ideas, which he thought would frighten off the traditional clientele of northern day-trippers, but the aim was to attract a new and younger set with greater sophistication.'[34] The hotel was also notable for the art works it contained, with a wall relief and murals by Eric Gill and a further mural by Eric Ravilious. Such was Hill's success in Lancashire in putting up a modern building, quickly and cheaply, that he was also invited to modernise the Euston Hotel in London at the other end of the line.

As for Euston Station itself, its long overdue rebuilding should have been the LMS's flagship architectural project. Again paying the penalty for being a pioneer, Euston had rapidly become inadequate as a muddle of buildings grew behind Hardwick's noble Doric propylaeum and any clarity in the original terminus of the London & Birmingham Railway was expunged by expediency and alteration. Worse was to come when the 'Arch' itself was hidden from Euston Square by the London & North Western Railway's Euston Hotel crossing over the street. 'Someone said that when the L.M.S. was formed in 1923, it didn't deserve to get Euston,' wrote Hamilton Ellis in 1950; 'Have its heirs ever been worthy of it?'[35] By the 1920s when, by default, it had become the principal LMS station in the capital, Old Euston was an inconvenient mess, ripe for rebuilding on a grand scale — if the money could be found.

The long-rumoured rebuilding of Euston was at last decided upon in 1935. Two years earlier, Sir Josiah Stamp, the dynamic president and chairman of the LMS, had addressed the RIBA's Annual Dinner on the subject. But he first dealt with another inherited problem.

> How would you gentlemen like to be in my place with the responsibility for St Pancras Hotel? I was nurtured in the faith of the architectural text-books of my youth, for I read them all. The faith proclaimed that this noble building of Scott's was the very last word in the happy association of purist Gothic forms with modern industrial requirements; a veritable object lesson, and still described as one of the wonders of London. Well, I understand I am the last remaining man, with the mid-Victorian spirit, who is sufficiently philistine and bourgeoise and altogether out of the running, to be an unashamed admirer of the Albert Memorial. . . . Here am I responsible, in less than 60 years, for a building which is completely obsolete and hopeless as an hotel, and even worse than useless as offices; will it be vandalism of the worst order to destroy it? . . . We can either keep it for a revival of appreciation, with a dead economic loss for the site that it occupies and the use to which it is put, or we can pull it down and impose on the site something that can be equally condemned in its turn in 60 years' time.[36]

But in 1933 few shared his taste for Victorian Gothic (five years later Albert Richardson could recommend the demolition of the hotel), and what interested the assembled architects was Euston. 'I am told,' complained Stamp, 'that I must on no account, in scheming out ideas for a great new terminal, touch the noble proportions of the Great Hall at Euston. Vain are my struggles to invent any plan for a new Euston which will not involve the destruction of that Hall!' As for the Arch, 'I do not know what its ultimate fate will be. I do not know whether it will always stand in its present spot.' That admission, for those who cared about Philip Hardwick's still magnificent if abused propylaeum, might have been cause for optimism.

That same year, 1933, the young John Betjeman published an article in the *Architectural Review* entitled 'Dictating to the Railways' because 'Railways have so long dictated to the public, that one of the public, after years of indolence in gas-lit waiting rooms, takes this opportunity of dictating to the railways.' He then deplored how the railways had abandoned the 'civic principles' to which they had conformed in the designs of stations, bridges and viaducts in the early days.

'From a purely aesthetic standpoint, railway architecture, always excepting recent developments of the London Electric Railways, cannot be said to have improved. It is a far cry from such buildings as the viaducts between Saltash and Lostwithiel, Newcastle station, the Forth Bridge, Broadstone, Harcourt Street and Kingsbridge in Dublin, Cannon Street from the river and the pier at Holyhead, to Crewe, St Enoch's or Marylebone—this last building is unworthy of a provincial Temperance Institute.'

'Obviously something must be done for Euston,' he continued.

> But whatever is done let it not be done in the all too familiar railway manner. If the directors of the L.M.S. decide to rebuild Euston let us hope they will make a clean sweep of the building behind the Doric portico, and employ outside advice and assistance. As has been shown already, a new Euston is not a matter to be decided by old gentlemen in the mahogany confines of Hardwick's imposing Boardroom. Nevertheless the Directors of the L.M.S. have made one splendid gesture in sanctioning the erection of a first-rate piece of architecture in the form of the Midland Hotel. . . . If their public spirit and enterprise have allowed them to do this for Morecambe, how much more should they do for London? The first duty of the Directors is to employ a good architect who will not ruin an excellent chance of the improvement of London, as did the London and South-Western when it created that mean and ostentatious building, Waterloo. Let the L.M.S. employ what is publicly known as a 'proper architect' (not necessarily a knighted one).[37]

Perhaps the directors took notice. In February 1937 it was announced that the architect of the New Euston was to be not Oliver Hill, or even Sir Edwin Lutyens (who had renovated the Great Hall in 1927 and had been working on a scheme for rebuilding that same year[38]), but Percy Thomas (1883–1969), the designer of Swansea Civic Centre and the Temple of Peace at Cardiff. He was certainly a proper architect who happened to be President of the RIBA at the time and who only later would become a benighted knighted one. Thomas later recalled how Stamp 'asked me to go to America to see the stations and hotels there—and so I went. . . . The American stations were, of course, totally unsuited to our country and, before I left, Sir Josiah said to me: "I don't want you to look at them as something for you to copy, but rather as something not to

23 Unexecuted design for rebuilding Euston Station by Percy Thomas, 1937; rendered perspective by William Walcot. National Railway Museum, York.

do!'"[39] Thomas's proposal for Euston was certainly American in its scale and in its stripped Classical style with Art Deco massing was certainly typical of its time (fig. 23). However, by having a large multi-storey building flanked by lower wings facing towards Euston Square, the contemporary railway project it most resembled was the design by Herbert Rimpel for the proposed huge new Süd-bahnhof at the end of the North–South Axis in Albert Speer's plan for Berlin.

As Thomas's design envisaged the removal of the whole of the old station (including the inconveniently placed Great Hall) and of the buildings in front, which separated it from Euston Square, the new Georgian Group, founded in 1937, campaigned for the retention of the propylaeum. At first Thomas insisted that the 'Arch' could not be moved 'without smashing it to bits' but Josiah Stamp indicated that there was hope of saving it and Albert Richardson and Lord Gerald Wellesley, on behalf of the Group, persuaded the architects of the LMS that it could perfectly well be re-erected further south. Despite the objections of the Metropolitan Police on traffic grounds, this was the likely fate of the greatest architectural monument of the Railway Age when, on 12th July 1938, Lord Stamp, sitting in the Shareholders' Room designed by the younger Hardwick, 'turned a switch which closed a circuit and blasted out some 100,000 tons of limestone far away in the Caldon Low Quarries.'[40] But that stone was never to be used in Euston Square. At the end of the year, the committee of the Georgian Group was informed that 'financial stringency' made it unlikely that the rebuilding would proceed immediately.[41] And then war came. It was left, therefore, to the nation-alised railway industry, abetted by a cynical and philistine Prime Minister, to do the dirty deed. In 1961, having declined even to consider re-erecting Hardwick's 'Arch' elsewhere, the British Transport Commission, began to replace the old Euston by something much, much inferior to Percy Thomas's grand design.

The Second World War put a further heavy strain on the railways which, while contributing so much to the war effort, sustained considerable damage from enemy bombing. After, again, coming under central government control and with a Labour government elected in 1945, the ultimate fate of the Big Four was never really in doubt. At the very end of 1947, those emotive acronyms — LNER, LMS, SR and, above all, with its history stretching back over a century, GWR — officially became extinct. The future lay with the nationalised British Railways. It was a future which, arguably, saw the creation of some genuinely modern and thoughtful examples of railway architecture as well as the destruction of so many sound and serviceable Victorian buildings in favour of cheap and inefficient replacements. For mistakes, huge mistakes, were also made which, exacerbated by the malevolent indifference of successive governments, both Labour and Conservative, in the thrall of the powerful road lobby and its associated financial interests, merely encouraged further decline and demoralisation.

Only now, at the end of one (disastrous) century and the beginning of another, does there again seem to be a new railway architecture in Britain which reflects a new optimism about the continuing future of the most civilised and efficient mode of transport known to man.

I am grateful to Roger Bowdler, Elain Harwood and Alan Powers for their help during the preparation of this paper.

1   'Points from Papers and Addresses', *Architect & Building News* (28 April 1939), p.101.
2   Adrian Vaughan, *Railwaymen, Politics & Money. The Great Age of Railways in Britain* (London: 1997), p.223.
3   Illustrated in *The Liverpool Architectural Sketch Book*, vol.3 (London: 1913), and *Designs in Architecture by J.M. Whitelaw* (London: 1916).
4   William Haywood, *The Development of Birmingham* (Birmingham: 1918).
5   John Betjeman with John Gay, *London's Historic Railway Stations* (London: 1972), p.117.
6   Hamilton Ellis, *British Railway History 1877-1947* (London: 1959), p.369.
7   John Betjeman, 'London Railway Stations' in *First and Last Loves* (London: 1952), p.85.
8   *London's Historic Railway Stations*, p.78.
9   Vaughan, *Railwaymen, Politics & Money*, p.326 ff.
10 'Our Railway Stations', *Architect & Building News*, vol. 123 (7 March 1930), p.324.
11 Extract from Frank Pick, 'The Design of Modern Railway Stations in Europe and America' in the *Architect & Building News*, vol. 123 (7 March 1930), p.331.
12 William Walcot's 1926 scheme to replace Charing Cross Station by a grand Classical structure carrying a road bridge connecting County Hall and Trafalgar Square is illustrated in *Getting London in Perspective*, Barbican Art Gallery (London: 1984). For the Charing Cross Bridge and Waterloo Station rebuilding saga, see Gavin Stamp, 'The South Bank site', *Twentieth Century Architecture 5: The Festival of Britain*, Twentieth Century Society, 2001, p. 22ff.
13 Carroll L.V. Meeks, *The Railway Station. An Architectural History* (London & New Haven: 1957), p.148.
14 *British Railway History 1877-1947*, p.370.

15 'Our Railway Stations', p.324.

16 Gavin Stamp, 'Conversation with Ernö Goldfinger', *Thirties Society Journal* no.2 (1982), p.20.

17 Vaughan, *Railwaymen, Politics & Money*, p.335.

18 Like many architects anxious to establish their progressive credentials, Fry rewrote his own history or, rather, left it vague. His Fellowship nomination form (1938) states that he commenced practice as a partner of Adams & Thompson in 1927, but his Associateship form, written in November 1923, reveals that, on 1 September 1923, he had become 'Designer to Southern Railway.' This, combined with the information he chose to vouchsafe in his autobiography, suggests that he might have worked under J.R. Scott at the Southern for up to four years. The information given in some reference books that Fry worked for the Southern Railway during the years 1927 to 1930 is clearly incorrect.

19 Maxwell Fry, *Autobiographical Sketches* (London: 1975), p.125.

20 Information on Scott from J.L. Harrington via Michael H.C. Baker via Dr Roger Bowdler. Scott was the son of Andrew Scott, the partner of W. Hamilton Beattie, and articled to Leadbetter & Farley of Edinburgh before working in the office of John Belcher. Scott remains obscure as he was not a member of the RIBA. Notices in the architectural press of new Southern Railway stations sometimes omit his name as architect, possibly suggesting that the writers knew he was not responsible for the buildings designed under his name.

21 'Patrons of Architecture. No.III.- The Southern Railway', *Architect & Building News*, vol. 123 (7 March 1930), p.321.

22 All these stations are illustrated in Gordon Buck, *A Pictorial Survey of Railway Stations* (London, New York, Sydney, Toronto: 1992).

23 John Betjeman, 'London Railway Stations' in *First and Last Loves*, p.81.

24 John Betjeman, 'Antiquarian Prejudice' (1937) in *First and Last Loves*, p.60. In his obituary, Culverhouse was described as 'architectural assistant to the chief engineer of the Great Western Railway.'

25 *Builder* (3 February 1939), pp.247–48. Other examples include the new office building above the station at Newport of 1928 (Classical) and the small building at Parson Street, Bristol (modernistic): see A. Vaughan, *A Pictorial Record of Great Western Architecture* (Oxford: 1977).

26 *The Architects' Journal* for 2 February 1948 and 29 September 1949 record that Stratford and Maryland Stations had been given new booking offices, T.P. Bennett & Son acting as architectural consultants.

27 Vaughan, *Railwaymen, Politics & Money*, p.329.

28 Nikolaus Pevsner, *Buildings of England. London, except the Cities of London and Westminster* (Harmondsworth: 1952), p.370.

29 The nameboard, manufactured by G.C. Hawkes of Birmingham, is explained and illustrated at plate 291 in Roy Anderson and Gregory Fox, *A Pictorial Record of L.M.S. Architecture* (Oxford: 1981).

30 Hamlyn's RIBA Associateship nomination form (1920; sponsors: Reginald Blomfield, Ernest Newton and Aston Webb) reveals that he entered both the R.A. School of Architecture and the service of the L&NWR in 1911 and that he qualified in 1920. His Fellowship nomination form (1934) cites the new station buildings and offices at Shoreditch, 1928, the conversion of Welcombe House, Stratford-upon-Avon into an hotel, 1931–33, the LMS office building in Seymour Street, now Eversholt Street (with Victor Heal), 1933, and the new station buildings at South Kenton, 1933.

31 Shown under construction in Anderson and Fox, *A Pictorial Record of L.M.S. Architecture*, pl. 285. Also see Peter Carolin & Trevor Dannatt, eds., *Architecture, Education and Research. The Work of Leslie Martin: papers and selected articles* (London: 1996), pp.18–19.

32 Anderson and Fox, *A Pictorial Record of L.M.S. Architecture*, fig. 92.

33 *Builder* (30 June 1939), p.1234. The holiday camp has been demolished.

34 Alan Powers, *Oliver Hill. Architect and Lover of Life 1887–1968* (London: 1989), p.34; also see Alan Powers, 'The Stone and the Shell — Eric Gill and the Midland Hotel, Morecambe', *The Book Collector*, vol. 47, no.1 (Spring 1998).

35 Hamilton Ellis, *Four Main Lines* (London: 1950), pp.15–16.

36 *RIBA Journal* (25 March 1933, p.407.

37 John Betjeman, 'Dictating to the Railways', *Architectural Review*, vol. 74 (1933), p.84.

38   Lutyens wrote to his wife 16 July 1927: 'You ask me what I do. I am busy on a scheme for rebuilding Euston Station. Don't talk about it or say anything, it is a 7,000,000 project if it comes off': Clayre Percy and Jane Ridley, eds., *The Letters of Edwin Lutyens to his wife Lady Emily* (London: 1985), p.408.

39   Sir Percy Thomas, *Pupil to President* (Leigh-on-Sea: 1963), p.37, in which William Walcot's perspective drawing of his design is illustrated. Thomas's scheme was not published at the time, nor did he exhibit at the Royal Academy his rendered elevation by Walcot (reproduced in *All Stations. A Journey though 150 years of Railway History* (London: 1981), and in Anderson and Fox, *A Pictorial Record of L.M.S. Architecture*, and preserved at the National Railway Museum, York). The *Builder* (28 April 1939), p.792, records that after the lecture on 'Railway Stations', Thomas stated that 'he was disappointed that in dealing with American stations Professor Richardson dealt only with those that were out of date 20 years ago. The two modern stations he had in mind were the new Cincinnati station and the one at Philadelphia.'

40   Ellis, *Four Main Lines*, p.21.

41   Minutes of the committee of the Georgian Group, 5 January, 11 May, 25 May, 24 August, 12 October, 7 December 1938, see Gavin Stamp, 'Origins of the [Georgian] Group' in the *Architects' Journal*, vol. 175 (31 March 1982).

'A Little Grit and Ginger': The Impact of Charles Holden on the Architecture of the London Underground, 1923–40

Susie Barson

T HERE ARE 275 stations currently in use by passengers travelling on London's underground railway network. Of varying dates and architectural styles, they are easily recognisable primarily by the logo of a red circle intersected with a horizontal blue line representing station and track. This corporate symbol was created in 1908, in a slightly different form, for the London Underground Electric Railways Company, and adopted by the company's founder, Chicago financier Charles Yerkes, to brand the tube system as a unified one. Yet it is important to remember that the underground network evolved through the disparate activities of many private companies. Family resemblances between stations built in the late nineteenth century can still be identified, while the first decades of the twentieth century saw the emergence of a conscious corporate style for some of the lines and their stations.

Many examples of early underground stations survive and feature prominently in London's high streets. They show the hands of different architects: Harry Bell Measures's terracotta-faced stations on the Central Line of 1900; Leslie Green's 'oxblood' coloured stations for the Great Northern, Piccadilly and Brompton, 1903–07; Harry Ford's District Line stations in a similar vein at Earl's Court and Fulham Broadway, both of 1906. Green's jolly Edwardian-Baroque style was perpetuated by his assistant and successor Stanley Heaps at Maida Vale and Kilburn Park, of 1915 and 1916 respectively. Something consciously different was attempted by Charles Clark, the architect to the Metropolitan Line — the only sub-surface railway company not under the umbrella of the Underground group — with his white faience-clad stations of the 1920s, such as Farringdon, Willesden, Aldgate, and Great Portland Street. All these varied architectural approaches relied heavily on reinterpretation of classical idioms, and although they were successful at creating an immediately recognisable corporate identity, they were not always able to address the practical and functional problems of underground travel after 1918.

24 Frank Pick (1878-1941) worked for the railway companies from 1902. He became chief executive of the London Passenger Transport Board, 1933-40. Photograph © London Transport Museum.

25 Charles Henry Holden (1875-1960), at Frank Pick's invitation, designed a range of buildings for London Underground Group between 1924 and 1948. Photograph © London Transport Museum.

With the basis of the network established by 1920, the primary concern of the former L.U.E.R. Company, now renamed London Underground Group, was extension and modernisation of existing lines rather than the construction of brand new ones. Frank Pick (fig. 24), the Group's publicity manager, together with the chairman Albert Stanley, later Lord Ashfield, were determined that advertising on the Underground would contribute to the modernising process, as well as raising the public profile and glamourising the image of the London Underground Group. Frank Pick (1878–1941) was educated in York, qualified as a solicitor, and joined the North Eastern Railway Company in 1902, and the London Underground Group in 1906. As early as 1908, Pick had been involved in the design for a symbol or logo that would define the image of the London Underground Group. He was critical of the lack of clear signs on the stations, and of the way that station names and signs had often been painted on the tiles as a clumsy afterthought. Pick thus conceived of the idea of station name plates. Christian Barman's biography of Frank Pick, *The Man Who Built London Transport* (1979), explains his experimental approach:

26 Stanley Arthur Heaps FRIBA (1880-1962), appointed architect to London Underground in 1910 and worked with Charles Holden throughout the 1920s and 1930s. Photograph © London Transport Museum.

After a trial run it was felt that something a little more forceful was needed and experiments were carried out with sheets of paper overprinted in bright red colour, cut out in a near semi-circular shape. The red segment was pasted on a white background panel, one above and one below the name plate to make a full disc pattern. This time Pick was more satisfied; the bright red disc made all the difference to the name plate which now became quickly recognisable for what it was.[1]

Thus the 'bull's eye' was born. The architect Harry Ford later claimed that it was he who introduced the blue bar to form the roundel symbol that we know today, an early version of which was a blue bar on a solid red disc. From 1911, the Underground logotype with its large U and D appeared across the bar, and marked the tentative beginning of the Underground roundel as a company trademark. Versions of this symbol were incorporated into the decorative schemes of subsequent new stations such as Stanley Heaps's booking hall at Maida Vale of 1915.

Increasingly passionate about design in the environment in general, and still dissatisfied with the overall appearance of signage and advertisement on the Underground in particular, Frank Pick was soon deeply involved with the newly founded Design and Industries Association. This body concerned itself with new industrial design and manufacture, and its guiding principle, 'Fitness for Purpose', was adopted uncompromisingly by Frank Pick. Through the Association Pick met the calligrapher Edward Johnston, and in 1916 commissioned him to design the famous sans serif typeface, Johnston Sans, which Pick used throughout the network on signs and posters. These posters, by artists such as Fred Taylor, Edward McKnight Kauffer and Charles Nevinson, were also a result of Pick's enlightened patronage, and aimed to project an *avant-garde* image of the London Underground. Johnston's version of the roundel was registered as a trademark in 1917.

In the early 1920s, the Northern Line was extended from Golders Green to Edgware. The new stations, completed between 1923 and 1924, were designed by Stanley Heaps (fig. 26), by now staff architect of the London Underground Group. They were single storey, stone-fronted buildings whose front elevations were dominated by a classical colonnade. Frank Pick's biographer Christian Barman described the stations as 'a series of simple, unassuming designs having an air of cosy domesticity ... good neighbours to the homes of the commuters for whose travel they were built.'[2] Stanley Heaps himself later described the thinking behind his designs:

> As the line traversed a dormitory district it was thought that station architecture having a touch of domestic feeling about it would be in harmony with the environment. The stations of the Edgware line were dignified to command respect and sufficiently pleasing to promote affection; it helped the daily round of life if the first step in the morning inspired pleasant thoughts.[3]

Pick, however, eschewed Heaps's cosy classicism for stations on the southern branch of the Northern Line to Morden. According to Barman, Pick discussed the matter with connoisseurs of contemporary architecture (no names given) and was 'interested to find that among the names of architects mentioned with special respect was that of Charles Holden.'[4]

Since meeting Holden (fig. 25) in the early days of the Design and Industries Association, Pick had followed his work with the firm Adams Holden and Pearson with interest and 'liked him for his energy in pursuing the simple, honest, functional approach to design which the Association had made itself an advocate.'[5] Bypassing Stanley Heaps as worthy but uninspired, Pick asked Holden, in 1923, to improve the entrances at Westminster, Oval, Stockwell and Bond Street stations. Little more than shop fronts, these 'timid efforts', as Holden was later to call them, were the beginning of the revolution in design and architecture of the London Underground created by the partnership of Frank Pick and Charles Holden.

Holden's first job was to design an entrance to Westminster underground station next to Parliament Square in 1923 (fig. 27). It was a modest affair, a simple structure in concrete and render, a geometric fascia with a stepped lintel. There were no

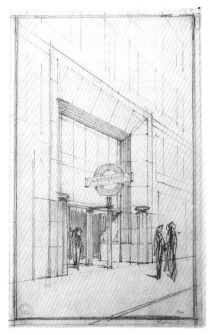

27 Entrance to Westminster Station, Holden's earliest design for London Underground in the modern style (1924; demolished). Photograph © English Heritage.

28 Holden's drawing of Morden Station entrance, 1924. Photograph by Geremy Butler. ©RIBA Library Drawings Collection.

columns, no swags, no egg-and-dart mouldings, no arches; merely a simple abstract form comprising a stepped parapet, an illuminated fascia and a doorway. Nothing architectural on the underground had resembled this before. Pick recognised in this elemental facade a new architectural idiom which, according to his biographer, constituted a 'step in the right direction'.[6] More jobs for Holden followed swiftly, notably the improvement of the booking halls at Clapham Common and Stockwell stations on the Northern Line, and on the Central Line. Huge skylights were inserted in the ceilings of the booking halls to increase daylight; ticket machines and escalators were installed, and modern facades were added.

Pick and Holden then turned their attention to the design of proposed new stations on the Morden extension of the former City and South London, now the Northern Line (fig. 28). Heaps, by this time London Underground's chief architect and still engaged on the project, later told of the consensus to adopt a style that would 'distinguish the stations from all other buildings,' and tantalisingly referred to a visit to the Exposition des Arts Decoratifs et Industriels Modernes in Paris in 1925 to 'obtain new ideas with the ultimate result now in evidence.'[7]

29 Station model, 1925. The stations on the Morden extension were to be built on corner sites of varying angles and the idea of a three-leaf folding screen was arrived at, the sides 'bent back' as far as necessary. Photograph © London Transport Museum.

30 Morden Station, 1926, by Charles Holden, the screen fully extended. Photograph © English Heritage.

Most of the new stations were to occupy corner sites in built-up streets. The problem of how to deal with entrances at corner sites of varying width and angles was solved with the principle of the three-leaf folding screen. This tripartite frontage could remain flat, as at Morden, or with the outer sides bent back to form a corner, as at Tooting Bec and Clapham South. A full-sized three-dimensional model or mock-up was set up in an engineering workshop in Earl's Court in 1925 (fig. 29), and Pick and Holden experimented with various forms of canopies and lighting. It was clearly an exciting, creative time, as Pick made clear in a letter quoted in Barman's biography:

> By way of an exciting finish, I may say that we are going to build our stations upon the Morden extension railway to the most modern pattern. We are going to discard entirely all ornament. We are going to build in reinforced concrete. The station will simply be a hole in the wall, everything being sacrificed to the doorway and some notice above to tell you to what the doorway leads. We are going to represent the DIA gone mad, and in order that I may go mad in good company I have got Holden to see that we do it properly.[8]

Seven new stations were built and completed by 1926, all treated in a similar architectural manner (figs. 30-32). The reinforced concrete frames and brick walls

31 Balham Station, 1926, by Charles Holden. This station illustrates the screen still opened out but with the wings pulled back to create two entrances. Photograph © London Transport Museum.

32 Tooting Bec Station, 1926, by Charles Holden, the screen wings pulled right back to form an acute angle, creating two large windows. Photograph © London Transport Museum.

were faced with Portland stone, and each had generous entrance halls lit by a huge window with an integral blue-and-red roundel in the glazing. The windows were divided by columns which were square in section and surmounted by a sphere intersected by a small horizontal slab: a three-dimensional London Underground roundel. Coloured mast-mounted roundels were also placed above the entrances and the map and posters clearly positioned. Inside, polygonal top-lit booking halls were decorated with narrow grey tiles with blue-black and green tiled borders, indicating the position for publicity posters.

Pick's idea of a giant doorway dominating the facade is shown in Charles Holden's drawings for Tooting Broadway on the Morden extension, showing the opening with glazed area above, and advertised by a standard bearing the roundel. The glazing allowed the entrance to be flooded with light at night. Describing the stations in 1927, Stanley Heaps emphasised the importance given to illumination:

> Special regard to the requirements of flood lighting determined the main features. The reinforced concrete canopy with enamelled iron fascia supplies the supports and cover for the lamps which project the light onto the walls above and below. The large window to accommodate the bull's eye device is the motive for the two storeys, the upper or window storey being given more height and importance than the lower or doorway storey. The projecting 'Underground' silhouettes with masts, which are also flood-lit, provide the necessary advertisement when the station is approached from the side.[9]

Between 1927 and 1929 Charles Holden was engaged on the headquarters building for London Underground on the south side of St James's Park, a giant office block incorporating an underground station. Holden's solution for the site was an ingenious cruciform plan that obviated the need for corridors on the outer edge of the building, and the strong steel frame enabled him to build high. The frame was clad on the exterior with Portland stone dividing the floor levels horizontally and the window bays vertically, with no mouldings or projections. At a later stage, despite fierce criticism, Holden was able to include works by famous sculptors of the day: Eric Gill, Jacob Epstein, Eric Aumonier and the young Henry Moore, on the exterior of the building. Norway granite was used for the main doorways, and for the plinths and bases of the ground floor columns. The capitals were made from black Belgian marble. The interior was also fitted out with high quality materials: travertine stone walls and floors, bronze-finished metalwork and fireproof teak. Concealed lighting and illumination from opaque glass shades enhanced the calm, elegant mood of the interior.

This attention to detail and materials was evident in Holden's contemporary recasting of the subterranean interior of Piccadilly Circus station between 1926 and 1928. In the space of twenty years the number of passengers using the station had increased from 1½ million to 25 million per year, and a more spacious station was desperately needed. Holden's idea was to emulate the shape of Piccadilly Circus below ground by creating a circular chamber, reached via short

33 Ealing Common station by
Charles Holden, 1931. Basil Ionides
(1884-1950), a leading interior
designer, created friezes of
coloured tiles with a jazzy ziggurat
pattern to line the polygonal booking hall. Photograph © English
Heritage.

passages tiled with matt dun-coloured tiles with dark borders. Part of the chamber was the open landing for the escalators; the other half was divided by a
double row of fifty columns forming a curved route; lining the outer sides were
bookstalls and shops, with wide plate glass windows. Lanterns at the tops of the
columns provided low-level calm and elegant lighting, enabling the finishing
materials, the travertine limestone wall panels and the red scagliola columns
with bronze-finish bases, to glow and twinkle. Bronze-finished escalators took
passengers down to platform level in tunnels lit by uplighters. Re-opened in
1928, the sub-surface booking hall was widely acclaimed and visited by engineers
from Moscow, and the German architect Erich Mendelsohn.

    A year later new stations were built on the western section of the Piccadilly
Line, Hounslow West and Ealing Common. In these buildings Holden developed the geometric form further, encasing the booking halls in heptagonal

envelopes with open entrances in the sides, sheltered by a long blue-glazed and back-lit canopy. The dark vestibule, favoured by Heaps on the Edgware line, had been dispensed with and the booking hall plan further refined. The walls were of load-bearing brickwork, with a reinforced concrete roof cast in situ. The exterior was faced in Aberdeen granite and Portland stone; the lively interiors (fig. 33), with colourful tiled friezes in a jazzy, stepped pattern, were designed by interior designer Basil Ionides (1884–1950). These stations represent the Morden style fully realised in a freestanding building.

The Morden extension was completed in 1929. Contemporary comment on Holden's stations for London Underground was highly favourable. Peter Morton Shand noted in the *Architectural Review* that:

> Built in the present decade for the present decade the stations constrain those who behold them to pass in rapid review all that differentiates it, in a structural sense, from preceding ones. There is a complete absence of the periodicity of that façade architecture which necessitates closer inspection of the building before one can be quite clear whether the building is a library or a public house. They look like tube stations and nothing else. Their only ornament is such as serves an immediate and practical purpose. Lovely in the glistening whiteness of their flooding at night, they stand prophetic beacons of the new age amidst a drab wilderness of Victorian edification ... it inculcates a proper pride in our own particular *zeitgeist*.[10]

Unfashionable as the notion of *zeitgeist* might be today, there is no doubt that Frank Pick and Charles Holden, together with a small circle of artists, designers and architects, shared a similar vision in which clarity of form expressed the clarity of purpose. As Shand concluded:

> The Underground Company stands for good engineering, good architecture, good posters, good design and good workmanship. Thank you Lord Ashfield and Mr Pick, or whoever is directing and inspiring genius, who is not afraid of being alive and giving us a little grit and ginger mixed with the pulp of publicity.[11]

Peter Morton Shand emphasised the point with a telling juxtaposition of photographs of Victorian stations with Holden's new architecture for the Underground.

Architectural magazines such as the *Architectural Review* and books on architecture published in England in the late 1920s and early 1930s reflected a new interest in contemporary European architecture. In 1927 the English translation of Le Corbusier's *Vers Une Architecture* appeared; in 1929 Henry Russell Hitchcock published *Modern Architecture*, extensively illustrating the works of Gropius, Oud and Dudok.

The journals published articles on topics such as suitability of new materials to particular purposes. Reporting on the Swedish and Paris exhibitions the journalists noted architects using materials such as glass and steel as a substitute for ornament, for example in the Tugendhat House (1929) by Mies Van Der Rohe. The all-glass Van Nelle factory at Rotterdam by J. A. Brinkman and L. C. Van der Vlugt was also well publicised in the press. These buildings were described as 'flexible, interesting and in genuine accord with modern needs'.[12]

F. R. Yerbury, secretary of the Architectural Association, published three seminal books in the late 1920s: *Dutch Architecture of the 20th century* (1927), *Modern European Buildings* (1928) and *Modern Danish Architecture* (1927). Yerbury was an excellent architectural photographer and his book *Modern Dutch Buildings*, published in London in 1931, excited warm praise. Among the buildings illustrated was the Volkandinj Co-operative Society building in the Hague, with a glass tower and strong verticals and horizontals. There were twelve pages of illustrations of the schools designed at Hilversum by Willem Marinus Dudok (1884-1974). With their blocky massing and relishing of the plain brickwork, these buildings were often selected for praise in reviews of the book.

Directly relevant to Pick and Holden's interest in underground stations was the publication of an article by the modernist champion Peter Morton Shand in the *Architects' Journal* of 1929 on the newly completed Berlin underground stations. The text and photographs paid tribute to the stations designed by Professor Alfred Grenander, the chief architect to the Berliner Verkehrs-Gesellschaft, the central traffic authority which operated Berlin's unified underground, tram and motor bus services. Morton Shand admired the clear signs, open spaces, and soft lighting inside the stations. He concluded: 'The general impression is one of orderliness, spaciousness and fitness for function expressed in a severe economic use of the best, most rational and durable materials.'[13]

Architects in Britain in this period were revelling in new structural techniques, 'light airy skeletons of steel weighing less, costing less and proving far more practical than the pre-First World War type of steel buildings veneered with ponderous stage scenery of expensive stone'.[14] Finishing materials such as bronze metal alloys and stainless steel grilles were becoming widely available.

This sense of a new spirit and fresh approach from the Continent interested and excited Charles Holden and Frank Pick. The two were focusing now on a new programme of extension works to the Piccadilly line and looking for inspiration.

34 The Naarden-Bussum railway station was completed in 1917 to the designs of H.G.J. Schelling. Holden admired its blending of new forms with traditional building materials.
Photograph © London Transport Museum.

Pick agreed to make a trip with the chairman's secretary, a young man called Edwards, and Holden, to see the new buildings on the Continent at first hand.

Writing many years later, W. P. N. Edwards, Lord Ashfield's former secretary, wrote that:

> Frank Pick was insistent that the new stations should be outstanding in every way, that they should be functional above all, capable of dealing with vast numbers of passengers with the maximum ease, comfort and safety, but that they should be architecturally first class. About this time there was a great deal of talk going on about the new functional movement in architecture in Europe. Since Frank Pick could never normally be persuaded to take a holiday, Lord Ashfield suggested to him that before we embarked on the Piccadilly line extension we ought to go and see for ourselves the latest architectural development in Europe. So it came about that Frank Pick took a busman's holiday in northern Europe, accompanied by Charles Holden with me acting as secretary and general dog's body.[15]

In two and a half weeks in the summer of 1930 the three men saw a variety of public buildings in Denmark, Sweden (including the Stockholm library by Gunner Asplund), and the German cities of Berlin, Hamburg, Dusseldorf and Cologne. At the end of the trip they visited towns in Holland, including the complex of civic buildings at Hilversum by Willem Dudok which Pick and Holden admired for their use of plain brickwork. They saw stadiums, factories, schools, town halls and, significantly, railway stations, including the earlier station at Bussum in Holland (fig. 34). This blocky, chunky, purely geometric and symmetrical building with its horizontal canopy and tall, gridded windows must have had a powerful impact on Holden.

An account of the tour was published in 1931 entitled *Note on Contemporary Architecture in Northern Europe*, and was circulated internally in London Underground. This document was signed by W. P. N. Edwards, but it is clear from the penetrating and thoughtful observations on the buildings that were visited, and the tightly argued conclusions, that the intellectual content is Charles Holden's. The key points in the document that formed the basis for Holden's mature approach to architecture concerned the use of modern structural techniques and the possibilities and freedoms that would result, together with the need for an aesthetic discipline to provide a framework within which to solve the particular architectural problem in hand.

Holden enthusiastically welcomed the freedom promised by the widespread use of both steel and the reinforced concrete frame. It meant that supporting arches were no longer necessary, that lighter coverings on the building could be used, and that fenestration was no longer restricted by load-bearing supports. Stylistically the impact would be felt with a tendency to rectilinear buildings and the increased use of cantilevered canopies of steel and concrete 'that can be projected from the side walls of shops or railway stations without visible support from below.'[16] He immediately identified the possibilities of building tall and wide, with flat roofs emphasising the horizontal. Reinforced concrete, he noted, would allow for more plastic or irregular shapes which could achieve an interesting contrast with the rectilinear steel-framed building, but pointed out that although it gave a finished surface it was as yet difficult to make the surface appear aesthetically pleasing. Perhaps the most important point for Holden when advocating the use of these new structural techniques and materials was to use them truthfully, that there was a need for *veracity* in architecture.

Charles Holden was no doubt familiar with the writings of Pugin and Ruskin and the passionate plea of those earlier writers to reject meaningless applied ornament and to allow the materials to visibly perform a particular function without the need to disguise them as something else for the sake of show or convention. New structures, according to Holden, require new forms; the architect could no longer rely on tradition to dictate them. But he believed, equally passionately, that a nation's traditional way of building should not be completely ignored by the architect. Rather, tradition was to 'act as a guide rather than as a medium for imitation'.[17] New liberty without discipline merely resulted in the bizarre: Erich Mendelsohn's observatory at Potsdam was cited as an extreme example, where exterior and interior bore no relation to each other.

Holden foresaw the necessity to take great care with massing of tall buildings, particularly with the need to set back the upper storeys to increase light and avoid external projections in densely built-up sites. Such lucid rational thinking does not, however, indicate a purely functionalist approach. Reduced to its essential function, argued Holden, a building could not necessarily claim to be beautiful. He welcomed the emphasis on function, declaring that 'Fitness for Purpose is a necessary tribute of all good design', and that functionalism was 'a sure foundation for the development of a new architecture',[18] but that for *beauty* a sense of unity, proportion and line was essential: qualities that were vital to architecture of all periods and cultures. The horizontal line, for example, lent itself well to modern architecture and was particularly appropriate for 'low lying buildings such as railway stations',[19] but the horizontal and vertical lines had to be controlled and held in tension by the architect. The new station at Hamburg was cited as a pleasing way to handle a horizontal canopy. The Hilversum schools by Dudok he loved, too, for this balance of horizontal against vertical and climactic massing, as well as for their use of traditional materials of brick, and their 'mental alertness'.[20]

Holden had already incorporated this sense of mental alertness in his underground stations of the 1920s. Holden's approach to construction and aesthetic forms, however, changed direction following his Continental trip. In the Piccadilly extension stations there is a marked decrease in the use of Portland stone facing, and an increased use of exposed concrete, glazed metal frames and concrete cantilevered roof canopies. Precedents for these forms can be found not only in the buildings that he saw abroad but also in the drip-feed of Continental examples published in the architectural weeklies between 1930 and 1932. The *Architects' Journal* for 29 July 1931 illustrated a concrete tramway shelter and kiosk at Brunn in Czechoslovakia, the shelter roof supported by a concrete pillar around which was a wooden seat, and positioned at a higher level was a timetable display case. In its simplicity, clarity and enjoyment of the possibilities of reinforced concrete, this latter structure is strikingly similar to shelters subsequently built by Holden for London Transport. The stadium cafe at Nuremberg, illustrated in the same issue, shows a circular concrete roof and central pillar immediately reminiscent of the stations at Sudbury Town (1931) and Arnos Grove (1932).[21] Subsequent editions of the *Architects' Journal* published seductive photographs of recent buildings such as Herpichs fur store in Berlin, by Erich

35 Sudbury Town Station, 1931, Charles Holden, showing, in the influence of contemporary European architecture. Photograph © London Transport Museum.

Mendelsohn, with its lighting troughs in the base of windows, and the Garage Marboeuf by night with light flooding through the glass walls.

Naturally one must beware of attributing all Holden's ideas to these examples, or, indeed, the other way around (for example, Mendelsohn's Herpichs store was built after his visit to London in 1928). There is not much point in trying to identify which came first, but it seems clear that a mutual inspiration and use of a common architectural vocabulary was taking place in the early years of the 1930s.

Shortly after returning from the Continent, Holden was engaged by Frank Pick to design stations for the new railway extensions at either end of the Piccadilly line, to Uxbridge in the west, and to Cockfosters in the north east of London. Charles Holden worked intensively on this project between 1930 and 1933. The first to be built was Sudbury Town (fig. 35), and this was the first appearance of 'the brick box with a concrete lid'. With its clear, high, open and rationally organised space, its tall glazed openings that served as both windows and entrances, its proximity to a bus forecourt, Sudbury Town was truly modern. It was designed in an abstract style where the emphasis was on form rather than applied decoration, and exploited modern materials: glass, mass-produced metal components and new technology, concrete cast in situ. The geometry was sophisticated and balanced. Peter Morton Shand referred to these stations as 'a

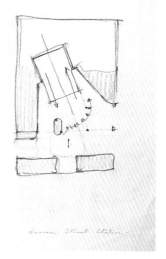

36 The striking circular ticket hall of Chiswick Park station, 1932, Charles Holden. Photograph © London Transport Museum.

37 Holden's diagram to show passenger flow at Warren Street station. © RIBA Library Drawings Collection.

standard type, a purely functional design that would be hard to improve on'.[22] Sudbury Town represented not only Holden's newly formulated architectural ideas based on contemporary Continental examples he had seen abroad, but also a synthesis of his and Frank Pick's ideas for a functional model for subsequent stations.

Three stations were built on the Sudbury Town model: Sudbury Hill, Northfields and Chiswick Park. Their prominent geometric and spacious booking halls allowed ease of movement between entering, buying a ticket and moving down onto the escalator (fig. 36). This was another example of Holden's rational thinking, his own 'mental alertness', which had an impact on the design of his stations and those designed subsequently by other architects.

What was more important to Charles Holden than the question of style was the interrelationship between the booking hall and the connecting spaces to the platforms, in short, the efficient use of the building. This was made clear by Holden's many architectural sketches for stations that concern themselves with passenger movement (fig. 37). Even the plan was dictated by the function, as can be seen in these diagrams. Using simple geometry, he aligned openings to control the flow and direction of movement in a manner that Leslie Green and even Heaps had not really addressed in a coherent and rational way. His approach is further illuminated by his published thoughts on the subject. Holden's theory was most clearly expressed in an article titled 'Designing a Passenger Station', published in 1933 in *Design for Today*. 'The first principle in planning a building for any purpose', Holden began, 'is for the architect to put himself in the place of the user, and this still holds in the case of the pigsty.'[23] Holden accordingly 'became' a passenger and took the reader through the journey on the Underground, identifying the necessary elements to a smooth, safe journey on the way. The principal factors he identified included a clear sign to tell you the location of a station and an entrance 'that could not be anything else';[24] a map of the system, illuminated at night; the cost of the journey clearly displayed close to the ticket machines, themselves widely spaced so as not to be obstructive; a centrally placed ticket office or 'passimeter'; and easy and unobstructed access to the platforms, 'without the danger of clashing with the incoming passengers.'[25]

Holden concluded that: 'It all seems so simple if you think of architecture in terms of service instead of in terms of design by formula based on this or that precedent.'[26] This clearly expresses the importance to Holden of thinking around the problem afresh.

This was by no means a wholly original approach. Holden and Pick had considered the passengers when working on the Morden extension and the Piccadilly Circus booking hall, where Holden had rejected the accepted classical spacing of columns in order allow freer circulation around and between them. What was new, following the Continental tour, was the way in which function and form had become even more closely integrated in Holden's stations, and the tighter relationship of the booking hall to the platforms and track. Symmetrical, rational, comprehensible inside and out; these were the qualities that distinguished Holden's stations from the muddles of entrances, warrens of tunnels and passages of earlier stations.

The northern extension of the Piccadilly line grew out of a demand for transport north of Finsbury Park. Following an enquiry of 1925, the extension was approved and was to be funded by the Government and the Treasury, with £12.5 million being allocated for building and improvements over the next fifteen years. The new programme was to include new improvements across the board: no sharp curves on the tracks for speed and smoothness, wider trains, wider tunnels, more efficient ventilation with more shafts in between stations. The first part of the journey was to be in a tunnel; the rest in the open with three viaducts. The viaducts, platforms, bridges, and retaining walls were the province of the engineer.

Holden was to be responsible for the design of eight new stations to be built over the next two years: Manor House, Turnpike Lane, Wood Green, Bounds

Green, Arnos Grove, Southgate, Enfield West (later renamed Oakfield), and Cockfosters. He had to take into account access at road level or below; the location of stairs and escalators; the provision of interchange with buses; the need for forecourts, car depots, signal boxes, electric sub-stations, and cabins for the rail men. Never before had so much become the domain of the architect. Holden concerned himself with the design of the stations, Stanley Heaps supervised the design and building of sub-stations, depots, and staff canteens.

Each station varied according to requirements. Standardisation was possible only in so far as questions of detail and finish were concerned: the result was a family resemblance rather than being identical. This was deliberate policy on Holden's part, expounded in his article on station design. Having listed the necessary functions of a station, he noted that:

> It might be supposed that if all considerations were worked out on paper a standardised station of monotonous uniformity would result, especially as a certain family resemblance is desirable in the treatment of the stations; but fortunately we have other considerations which make each and every station a new adventure in the design while yet fulfilling these several requirements: some local peculiarity of the site such as a corner site, a curved or flat frontage, the alignment of the booking hall in relation to the escalators or the railway track. There is no need to go out of one's way in search of novelty; a proper sense of fitness for purpose will supply all the material for adventure.[27]

The stations themselves illustrate this. At Arnos Grove, for example, the station was built in an open cutting, with a wide bridge on one side and a car park on the other. The circular hall, erected out of prefabricated concrete members, was to counter the fall in the roadway; the horizontal base took its cue from the parapet wall of the bridge. At Wood Green Station the curved façade echoed the bend of the road in front of it. The booking hall at Turnpike Lane was planned to be visible from many points of view at a busy road junction, with a large ventilation tower serving for greater publicity. Tramway island shelters with curved canopies of reinforced concrete were designed as part of the group; the ensemble was one of Pick's favourite compositions. Another was the Underground and bus station interchange at Southgate, where the low circular booking hall was sited within the long curve of the bus station on one side and traffic-controlling roundabouts on the other (fig. 38). This tightly planned group was finished in 1933, the year that the London Passenger Transport Board came into being, and the services of buses and trains could be integrated in the manner of the contemporary German

38, 39 Southgate Station, 1933 by Charles Holden, exemplifying Pick's vision of an integrated transport system. Photograph © London Transport Museum (38). Photograph © English Heritage (39).

system. Every detail on the escalators, shop fronts and electric light fittings were either designed by or specified by the architect; Pick was adamant that the architect should have this supreme control. The escalators, uplighters and freestanding lamp stands designed by Holden are particularly well preserved at Southgate Station (fig. 39) which, along with Oakwood and Arnos Grove, was, in 1971, one of the first twentieth-century stations to be included on the national statutory list for its architectural and historical interest.

Charles Holden took great care to please Frank Pick and incorporate places for advertisements on every station. A T-shaped concrete post on the platform could serve as both a station name stand and poster stand in one. Stripped of classical ornament and applied decoration, the beauty of the stations were to be enhanced by the strategic placing of eye-catching and didactic posters. The importance of a good relationship between the architect and the publicity manager was stressed by Holden in his article, with a sly reference to Pick:

> The publicity manager is another dreadful creature who is out for the architect's blood, and if the architect is a wise man he will make the publicity manager his friend for life by sublimating the poster into the principal decoration of the station. But apart from the matter of policy, the poster is in fact a power for decoration, and all other decoration must be made to assist in its effective display so that it is not only good as decoration, it is good as an attraction to the potential buyer; it is good publicity for the advertiser and it is good as a revenue producer.[28]

The hearts of Pick and Holden were beating as one.

Charles Holden took great care with the construction of the stations and later noted how well the stations were built:

> On these stations we have taken infinite trouble in the choice of suitable bricks for colour and weathering qualities and for good appearance over a number of years. The bond, the mortar and the method of striking the joints were also carefully considered. The concrete mix was the outcome of the experiment and test with a view to satisfactory weathering without sacrifice of strength. The shuttering was a work of art in itself, firm as a rock, clean and true as was the concrete itself. The foreman in charge was a great man and I take my hat off to him. Architecture is not a one-man show.[29]

In the London Transport Archives there is an informative letter from Charles Hutton (1905–95), Charles Holden's chief assistant from 1929 until 1936, concerning the construction of the stations in this period. He described how the fore-man referred to by Holden, a man called Mr Bye, had cast the concrete in situ at Arnos Grove, but that the unset concrete slurry had run down the sides of the brickwork and stained it. In order to avoid this problem, the concrete was cast first and the components assembled on site around the steel frame in subsequent stations. Once the concrete roofs were in place, brick infills between the columns came next, and internal finishes and glazing were carried out under cover.[30]

Hutton is also interesting on the relationship between Holden and his team, who were encouraged to work up an idea from the architect's own small sketch. This allowed the assistants a certain amount of original input. Boston Manor tower, for example, was Charles Hutton's own idea, which he claimed was based not on a Dutch precedent but on that of a simple organic form, a cactus, to advertise the presence of the station. When the work increased beyond his capacity, outside architectural firms were employed to follow Holden's ideas through, even though this was not always popular with Frank Pick. A sketch by Holden or one of his assistants was worked up by the consultant architects to a scaled drawing for approval by Pick, who liked the drawings to focus on essentials and distrusted large elaborate perspectives.

Holden was clearly regarded with affection and respect by his colleagues; his authority or architectural judgement was seldom challenged, and his influence could clearly be seen in the stations designed in collaboration with the other architects. On one occasion he was crossed by the engineer Harley H. Dalrymple-Hay. Dalrymple-Hay had transported some cast-iron Gothic capitals to the site at Arnos Grove, to hide the steelwork used in the construction of the bridge. Holden objected, maintaining that the steelwork had been beautifully designed and should be left exposed. Dalrymple-Hay appealed to Pick who refused to get involved, saying that they must sort it out between themselves. Charles Hutton, relating this story, concluded it by drily observing 'As far as I know they were never fitted.'[31]

Holden had a particularly sympathetic relationship with the architect C. H. James, who had worked up the design for Enfield West Station (now Oakwood). James accompanied Holden in leading a tour of the newly completed Piccadilly line extension in November 1933. Around fifty architects from the Royal Institute of British Architects went out for the day to look at the results. Their views were reported in the *RIBA Journal*:

Perhaps the most impressive thing about the work of the Underground railway is that every detail so clearly expresses one unifying influence. That the

40 St. John's Wood, 1939. Photograph of interior © English Heritage.

41 Park Royal exterior, designed by Uren, follows Holden's brick box style. Photograph © English Heritage.

directors of the railway should have correlated every part of their organisation, that everything from a poster or a doorknob to a completed railway station should so clearly express Underground is an achievement of which they have reason to be proud.[32]

Throughout the inter-war period Stanley Heaps had been working on buildings other than the passenger stations designed or supervised by Holden. Between 1935 and 1940 a new works programme was begun on the Bakerloo line to Wembley Park, and Heaps became the superintending architect of this campaign which included new stations at St. John's Wood, Swiss Cottage, Finchley Road and Harrow on the Hill, Uxbridge and Rayners Lane. St. John's Wood (1938–39), a station for which Heaps is credited, clearly shows Holden's influence in the use of steel frame with reinforced concrete panels for the circular booking hall, brick walls with rounded corners, concrete cills and cornices, internal finish in tiling, faience and glazed brick, shop fronts and poster panels in bronze, and uplighters on the escalators (fig. 40). Despite the development of flats above, much of the original station is still there. Warren Street (1939) was also designed by Stanley Heaps, but with Holden's direct involvement in arriving at a solution to the booking hall layout, as the latter's passenger flow diagrams testify. One senses a complete absorption of Holden's modernism by Stanley Heaps, which had begun with the Morden extension and ended with his Bakerloo line stations. Heaps retired in 1943.

Holden's collaborators at Rayner's Lane (Reginald Uren, 1938), Park Royal (Welch and Lander, 1935–36) and Uxbridge (L.H. Bucknell, 1938) utilise many Holdenian characteristics, particularly in the use of common materials, brick and concrete, and the massing of geometric forms. Park Royal is in a strong Dudokian idiom (fig. 41), and encases the staircases linking bridge to platforms just as Holden had done at Sudbury Hill, while Uxbridge employs the same concrete and glass train shed as Cockfosters. Charles Holden also worked with Bucknell on the Northern line stations at East Finchley (1939), distinguished by the Gropian glazed staircase towers and the sculpture of the archer by Eric Aumonier, and Highgate (1941). Holden's last work for London Underground were the stations on the eastern extension of the Central line: Redbridge, Wanstead and Gants Hill, with its famous sub-surface booking hall in the Piccadilly Circus vein, and a wide, tiled vaulted hall between the platforms. The above-ground buildings for these stations were not, however, particularly successful, especially the crudely sited ventilation shafts in the roundabout at Gants Hill. This is partly because they were completed in a hurry after the Second World War to revised, simpler plans that matched the financial and aesthetic austerity of the immediate post-war years.

Frank Pick, with an association with railways going back to 1902, unwillingly retired as vice-chairman of the London Transport Board in 1940, a post which he had held since 1933. Correspondence between Pick and Holden on this occasion is moving; each acknowledged the debt to the other and both clearly immensely valued the colloboration. Charles Holden subsequently directed his energies into town planning and carried out very little for London Underground after the war.

The achievement of the Frank Pick–Charles Holden collaboration was visible in the bus and tram shelters, stations, signs, fixtures and fittings all over London, all touched by the shared belief in a rational aestheticism. Frank Pick's role, of course, had been crucial in this. From the 1920s he had fixed on forward-looking, uncompromisingly modern designs. By the mid-1930s Frank Pick was probably more of a rampant modernist than Holden. Pick greatly admired the work and thought of Walter Gropius, and, following a visit from the famous German architect and founder of the Bauhaus to England in 1934 for an exhibition of his work at the RIBA, Pick wrote an introduction to a book by Gropius published in 1935. *The New Architecture and the Bauhaus* was based on the lecture Gropius had given

42 Croxley Green
in C. W. Clark's
vernacular style, 1925.
Photograph ©
London Transport
Museum.

43 Stanley Heaps's
neo-Georgian
Hendon Central
Station, 1923.
Photograph ©
London Transport
Museum.

to the DIA. Pick passionately endorsed Gropius's faith in new materials — steel, glass and concrete — as the materials for the future, from which a 'true architecture can be established',[33] and the benefit to both architects and industrial designers from a common and wide-ranging training. Both Pick and Holden shared Gropius's vision for something beyond pure functionalism, an 'aesthetic satisfaction of the human soul'.[34]

How has the reputation of the architecture fared since the 1930s? The Danish architectural writer Steen Eiler Rasmussen devoted a whole chapter to the London Underground in *London: The Unique City*, written in 1934 and published in English in 1937; Pick was invited to America soon afterwards to advise the Department of Street Railways in Detroit, Michigan. Some years later Nikolaus Pevsner praised the new stations in *The Buildings of England, Middlesex* published in 1951, as representing 'the style of today … outstanding examples of how satisfying purely by careful detailing and good proportions such unpretentious buildings can be.'[35] London Underground was internationally famous, envied and admired.

Holden's unique achievement was in the realisation of a philosophy in built form. His stations functioned well, and still function well; they are striking pieces of architecture and, to echo architectural writer and critic Ian Nairn, as fresh today as when they were built. Arnos Grove, Cockfosters, Oakwood and Southgate are stations that embody theory and practice in an exceptionally pleasing way, whether it be the relationship to the site; the visual tension between vertical and horizontal; the quality and appearance of materials; the clarity of composition and ease of passenger movement. All these considerations come together in these fine buildings. What is not there — unless you count the use of brick in the suburban stations — is the love of native tradition that Holden claimed to hold dear. For neo-vernacular one must look to the pre-First World War Metropolitan Line stations designed by Charles W. Clark at Croxley Green (fig. 42), Watford, Kingsbury and Stanmore; for neo-Georgian, the inter-war colonnaded stations on the Northern Line by Stanley Heaps at Brent Cross, Hendon Central (fig. 43), Colindale, Burnt Oak and Edgware.

The style of stations on the underground built since the war has inevitably evolved from that of Holden's iconic buildings, although a few post-war stations of the 1940s, such as Loughton, White City and Hanger Lane, pay homage to the Holden style. The firm Adams, Holden and Pearson completed their last work for the Underground in 1961, the year after Holden had died, with the reconstruction of Mansion House station. When the Victoria Line was constructed in the 1960s, the work was carried out by London Transport's in-house design team, led by chief architect Kenneth Seymour and Misha Black. Blackhorse Road's opening inaugurated the first section of the line from Walthamstow to Highbury and Islington in 1968, and its glass and brick-clad booking hall, decorated on the exterior by a fibre-glass relief of a black stallion by David McFall RA (1919–88) with mosaic by Trata Drescha (b.1928), is decidedly reminiscent of Holden's style.

Thirty years later, the influence of Holden and Pick on the principles of design and construction of underground stations on the recently extended Jubilee Line has been plainly evident. At Canary Wharf, for example, designed by Norman Foster's architectural practice in 1992 and opened in 1999 as part of the Jubilee extension, three dramatic curved and steel glass canopies rise from the ground to form the envelope of the station (fig. 44). They are more than shelters from the weather: the elliptical glass canopies act as lanterns to beam as much light as possible deep into the station below. Reinforced concrete columns weigh the building down as it lies below the waterline. Concrete is left exposed. Nothing in the building has been staged for effect; everything has been done for load-bearing, mechanical-engineering or acoustic reasons. Cabling is hidden away leaving clear, open spaces for the expected thousands of passengers, and directional flow is unencumbered. It stands the DIA test of 'fitness to purpose'. The spirit of Charles Holden and Frank Pick lives on.

44 Canary Wharf, Foster and Partners, designed 1992, opened 1999. The glazed canopy covers the entrance to a hole in the ground rather than Pick's idea of 'a hole in the wall'.
Photograph © Susie Barson.

1   C. Barman, *The Man Who Built London Transport, A Biography of Frank Pick* (London: David & Charles, 1979), p.30.

2   Barman, *The Man Who Built London Transport*, p.113.

3   S. Heaps, *Design of Stations*, T.O.T. Staff Magazine (February 1927), London Transport Museum Library, p.36.

4   Barman, *The Man Who Built London Transport*, p.114.

5   *Ibid.*, p.114.

6   Barman, *The Man Who Built London Transport*, p.115.

7   Heaps, *Design of Stations*, p.37.

8   Barman, *The Man Who Built London Transport*, p.118.

9   Heaps, *Design of Stations*, p.37.

10   *The Architectural Review* (November 1929), p.217.

11   *Ibid.*, p.235.

12   *The Architects' Journal* (July 1931), p.102.

13   'Order on the Underground in Berlin,' *The Architects' Journal*, vol.70 (1929), pp.302-09.

14   *The Architects' Journal* (July 1931), p.102.

15   Quoted in D. Neumann, *The European Influence on Charles Holden's Architecture of the 1930s*, Architectural Association Thesis (1980), London Transport Museum Library G811.265/1996, 77.

16   W. P. N. Edwards, *A Note on Contemporary Architecture in Northern Europe* (London: London Transport 1931), p.2.

17   *Ibid.*, p.3.

18   *Ibid.*, p.5.

19   *Ibid.*, p.10.

20   *Ibid.*, p.11.

21   These buildings are illustrated in *The Architects' Journal*, 29 July, 5 August, and 16 December 1931.

22   *The Architects' Journal*, 25 November 1931, p.694.

23   C. Holden, in *Design for Today*, vol.1 (August 1933), p.135.

24   *Ibid.*, p.135.

25   *Ibid.*, p.135.

26   *Ibid.*, p.135.

27   *Ibid.*, p.135.

28   *Ibid.*, p.135.

29   RIBA Library Holden Papers AHP/4/6/ i (ii).

30   London Transport Museum Library Archives: Frank Pick Collection, letters F18.

31   *Ibid.*

32   RIBA Journal (11 November 1933), p.28.

33   W. Gropius, *The New Architecture and the Bauhaus* (London: Faber and Faber, 1935), Introduction by Frank Pick, p.7.

34   *Ibid.*, p.20.

35   N. Pevsner, *The Buildings of England, Middlesex* (London: 1951), p.151.

Reappraising British Railways

Elain Harwood

THE POST-WAR STORY of Britain's surface railways is a frustrating one of ill-focused management and wasted opportunity within a climate that grew ever more favourable to road transport. This was not foreseen in the early 1950s, since there was an initial growth in railway journeys, both of passengers and freight.[1] The lack of scientific economic forecasting, close regional loyalties, and an inherited belief in providing a public service that conflicted with the new ideology of business planning are deep-rooted features of post-war railway management. In this it took the naivety then found in much British industry to exceptional lengths. It is, then, remarkable that in the short period when considerable investment was made in new station buildings and signal boxes, sophisticated attempts were made at standardisation and buildings of striking quality were produced. It is a story not told in the many general histories of railway nationalisation.

The 1947 Transport Act founded a wide-ranging British Transport Commission, with a Railway Executive to take over the four main-line railway operators and fifty-four smaller 'undertakings'. The 'Big Four' private railway companies, the London & North Eastern Railway, London, Midland & Scottish Railway, Southern Railway and Great Western Railway, had been created in 1921–23 after a brief period of government control in the First World War. There had been heated arguments for nationalisation in 1919. By 1945 nationalisation was Labour Party policy, envisaged by Herbert Morrison as the centrepiece of an integrated transport system of road, rail and water of the kind he had proposed for London in the inter-war period. The principle of nationalisation also enjoyed considerable support from a Conservative Party who, as the dominant partner in the pre-war National Government, had already set up the British Overseas Airways Corporation in 1939.[2]

The organisations of the Big Four were strong, distinctive and loyal. The most progressive in the inter-war period was Southern Railways, which under the leadership of Sir Herbert Walker intensified a programme of electrification begun in 1909 and which made it by 1939 one of the largest electrified systems in the world.[3] The other big companies had more mixed fortunes in the inter-war period, particularly as freight income from coal and heavy industry fell away in the 1920s. Their development of more efficient locomotives and investment in catering services made for faster and more commodious long-distance passenger services, but masked a general stagnation and disinvestment. By 1939 it was becoming clear that the London & North Eastern Railways would not be able to live off its reserves for much longer.

An exceptional enterprise was the Scientific Research Department established by the LMS in 1932. The LMS, created in 1923 from two relatively large and thirty-three smaller companies, had 38% of the total railway mileage in Britain and was much the largest of the Big Four, with interests in Northern Ireland and Wales as well as in Scotland. It was, moreover, by far the largest non-government business enterprise in the United Kingdom, with a stockholders' capital of £414 million that compared, for example, with just £74 million held by ICI. Its management system was akin to those of many American companies (though not specifically railway companies) in having a Board formed of a President and Vice Presidents; the operating and commercial departments were managed by a single Vice President, who was a mechanical engineer. The Scientific Research Department seems to have been the personal interest of the President, Sir Josiah (later Lord) Stamp, who opened specialised laboratories and testing facilities at Derby in 1935. The Scientific Research Department was divided into six main sections: engineering, metallurgy, paint technology, physics, textiles and chemistry. With a staff of 150, of whom sixty were graduates, it could 'give advice or conduct investigations on probably a wider range of subjects than any research organisation in the country', as well as foster close links with universities and government organisations.[4]

The Architect's Department was independent of this structure, being part of the engineering and planning division at Watford. But the same spirit of research was present in the first specifically termed 'development group' of any architectural service in the country. This had close links not only with Derby but with the British Research Station (now Building Research Establishment) founded at Garston just outside Watford in 1918. Leslie Martin joined as Principal Assistant Architect in 1939:

> I joined a public office ... precisely because I realised that a change was taking place in the whole range of building work and the scale of its production. It seemed obvious that developments of this kind should be preceded by some investigation of the problems involved.[5]

The LMS was very conscious of the work of Frank Pick, Charles Holden and others for London Transport, who had established a consistent design policy

45 Hoylake Station. LMS Architect's Department, 1938. Photograph: Elain Harwood.

evident in everything from the rolling stock to the buildings and the posters that adorned them. For Steen Eiler Rasmussen, visiting London for the first time in 1927–28, 'the only true modern construction is, taken as a whole, not architecture: the Underground'.[6] Rasmussen was quick to draw comparisons between the Underground and the traditional railways. 'Nothing on earth is as dirty and depressing as the "real" London stations. Everything seems to be coated with soot, and the old-fashioned edifices with their many grooved spaces of brick wall, their gimcrack ornamentation and the iron framework of the roofs, seems made on purpose to collect the dust. It would be an absolute impossibility to clean them. No one could ever feel attracted by the stations which are a necessary evil, a filthy connecting link with the journey. On the other hand it is a pleasure to go down into the stations of the Underground, bright clean and orderly as they are.'[7]

The LMS had only a limited opportunity to demonstrate a new approach before the war, with the electrification of the 'Wirral lines' between Birkenhead Park, New Brighton and West Kirby in 1938. Here they developed a series of distinctive station buildings, responding to the different sites but with considerable standardisation in the smaller shelters. The largest station, at Hoylake (fig. 45), shows the north European influence seen in Charles Holden's London Underground stations. Apsley (1935) was also built of concrete, its smooth lines again reminiscent of London Underground work. At South Kenton (1933), the Architect's Department under W. H. Hamlyn experimented with the use of enamelled iron panels, on a timber frame. Not only was smoke a problem, but the cast-iron brakes created magnetised brake dust and Hamlyn's team sought a finish which could be wiped clean.[8] In 1940 a Building Research Committee was set up under the engineer Sir Alfred G. C. Egerton to consider the production of a durable, quickly erected, yet flexible modular station building to replace those destroyed by enemy bombing. The architect members of the Committee were W. H. Hamlyn (the chief architect), Leslie Martin, and Richard Llewelyn Davies, who acted as secretary and co-ordinator. There was also a structural engineer, a heating and lighting consultant, and a medical officer. Though much of their wartime work was devoted to building hostels and temporary facilities, the team made a full study of station planning, and looked at the performance of structures and finishes. Martin considered that their emphasis on prefabrication continued a railway tradition of using iron, glass and timber in standardised designs, such as the London & North Western Railway had built at Boxmoor, Hertfordshire, in 1875, and indeed Fox and Henderson had built at Oxford as early as 1851.[9] It was soon decided to erect a full-size prototype, which was constructed at Queen's Park as early as December 1945. That the system was a success is shown by the way this was moved to West Hampstead in around 1950, modified, and still stands today (fig. 46).

The Queen's Park building predated Hertfordshire County Council's system-built schools by a couple of years. Llewelyn Davies and his assistant, John Weeks, developed close links with Ernest Hinchcliffe and Hills and Company of West Bromwich well before this firm began working with Hertfordshire on school buildings. The LMS work had a mature sophistication, for although the main frame supporting the roof was on the 8'3" grid already used for schools in Sussex and Middlesex, the separate wall frame pioneered the neat and flexible 3'4" grid based around the size of a door and the metric unit. Davies was sitting on a RIBA Committee for 'Dimensional Co-ordination' at the time. The system was a parallel grid, with the principal posts and those for the secondary walling following separate though parallel modules. This was well seen in the waiting room at Stonebridge Park station, erected in 1948 entirely to Llewelyn Davies's design and demolished in 1998.[10] Although it had been championed by Walter Gropius with his 'General Panel System' between 1943 and 1947, 3'4" was not developed by Hertfordshire County Council until 1950, while the concept of the parallel grid, used by Leslie Martin and his team at the Royal Festival Hall, was

46 West Hampstead (now Thameslink) Station. LMS Architect's Department 1945, moved in 1950 to present location from Queen's Park. Photograph: Nigel Corrie, English Heritage.

not fully explored until the 1960s, when it became fashionable as a means of concealing large service ducts in university research buildings and laboratories and was developed as the 'tartan grid'.[11]

Although Queen's Park was a tiny building, comprising just a waiting room, heating chamber and lavatory, every detail was carefully thought through. It featured the enamelled metal panels pioneered in the 1930s, set over a dado-height wall of concrete blocks textured with a tough granite aggregate and set forward as a buffer to railway barrows. Behind the walls the main steel frame carried the stepped, cantilevered roof canopy. Windows and doors were either of steel or were 'bronzed': those originally installed at Queen's Park experimented with both finishes. As re-erected at West Hampstead the lavatory was omitted and bronzed fenestration adopted throughout.

Queen's Park was rapidly followed by the larger Marsh Lane and Strand Road Station, now Bootle New Strand, with a ticket office, waiting room and porter's den. John Weeks recalls how the big sheets of glass attracted local youths, who peppered them with air gun pellets. The station was demolished in the 1980s.

47 Stonebridge Park Station. LMS Architect's Department, 1947, demolished. Photograph: Nigel Corrie, English Heritage.

At Stonebridge Park (fig. 47) the quirky, two-stepped roof canopy of Queen's Park and Marsh Lane was abandoned in favour of a sharply angled monopitch roof, while Davies revised the cladding system and found money for hardwood windows, given a thick varnish.[12] However, there was neither money nor enthusiasm for an extended building programme upon nationalisation. Martin went to the London County Council, while Llewelyn Davies and Weeks joined a multi-disciplinary research team set up by the Nuffield Provincial Hospitals Trust.

Though road transport's challenge to the railways' position as the principal carrying service was not made until the 1950s, there had been warning signs since the 1920s. The operating ratio, or the working costs as a percentage of revenue, had increased from 51% in 1870–74 to 62% in 1900, where it stayed until 1914, and rose steadily thereafter. After the First World War, road vehicles took over many short-distance passenger and freight services, while coal haulage remained well below pre-1914 levels even in the 'recovery years' of 1934–38. The Big Four were obliged to accept even the most unprofitable traffic on an inflexible, published rate structure fixed by government, who also regulated wages and conditions. The worst controls were challenged by the companies' 'Square Deal Campaign' in 1938, but the war prevented any changes becoming law and instead more restrictions were placed on their charges. An agreement made in September 1941, and backdated to 1 January, gave the railways a guaranteed net revenue of £43.5 million; the government took any surplus, but agreed to establish an accumulating trust fund to support deferred repairs and renewals. The result was that the companies saw little extra revenue from the 50% increase in freight mileage, by 1944, and 67% increase in passenger numbers. By 1945 there was a thirty-month backlog of repairs, while 39% of the engines were over thirty-five years old and the wagon stock was even older.

Nationalisation did not lead to an immediate investment in the railways, in spite of their poor condition after years of war and shortages. Why was so little done? The prospect of nationalisation, first publicly mooted in November 1945, concentrated the companies' energies into, first, a propaganda campaign for survival, then a battle to secure the best compensation for their shareholders. There seemed little point in long-term planning, when even day-to-day management was supervised by the Transport Minster, Alfred Barnes, and his staff. More severe speed restrictions were imposed on many routes — the result of materials shortages, exceptionally bad weather, and a spate of accidents that gave 1947 the second highest tally of fatalities (121) of any year in railway history. Delays to repair work and to the introduction of colour-light signalling were blamed for sixty-one of these deaths. But the biggest difficulty was rising costs. The government accepted an increase in rates in 1946, and a wage rise in 1947, but it preferred to make one-off payments rather than accept the potential inflationary consequences of a more open policy.[13] The only major projects were the completion of two schemes promoted in 1935 to alleviate unemployment: the electrification of the Liverpool Street–Shenfield line and the Manchester–Sheffield–Wath lines.[14] The reintroduction of prestige 'Pullman' services took place in 1948, but at lower speeds than formerly. And although the London–Norwich services were comprehensively reorganised with new locomotives in 1951, heavy loading and poor track maintenance meant that it was 1953 before the longer-distance services approached their pre-war speeds.

Outside the Southern Region there were only short electrified lines, mainly on Tyneside and Merseyside and around Manchester and Glasgow. In 1931 the Weir Committee reported that the net capital cost of electrifying all Britain's main lines would be almost £261 million, and the companies' return would only be some 2%. Such estimates, made at the height of the Depression and including the electrification of uneconomic as well as the most profitable lines, were not appealing. But the alternative of diesel traction was not explored, although it offered many advantages of efficiency and durability over steam without high capital outlay on track and wiring. Experiments in the United States, where by the end of the decade a quarter of all passenger miles were made behind diesel-hauled locomotives, showed the possibilities. By 1945 there were just 53 diesel engines out of more than 20,000 locomotives in Britain. One reason was the belief that Britain's reserves of coal made steam traction the most economic system, as was firmly believed by Alan Mount of the Ministry for War Transport and his colleague Sir Cyril Hurcomb, who went on to become the first Chairman of the British Transport Committee; another was the significant improvement made in the performance of steam locomotives in the 1930s.[15] Moreover, it was always recognised that in the long term electrification held advantages of faster speeds with lighter trains, greater efficiency and comfort over diesel.[16] Nevertheless the BTC were surprised to learn in 1948 that its Railway Executive had commissioned a programme of twelve new 'standard' steam locomotive designs suitable for use across the network. R.A. ['Robin'] Riddles, formerly of the LMS and working in the tradition of the engineers Stanier, Ivatt and Fairburn who had established the company's reputation for high-performance engines, developed 'standard' designs with gusto, with the research laboratories at his back. Between 1951 and 1960 there appeared 999 new steam locomotives, each with a life expectancy of at least 25 years. No wonder, then, that a powerful steam preservation movement emerged in the 1960s, for so many engines were new.

In 1953 the Railway Executive was abolished and the BTC assumed direct control, developing a limited regional structure for day-to-day operations. A more dynamic future seemed assured when in January 1955 the BTC announced a 'Modernisation Plan', aimed to 'exploit the natural advantages of railways as bulk carriers of passengers and goods' by means of an investment programme of £1,240 million over fifteen years.[17] Here at last was a comprehensive programme to renew track and signalling, to invest in diesel traction, and to modernise stations and rolling stock. It was also a portmanteau for the realisation of many long-cherished electrification projects, including the former LMS (now London Midland Region) lines between London, Manchester and Liverpool; the remaining Southern steam lines; and services between Liverpool Street and Bishop's Stortford. Sir Cyril Hurcomb was replaced by General Sir Brian Robertson, a distinguished administrator as well as a military leader and a friend of the Churchill government. He recognised that investment in the railways had lagged behind that in the other nationalised industries. When the government realised in 1956 that the BTC would require an even larger sum to implement this strategy, it asked for more detailed accounts and on the basis of these agreed to advance money to meet the outstanding deficits on current operations as well as to defray capital expenditure. It was not to know that 1955 was the last year that British Railways would show a profit on its running costs, and that investment would not stop a rapid acceleration into unprofitability.

The growth in the private ownership of cars and lorries increased threefold between 1947 and 1962. Yet such was the great increase in travel, both of people and goods, that the amount of railway traffic declined relatively little before 1960: 21,022 passenger miles were travelled in 1948, 19,772 in 1962. Total freight declined more sharply in the same period, from 21,457 to 16,104 net ton miles, of which the biggest reductions were in coal and minerals. This contrasts with the European situation, where there was an even greater growth of vehicle ownership, but also an increase in passenger and especially freight journeys by rail. Britain's old-fashioned wagon fleet and marshalling yards, as well as its relatively short distances, were major factors in rail's decline. The biggest problem, however, was that spiralling wage bills and maintenance costs were not met by comparable increases in fares and freight charges; by 1961 railway expenses were over 300% higher than in 1938, whereas rates and charges had risen by less than half. As traffic levels began to fall around 1960 operating losses became dramatic.[18] Even the *Architects' Journal*, giving a viewpoint from outside the industry, doubted whether the rapidly rising costs of construction were being countered by comparable increases in fares.[19]

Between 1948 and 1959 some of the most rural lines were closed, accounting for 5.3% of the system, and some 1,000 stations and freight depots were abandoned. Yet aggrandisement rather than curtailment was the feature of the Modernisation Plan, and when in 1959–60 escalating costs forced the Government to review the proposals it was shocked to find, for example, that electric and diesel options for the LMR line had never been properly compared. In 1960 the Transport Minister, Ernest Marples, demanded that the whole Modernisation Plan be reviewed by a Special Advisory Group under the chairmanship of Sir Ivan Stedeford. Most of its small membership came from private industry, and included Dr Richard Beeching — then of ICI, but who became chairman of BTC in May 1961. The hiatus in building while the Group met saw a loss of confidence and the imposition of financial restrictions from which the programme never recovered. Writing of proposed reorganisations and regroupings in 1961, the *Architectural Review* hoped that 'they and the general public will not, in ten years time, have to look back on the pre-Stedeford epoch as a golden age of railway architecture.'[20]

Electrification was not only a financial risk, but also a technical one. In 1927 a Railway Electrification Committee had recommended the use of either 750V direct current by means of a third rail, or 1,500V DC using overhead wires, and these were accepted as standard in 1932. One oddity was the Lancaster–Morecambe–Heysham branch, electrified as early as 1909 using a prototype 6.6kV AC system. When it was agreed in 1953 to modernise this line the Railway Executive chose the 25kV AC system then being pioneered by the French engineer Fernand Nouvion. His conversion of the mountain line between Aix-les-Bains and La Roche-sur-Foron in 1954, and of the line between Valenciennes and Thionville in 1954–55, owed much to a single German route, which had fallen into the French occupation zone in 1945, and had been electrified to this system in the 1930s. The higher voltages meant that there were reduced distribution losses, wider spacing of sub-stations and thinner cabling. In 1955 Stanley Warder, BTC's Chief Electrical Engineer recommended this 'undeveloped system which would probably be less costly and have greater future potential', and 25kV was selected for the LMR main line.[21] The pilot line between Manchester and Crewe was electrified between 1957 and 1960, and work on the line from Crewe to Liverpool began in 1959. Interference with signalling circuits and estimating the minimum clearances allowable between wires and bridges required further experimentation, and put extra demands on the LMR Architect's Department.

The Big Four's architects' departments were little altered by nationalisation. Their heads became 'Regional Architects', continuing to report to their respective Chief Engineers, but additionally a Chief Architect was appointed in 1950. Dr F. F. C. Curtis from Western Region was a German emigré, who had taught at the Darmstadt School of Architecture and had worked for the Southern Railway and for Charles Holden.[22] Although he had no day-to-day control over the Regions' output, Curtis's personal experience of London Transport design led him to seek a consistent design policy for British Railways. He established an Architects Study Group, which met three or four times a year and liaised with a Design Panel formed in 1956 to advise on 'the best means of obtaining a high standard of appearance and amenity in the design of its equipment', principally the new locomotives, coaches, ships and uniforms commissioned under the Modernisation Plan. Curtis also took an interest in advertising, alterations to older stations and, especially, signage. He recognised, however, the regions' strong individualism, admitting that 'if there is a family likeness among the buildings and projects . . . , this is more due to a common aim than to central direction.'[23] From the late 1950s there was also an annual conference with the architects' counterparts in the Netherlands, France and Switzerland. Paul Taylor and David Perkins also remember pilgrimages to see new Dutch stations at Schiedam, Rotterdam and Utrecht, and Paul Hamilton recalls that his railway pass took him to Holland for free.

Curtis was Chief Architect from 1950 until 1970, and the Regional Architects enjoyed similarly long reigns. Harry Pittaway, appointed Chief Architect to the Southern Railway in 1940, continued to serve Southern Region until 1965. The area of the LNER was split into two, with Harold H. Powell serving as Regional Architect to Eastern Region until 1967 when the area was reamalgamated with North Eastern Region under the latter's architect, Syd Hardy. Western Region saw the most changes, although H. E. B. Cavanagh served as Regional Architect throughout the 1950s. Most of those who worked for the railways appreciated the regional system, with its close-knit teams and traditional rivalries. Critics outside, however, felt that it limited the potential for good standardised designs and led to great variations in quality.[24]

The head of the LMR Architect's Department in its most important years, between 1956 and 1963, was W. R. ['Bob'] Headley, a graduate of the Architectural Association. Between 1956 and 1957 he recruited a team of assistants to work on the Modernisation Plan mainly from the Architectural Association and the London County Council. Members included Max Clendinning, Pat de Saulles, David Goldhill, Derrick Shorten, Michael Brawne, Roger Cunliffe, David Perkins, Paul Taylor, Maurice Wheeler, and Francis and Charlotte Baden Powell. It was an auspicious moment. The initial programme of eighteen new stations and three signal boxes had to be implemented quickly, and Headley was willing to encourage the more 'prima donna' types to fulfil their maverick talents. The young team realised that they were working in 'the cradle of prefabrication', in Paul Taylor's words, as the inheritors of the LMS work. Prefabrication for the small stations between Manchester, Crewe and Liverpool ensured a consistency of style by which the buildings could be recognised as the Midland Region's work, but Headley allowed each architect to take charge of a station and make variations within the vocabulary. A development group began in 1957 under Pat de Saulles, with one year in which to design the first four buildings of the new programme. Because of this pressure, the first two stations, at East Didsbury (fig. 48) and Burnage in south Manchester, used a proprietary 'modular' type of steel framework, resembling a Meccano set in that the sections were pre-drilled with holes to suit a variety of options. Into this frame could be fitted infilling panels to the architects' own design, here an asbestos-based slab for the

48 East Didsbury Station: London Midland Region Architect's Department, 1959.
Photograph: Nigel Corrie, English Heritage.

plinth and vitreous-enamelled sheet-steel panels. These two became known as 'Mark I', and gave the group time to refine a 'Mark II' for the next phase.

The Mark II system discarded the proprietary steel frame in favour of aluminium, which was lighter and did not need to be painted. The architects also experimented with lighter glass-fibre reinforced polyester finished panels, but when these delaminated at the prototype shelter at Heald Green they returned to an enamelled steel system. Only with the Mark IIa stations—Levenshulme, Heaton Chapel, Navigation Road, Cheadle Hulme and Holmes Chapel ('up' platform)—was an adequate compromise between weight and durability realised, with aluminium used to face the cladding panels. Mark III, used at the six new stations between Crewe and Liverpool, saw the panels hung instead of glued, so that they could be fixed on site rather than having to be transported ready installed. However, by the time these were being completed in 1961–62 the Stedeman Group had reported, 'capital investment was restricted', and much of the original finesse had gone from the project.[25] All the stations were based on a 3'4" grid, and the later versions were pin-jointed; that is, they relied for bracing on

49 Wilmslow Signal Box: London Midland Region Architect's Department, 1960.
Photograph: Elain Harwood.

their cladding panels. Three power-operated signal boxes, at Manchester London
Road (Piccadilly), Sandbach and Wilmslow (fig. 49), were also prefabricated.[26]

The BTC permitted smaller, 'intermediate' stations to be 'serialised', but
required that principal stations and termini should be 'special' and given a 'distinctive architectural treatment'.[27] Macclesfield was prefabricated and built in seven
months during 1960. Prefabrication was also to play a role in the construction of one
most unusual station, Manchester Oxford Road (fig. 50), because of exceptional site
conditions. A structure was needed that was light enough to rest on old viaduct
arches of limited strength, and which could cope with the awkward, wedge-shaped
site and curved track. The solution chosen by Max Clendinning was timber.

Britain's contribution to timber-shell roofing was both original and distinctive. No other European country appears to have had a committed programme
of research into the use of timber for bridging big spans. The Timber Development Association (TDA, later the Timber Research and Development Association) appointed Hugh Tottenham in 1956 as their consulting engineer for roof
development. His first experiment with conoid roofs, laminated timber boards
incorporating a 'north' roof light, was for the TDA's own new laboratory at
Tyler's Green, outside Beaconsfield, Buckinghamshire. Just two more examples

50 Oxford Road Station, Manchester: London Midland Region, Max Clendinning job architect, 1959–60.
Photograph: Nigel Corrie, English Heritage.

were built, at Yeovil Cattle Market (1960) and at Manchester Oxford Road (1959–60). Tottenham designed over a hundred simpler shell roofs, but considered that Oxford Road was the most important of his works in timber because it combined a new technology with good looks. The main building, set between two sharply angled platforms and reached via a steep driveway, covers a trapezium-shaped concourse with three north-lit conoids widening from 42 feet to 96 feet, and supported on a cruck-like frame of laminated hemlock. Similar crucks support the curved canopies over the platforms, most easily seen on the ancillary platform building over the southern tracks — the smallest canopy, over the northern tracks, has gone. The use of timber is continued to ground level, with the parcels office, booking hall, cafeteria and waiting room set in a kidney-

51 Oxford Road Station, Manchester: London Midland Region, Max Clendinning job architect, 1959-60. Photograph: Nigel Corrie, English Heritage.

shaped building framed in thick, highly varnished laminated sections and clad in the vitreous panels used on the suburban stations (fig. 51).[28] The roof itself was formed of 'second class' ¾" and ½" boarding, tongued and grooved on the underside to give a better finish. Cheap timber could be used because knots did not matter, but a skilled supervisor was needed to ensure that the boards were properly layered. The three layers of timber were set round a formwork, but the individual lengths did not need to be specially bent, and they were cut individually where they reached the edge beam. Thinner boards were used for the side canopies because of their greater curve. These were made up in a builder's yard in west Manchester and brought in on a Sunday morning to be installed while the overhead electric wiring was going up.[29]

52 Coventry Station: London Midland Region, Derrick Shorten job architect, 1960–62.
Photograph: Nigel Corrie, English Heritage.

A few other buildings were also constructed of timber for the LMR. The 300-foot maintenance depot for the new electric trains at Longsight, Manchester, was constructed of nineteen laminated timber arches 7½ inches thick. An elegant new glazed booking hall was added at Crewe, with an exposed roof of eight hyperbolic paraboloids like upside-down umbrellas. Hugh Tottenham was also responsible for a parcels depot at Coventry Station, completed in 1961 and made of five regular timber shells of laminated boarding.[30]

Coventry was the most successful 'special' station built by the London Midland Region (fig. 52). The difficulty was that it had to be built quickly, in time for the opening of the Cathedral by the Queen in 1962. General Sir Brian Robertson was the brother-in-law of Cuthbert Bardsley, appointed Bishop of Coventry in 1956, and made a personal promise that the station would be ready. The architect chosen was Derrick Shorten. Shorten had studied under Dr Curtis at Liverpool, and had gone to work for him at the British Railways' headquarters in Marylebone Road after a brief period with Hemel Hempstead Development Corporation. Most of the headquarters' work was on rolling stock, including modern carriage interiors, and eventually Shorten decided that it was time to move on. He chose London Midland because he 'liked the old LMS line', although he found working for the elderly engineers there initially disappointing. However, he designed a modern addition to Barrow Station, which Headley had likened to 'London Airport'. Shorten was not sure if this was a compliment, but assumed that he was thought to have talent, for late one Friday afternoon in the middle of 1959 he was one of three architects summoned to Headley's office, and asked to prepare a design for Coventry over the weekend. 'Headley was fond of giving out homework' or sending his staff off to look at stations over the weekend.

Many of the parameters had already been determined. Arthur Ling and Michael McLellan at Coventry City Council had already included a 'Station Square' in their masterplan for their rebuilding of the city, and there was to be a parcels depot and a car park. There were also to be four platforms instead of two. For the railways Mike Edwards had already turned this into a development plan with the concourse built at right-angles over the tracks, but it was Shorten's 'homework' project that formed the outline of what was eventually built in all its essentials. The key to the building is thus its section. Shorten gives his influences as Neutra, Breuer and American architects, though he had recently seen and admired Arne Jacobsen's Munkegårds School in Copenhagen, and new metro stations in Stockholm. A love of Scandinavian architecture was to pervade much of his later work, including his own house in Stevenage. He did not share the enthusiasm of many railway architects for Dutch station buildings, although he had had a fascinating meeting with the eccentric architect of Rotterdam Central Station, Sybold van Ravesteyn. There is something of the same big-boned quality of the latter's work in the design for Coventry, but its closest source is the unrealised design of 1954 by Pier Luigi Nervi for a concourse at Naples Central Station, with its high glass sides and open structure. 'In 1957 I had been to Naples Station to the first (erected) splayed columns, probably built to test the Nervi system. Italian state railways engineers showed me around.'[31] The difference is that Naples was to have been set parallel to the tracks, and its structure is much more expressive.

In his cleaner, simpler structure, Shorten was aided by 'a very remarkable engineer', Paul Beckmann of Ove Arup and Partners, who developed a system of stainless steel rods on which the connecting bridges were hung. He considers himself fortunate that architect and engineer were put to work together from the first. Shorten developed the scheme with Mike Edwards, transferred from designing Stafford Station, Keith Rawson, and a very able technician named John Collins. Edwards also designed the parcels office and staff association building next door, in conjunction with the timber parcels depot and slightly in advance of the main station.[32] They were fortunate in being 'left to get on with it' by Headley and the rest of the team; Paul Hamilton was Shorten's immediate superior, but was sufficiently trusting — and so preoccupied with designing signal boxes — that their discussions were usually about Le Corbusier. Much of the detailing was done by a firm of shopfitters and metal fabricators that Shorten knew in South London. He was also responsible for bringing in Jock Kinneir, whose lettering for the motorway system had much impressed him.[33] Coventry and Glasgow Queen Street were trial stations for a new version of his lettering, which being black on white is rather heavier than the reversed colour used on motorways.[34]

The new station is striking for its high, light concourse, at right angles to the tracks and the square at its front, the ease of circulation thence to the platforms. The structure is of reinforced concrete, sheathed in white Swedish glazed tiles and with large areas of external glazing, only made possible by the recent introduction of neoprene gaskets. There is a particularly careful discipline in the timber detailing of the handrails, dados and framed platform buildings. The balustrading was formed from unfinished glass, acquired cheaply from Pilkington's because of its imperfections and then toughened by heat, while the handrails are of afzelia wood and the ceilings of agba hardwood. The concourse is the building's heart, of double height, with the staircase leading over the tracks rising from within it, so that there are views across it and out to the city. 'It forms a noble gateway to the city and stands witness to the living traditions of railway architecture, grandiloquent, spacious, and clear.'[35] The high station ticket hall, with its walls of glass and marbled floor, has a public grandeur comparable with that found in the Cathedral at the opposite end of the central area, but its clean lines are a striking contrast to the building, so obviously conceived much earlier. The laminated teak panels and bold lettering remain the most distinctive feature at platform level. The last part to be completed was a flat over the ticket office, built so that the station's catering staff could live on site. Looking back after a career that ranged from designing a hospital, to local authority and private practice, Shorten considers that Coventry Station was the only building he designed that was consistent all the way through.

Other stations from the early 1960s were less fortunate. At Stafford Station there were lengthy delays while a decision was made to complete its rebuilding, although the resulting design by David Goldhill has clean lines and a pure section. Elsewhere on the southern arm of the LMR electrification, some economies were made by relaxing the clearances between wires and bridges, and by improvements in lightweight insulators and transmission gear; nevertheless there was a reduction in the pace of station rebuilding, and the regions were encouraged to make an economic return by incorporating offices into new designs, so that money could be invested instead in power signal boxes.[36]

A small electrification programme was also authorised for Eastern Region under the 'Modernisation Plan'. The line between Greenwood and Potters Bar was quadrupled and the lines from Liverpool Street to Bishops Stortford, and from Fenchurch Street to Tilbury and Southend, were electrified, with a consequent station rebuilding and resignalling programme. The first station to be rebuilt was Potters Bar, completed as early as 1955. It comprised a booking hall, signal box, goods office, and a series of platform buildings under flat concrete canopies deliberately made as thin as was possible; they were so thin, indeed, that they buckled.[37] The architect was James Wyatt, one of the few post-war architects to make a life-long career on the railways and who was then deputy to Harry H. Powell, the Regional Architect. Powell had been an architect in the LNER since before the war; Paul Hamilton remembers him as being most interested in an easy life, reading novels in the office, although he was supportive of his young staff. In early 1956 Powell was joined as Chief Assistant by Roger Walters, from the Timber Development Association and a dynamic organiser. Wyatt's girlfriend worked at the LCC, which proved a good recruiting ground for young architects looking to design real 'one-off' buildings, including Paul Hamilton and, a year later, John Bicknell. Hamilton — overseen by Walters — developed a prefabricated timber 'System C' that was used for about a hundred mess rooms, workshops and other 'back room' buildings, yet the Eastern Region's architects simultaneously recognised that the relatively small number of new station buildings required by the region could be designed more efficiently as 'one-offs', and that designing individual buildings was more fun than spending a long time developing a standard unit. Walters felt that there should be a 'development group' to examine this, and Hamilton recalls how he and Arthur Quormby visited Express Dairies to make a study of milk floats, which had fibre glass fronts, before devising a standard electricity relay station built of plastic, whose light weight made it a practical material for poor soil conditions.

The three most significant Eastern Region stations are Harlow, Broxbourne, and a new concourse at Barking set on a road bridge above older platform buildings. John Ward was the group leader for Barking (fig. 53), whose design closely resembles 'on an English smaller scale' the new concourse building erected between 1947 and 1951 to complete Rome's Termini Station of 1936, by Eugenio Montuori and Leo Catini (incorporating elements of a scheme by Castellazzi,

53 Barking Station: Eastern Region, John Ward, group leader, 1960.
Photograph: Nigel Corrie, English Heritage.

Fadigati, Pintonello and Vitalozzi).[38] With its thin, concrete beams forming a dramatic canopy and upsweeping roof, infilled with glass, the concourse at Rome Station was a model for modern rail travel, an enticing design that attracted the traveller with an expressionistic image of light and speed while keeping the actual locomotives and tracks out of view. Barking itself was widely admired. In 1962 a critic remarked that 'the satisfying simplicity of the building externally is not belied by its interior . . . a rare instance of "beton brut" being used with an air of austere elegance.'[39] Also indebted to Rome's Termini Station was the new entrance built at Crewe; this, sadly, has been demolished.

Hamilton considers that the planning of Broxbourne and Harlow was more distinctive than their architectural style. Hamilton himself headed the design team for Harlow (1959–60, fig. 54), which included John Bicknell and Ian Fraser. Harlow was the most prestigious new Eastern Region station, a rebuilding of Burnt Mill to serve the post-war new town. The marshy land required piling, so they decided to use as little of it as possible, placing the waiting room on the bridge and making a feature out of the lifts which then principally served the parcel traffic. This concept had been pioneered by Western Region in 1956–58 at Banbury, where the building of an additional line for through traffic resulted in a

54   Harlow Town Station: Eastern Region, Paul Hamilton, group leader, 1959-60.
Photograph: Steve Cole, English Heritage, National Monuments Record.

new station. With limited space on one side of the tracks and a high percentage of the passengers using the station as an interchange between trains, the Western Region Architects' Department, under H. E. B. Cavanagh, decided to place the cafeteria and waiting room on the bridge. Banbury also experimented with the use of precast prestressed beams, which could be dropped into place with a mini-mum of disturbance to train services below. But the rather flat facades and brick facings gave the completed station the rather static character of a contemporary office block—perhaps a reflection of the lack of a large-scale rebuilding pro-gramme in the region to encourage the development of a more distinctive style.[40]

Hamilton was concerned that Harlow's chunky detailing and robust finishes should be able to withstand knocks and expect little maintenance. Its distinctive image is a series of thick horizontal concrete and timber slabs, covering the glazed booking hall, brick offices and stairs from the platforms, which rise to the covered bridge building and are crowned by the lift towers. It is tempting to draw

55 Broxbourne Station:
Eastern Region, Peter
Reyniers and John
Ward architects, 1960.
Photograph:
Nigel Corrie,
English Heritage.

references to Hamilton's favoured Frank Lloyd Wright, although the *Architects'
Journal* preferred to compare the station with the detailing of the Japanese pavilion at the 1957 Brussels exhibition, which Hamilton also seems to have known.[41]

The concept of integrating the bridge to the platforms within the overall
design was repeated the next year at nearby Broxbourne, largely designed by a
South African, Peter Reyniers, working under John Ward. The pale brick and
timber that give Harlow its more delicate, oriental character is here substituted by
yellow brick and raw concrete. The flow from the entrance to stairwell, bridge and
platforms constituted a single, sweeping gesture, with broad steps, generous
handrails and a judicious use of big windows to draw the passenger through the
space (fig. 55). The greater simplicity and robustness of Broxbourne ensured its
critical appraisal was entirely favourable, and even ecstatic. Ian Nairn for one considered it 'honest, straightforward and far more successful' than Harlow.[42]

Paul Hamilton left Eastern Region in late 1959, headhunted for a more senior

56 Hackney Downs Signal Box: Eastern Region, Paul Hamilton group leader, 1960.
Photograph: Nigel Corrie, English Heritage.

job with London Midland, where his main work was on the power signal boxes required as part of the electrification programme. In order to enable higher speeds to be reached in safety by the new form of traction, and to prevent excessive wear, improvements in track and signalling apparatus were necessary. Initial progress was slow, however. By the end of 1963 multiple-aspect, colour-light signalling covered 3,600 single track miles, 1,650 of which had been installed since the inception of the Modernisation Plan. The new signal boxes covered far larger sections of the track than their predecessors, so that 1186 boxes were eliminated between 1955 and 1963.[43] The development of control technology and electrical relay interlocking also permitted a greater freedom of plan, though the new equipment demanded fire-resistant, air-conditioned spaces. Above these the continued desire for clear visibility was expressed by large, undivided windows under exceptionally deep eaves or 'sun screens' that were treated as powerful, sculptural slabs.

The prototype power signal boxes were built on the Eastern Region, at Tilbury, Sawbridgeworth and Stanford le Hope, designed by John Bicknell, and Harlow Mill. Paul Hamilton designed about five boxes, but most were produced by colleagues who adapted standard elements such as sun-screens and fenestration

57 Rugby Signal Box: London Midland Region, Paul Hamilton architect, 1964.
Photograph: Nigel Corrie, English Heritage.

which he had designed. The distinctive Eastern Region style was epitomised by the little platform-end box at Hackney Downs, its overhanging sun screen and forthright modernity a contrast to the cluster of late nineteenth-century buildings around it (fig. 56). Hamilton and Bicknell subsequently developed the idiom for the larger and more complex buildings required by London Midland, at Watford, Bletchley, Rugby and Birmingham New Street. As Hamilton himself wrote, 'to hold their own visually the scale of the building should be as large as possible, the massing simple, the materials modest but sturdy-looking. Power signal boxes are key buildings and should attempt to express that fact.'[44]

Because of their tight sites, a few of the boxes had to be three storeys high. First Rugby appeared in this guise (fig. 57), then, most dramatically, Birmingham New Street (fig. 58), commissioned in 1962, built in 1964–66, and set into the side of a railway cutting. The technical brief for New Street included standby power plant demanding exceptional sound insulation and very heavy floor loadings, while

58 Birmingham New Street
Signal Box: Bicknell and
Hamilton, 1964.
Photograph: Crown Copyright,
NMR.

sensitive electronic equipment had to be shielded behind blank walls. The main
accommodation was laid out on five levels around a central shaft which projects
above the rooftop control room. Because of a shortage of local materials and
bricklayers, and the difficulties of the cutting, most of the structure was made of
concrete precast off-site. A bold horizontal emphasis enhanced the sturdy massing and projecting sun baffle, and created an image of power and stability that was
appropriate to a new Railway Age.[45]

By the time that Birmingham New Street signal box was completed, Bicknell
and Hamilton had set up in private practice. A former colleague at the LCC
commissioned them in 1963 to build housing at the Royal Staff College at Cam-
berley, which was largely designed by Bicknell between teaching work at the
Regent Street Polytechnic. A fellow tutor there was Ken Jones, who was in charge
of the Greater London Council's motorway projects, and when the GLC realised
at a late stage that its development of the Westway would involve the demolition

59 Paddington Maintenance Depot: Bicknell and Hamilton, 1966–68. Photograph: Nigel Corrie, English Heritage

of British Rail's road vehicle maintenance depot at Westbourne Grove, an architect with experience of the railways was needed urgently to provide a replacement.[46] Hamilton had already designed a number of vehicle depots, for example at Stoke-on-Trent, so knew what was required, and this gave him the opportunity to finally leave Midland Region, taking the Birmingham job with him. Bicknell recalled that the budget for the depot was unrestricted, but that time was tight, so that eight assistants were brought in to work on the drawings. The final cost was £1,404,582.

The Paddington Maintenance Depot (figs. 59. 60) is perhaps the most sophisticated building erected by the railways in the 1960s. The site is an extraordinary one, a wedge of land bounded by two arms of the re-routed and raised Harrow Road and by the Regent's Canal, with in addition on its southern boundary the oversailing Westway. Work on the road began in 1964, but construction of the buildings had to await lengthy and expensive digging out to a new ground level, and although the design was published in January 1965 detailed planning permission was only granted a year later. Building work began soon after.

60 Internal staircase, Paddington
Maintenance Depot: Bicknell and
Hamilton 1966–68.
Photograph: Elain Harwood.

The Depot consisted of two buildings. The larger building on plan is little known: an oval-shaped maintenance garage tucked within the raised Harrow Road roundabout. Usually only seen from above, it is notable for its thick roof beams, cranked to allow a central raised clerestory and to give greater interest to the viewer. Across the gyratory system, the western office building poked a distinctive snout over the top of the Westway. Its specification is heavily industrial; it was designed to take 200-lb per square foot loadings and heavy services, while the awkward site imposed specially rigorous fire precautions and a disproportionately large sprinkler system. The second floor is at the level of the Harrow Road and houses repair workshops and stores; above it there were the machine shop, offices and extensive messes for what John Killick described as the railwaymen's 'antediluvian' tea drinking. The building resembles a dirty British coaster beating its way down the motorway, thanks to its two funnels emanating from the first-floor boiler room and the round staircase and square lift tower giving height to its stern.

The buildings are finished with exceptional care, with mosaic cladding to the office building and a generous central staircase detailed by Bicknell. 'The staircase well forms a superb curving sculpture in an icy mosaic sheath' wrote Killick.[47] The building won a Concrete Society Award in 1969 and a Civic Trust Award in 1970 for the qualities of its finishes. Its significance today, however, lies more in its value as an early and pungent example of a small group of buildings which, in the late 1960s, emulated the style of thirty years before, but with more muscle — much in the vein of Hans Scharoun's more nautical designs. 'I have found it difficult not to launch into superlatives over this design,' wrote Killick, 'but it is my bet that if British Rail continue to appoint talent of this quality, in AD 2968 a preservation society will nominate the Paddington Maintenance Depot one of the most significant railway buildings of its era and in its urban context.'[48]

However, by the time the Paddington Maintenance Depot was under construction the heroic era of railway building was over. The Stedeman Group's report was never published, but its proposals formed the basis of a White Paper and the 1962 Transport Act, which abolished the BTC in favour of a streamlined British Railways Board. Beeching became the symbol of this new era, appointed to give effect to government intentions for its largest loss-maker by a Minister, Ernest Marples, bent on redirecting resources into road transport. They looked at the railways from a purely economic point of view, rather than concentrating, as had the 1955 Plan, on technical modernisation. From December 1960 until June 1963 investment and, particularly, railway closures, were held up, while annual losses continued to rise. Beeching's report, *The Reshaping of British Railways*, published in March 1963, led to the closure of 2,000 stations, 3,700 freight depots and 4,500 miles of track by late 1966. However, by the time the effect of the 'reshaping' programme was felt, a Labour Government more sympathetic to rail had been returned to power, in 1964, and Beeching had gone back to ICI. Labour's White Paper of July 1966 attempted a moderate reversal of his policy, accepting social need for railways over economic arguments in remote areas.

In this uncertain climate modernisation proceeded more slowly. The electrification of the lines from Euston to Birmingham, Liverpool and Manchester was completed in 1967; electrification from Brookwood to Branksome was completed in July 1967, and from Clapton to Cheshunt in 1969. The British Railways Board began to exploit the economic possibilities of its station sites, with only limited success. The first 'Park and Ride' station, the ugly and utilitarian Bristol Parkway, opened in April 1972 and soon repaid the investment of £230,000; the second, Alfreton and Mansfield Parkway, was only moderately profitable. The rebuilding of Birmingham New Street in 1964–66 was followed by the construction of a shopping mall on a raft over the station, completed in 1972. There were numerous office and shop developments accompanying station schemes, for example at Cannon Street and Wembley Central in London and at Sheffield, Manchester, Cardiff and Southport. Expected returns for Cannon Street were estimated at just 3% before interest charges, while at Birmingham an expenditure of £8.3 million was expected to yield no more than 7%. What was to have been the flagship of the Modernisation Plan, the rebuilding of Euston Station, was not only vilified by campaigners for the Euston Arch, but became caught up in this 'stop-go' search for economic return and was successful neither architecturally nor commercially. But given the difficulties and expense of building over railway tracks, with complicated schedules and the need for over-sized members to resist vibration and heavy use, it is perhaps remarkable that a group of handsome buildings were produced at all. They are not a tribute to the railway managers of the day, but to an enthusiastic body of young architects who seized the opportunity still rare in the late 1950s to be creative and dynamic. Today their work is emerging as some of the best 'one-off' designs of the period.

1   Derek H. Aldcroft, *British Railways in Transition* (London: Macmillan, 1968), p.122.

2   James Gillespie, 'Municipalism, Monopoly and Management', in Andrew Saint, ed., *Politics and the People of London* (London: Hambledon Press, 1989), pp.116-25; T. R. Gourvish, *British Railways 1948-73, A Business History* (Cambridge: Cambridge University Press, 1986), pp.13-24. As Lord President of the Council Morrison was responsible for economic planning.

3   Aldcroft, *British Railways in Transition*, pp.71-72.

4   *The London Midland and Scottish Railway, 1923-46, A Record of Large-Scale Organisation and Management*, p.12, PRO ZLIB 6/153. Also, LMS Railway, *The Scientific Research Department at the London Midland and Scottish*, n.d. c.1947 (PRO ZLIB 6/159); Sir Josiah Stamp, 'Modern Developments on the London Midland and Scottish Railway', in *Modern Transport* (11 June 1932), (PRO ZLIB 6/78); *The Economist* (2 July 1938), 'LMS Supplement', p.3 (PRO ZLIB 6/81).

5   Leslie Martin, *Buildings and Ideas from the Studio of Leslie Martin and his Associates, 1933-83* (Cambridge: Cambridge University Press, 1983), p.204.

6   Steen Eiler Rasmussen, 'First Impressions of London or, Sir Edwin in Wonderland', in *AA Files*, no.20, (Autumn 1990), p.21.

7   Steen Eiler Rasmussen, *London: the Unique City* (Cambridge, Mass.: MIT Press, revised edition 1982), pp.347-50.

8   *Official Architect*, vol.5, no.4 (April 1942), pp.175-78. Information from John Weeks and Gavin Stamp.

9   Paul R. Taylor, *Buildings for the Railways, Report for English Heritage* (1994), unpag.; *Architects' Journal*, vol.102, no.2654 (6 December 1945), p.43; *Architectural Review*, vol.99, no.591 (March 1946), pp.77-78. Boxmoor was replaced by Hemel Hempstead station.

10 Information from John Weeks. Llewelyn Davies went on a tour of Germany as early as October 1945 studying constructional techniques with the British Intelligence Objectives Sub-Committee of the RIBA under Mark Hartland Thomas.

11   I am grateful to Andrew Saint for his help in charting the development of the tartan grid. See also his *Towards a Social Architecture* (London: Yale University Press, 1987), pp.102-4.

12   *Architectural Design and Construction*, vol.26, no.3 (March 1946), pp.82-85; *The Builder*, vol.170, no.5375 (8 February 1946), pp.137-39; *Architects' Journal*, vol.107, no.2774 (8 April 1948), pp.328-29; *Architect and Building News*, vol.216, no.13 (November 1959), p.395.

13   Gourvish, *British Railways, A Business History*, pp.6-13.

14   G. Freeman Allen, *British Railways Today and Tomorrow* (London: Ian Allan, 1959), p.68.

15   Gourvish, *British Railways, A Business History*, p.87. Aldcroft, *British Railways in Transition*, pp.74-77.

16   Allen, *British Railways Today and Tomorrow*, p.41.

17   British Transport Commission, *Modernisation and Re-equipment of British Railways* (London: 1955), para.6.

18   Aldcroft, *British Railways in Transition*, pp.123-46.

19   *Architects' Journal,* vol.132, no.3426 (15 December 1960), p.870.

20   *Architectural Review*, vol.129, no.771 (May 1961), p.312.

21   Roger Ford, 'Nationalisation's Unsung Success', in *Modern Railways*, vol.53, no.575 (August 1996), p.507.

22   *Industrial Architecture*, vol.7, no.1 (January 1964), pp.258-59.

23   *Architect and Building News*, vol.216, no.13 (4 November 1959), p.392.

24   *Architectural Review*, vol.129, no.771 (May 1961), pp.311, 316; *Design*, no. 171 (March 1963), p.67.

25   F. F. C. Curtis, 'British Railway Architecture', in *Official Architecture and Planning*, vol.25, no.9 (September 1962), p.539.

26   *Official Architecture*, vol.11, no.4, p.180. R. B. White, *Prefabrication* (London: HMSO, 1965), pp.263-65.

27   R. B. White, *Prefabrication*, p.236.

28   *Architect and Building News*, vol.216, no.13 (4 November 1959), pp.404-9.

29   Conversation with Hugh Tottenham, 4 July 1995.

30   *Timber Technology*, vol.69, no.2260 (February 1961), pp.40-1; *Wood*, vol.26, no.1 (January 1961), pp.16-17; *Architectural Review*, vol.139, no.771 (May 1961), pp.314-15.

31   Letter from Derrick Shorten, 16 January 2001.

32   Letter from Derrick Shorten, 19 January 2001.

33   Conversation with Derrick Shorten, 21 December 2000.

34   *Design*, no. 171 (March 1963), pp.72-77.

35   Grant Lewison and Rosalind Billingham, *Coventry New Architecture* (Warwick: 1968), p.21.

36   G. Freeman Allen, *British Rail after Beeching* (London: Ian Allan, 1966), pp.136, 151.

37   *Architect and Building News* (26 January 1956), pp.114-17. Information from Paul Hamilton.

38   *The Builder*, vol.202, no.6192 (19 January 1962, pp.121-24.

39   *Official Architecture and Planning*, vol.25, no.12 (December 1962, p.825.

40   *Architects' Journal*, 19 February 1959, vol.129, no.3338, p.297.

41   *Architects' Journal*, 15 December 1960, vol.132, no.3426, pp.869-78.

42   Ian Nairn, *Modern Buildings in London* (London: London Transport, 1964), p.90. The extensive coverage given all the stations in this little book is a testament to their importance.

43   Aldcroft, *British Railways in Transition*, pp.162-63.

44   Paul Hamilton, 'The Power Signal Box', in *Architectural Review*, vol.138, no.825, (November 1965), p.334.

45   *Building*, vol.208, no.6483 (18 August 1967), p.74. Notes from Paul Hamilton in Twentieth Century Society, *Sixties: life, style, architecture*, unpublished, April 1997.

46   Information from John Bicknell, 1994.

47   John Killick, *Official Architecture and Planning* (February 1969), p.154.

48   Killick, *Official Architecture and Planning*, p.157. The Maintenance Depot was indeed the first post-war railway complex to be listed, in April 1994 rather than 2968, and in 2002 it was adapted as offices for the fashion outlet Monsoon.

PLANES

THE
CEMENT &
CONCRETE
ASSOCIATION

52
GROSVENOR
GARDENS
LONDON S.W.I

AN ORGANISATION
FOR IMPROVING &
EXTENDING THE
USES OF CONCRETE

CONCRETE IN
AERODROME CONSTRUCTION

61 Gatwick Airport, Surrey, 1936. Hoar, Marlow & Lovett, architects. Aerial view illustrated on the cover of *Concrete in Aerodrome Construction*, c.1937. Author's collection.

Arrivals and Departures: Civil Airport Architecture in Britain During the Inter-War Period

Neil Bingham

Sweep away the refuse with which life is soiled, clogged, encumbered. Let us undertake the great tasks of the new machine civilition.

Le Corbusier, *Aircraft* (1935)

Aerodromes of the middle twentieth century shoud be as vital and redolent of their age as the Temples of Greece, the Public Baths of Rome, the Cathedrals of the Middle Ages, and the Palaces of the Renaissance.

Graham Dawbarn, airport architect (1932)[1]

DURING THE INTER-WAR YEARS, air travel emerged as a new form of transportation. Exciting, sophisticated and extremely modern, flying was to find its architectural expression in a new building type—the airport terminal.[2] Architects responded not only to the need to plan a building with a previously unheard-of set of requirements—control towers, viewing platforms and hangars—but also paid homage in their designs to the very machine around which the building revolved—the aeroplane. The airport terminal, it was believed, was a building form which was an extension of the flying machine aesthetic that, as Le Corbusier proclaimed, was the exemplification of 'the new machine civilisation.'

The sympathy between terminal buildings, aeroplanes and flight existed because many of the British architects who designed airports durings this period were either pilots themselves or very closely associated with flying men. This design harmony, linking terminal and aeroplane, was often clearly visible: for example, the interiors of earth-bound waiting rooms and airborn cabins were frequently complementary, using similar fixtures, materials and style. Moreover, like the symbolism of the cruciform plan of a church, many architects designed the terminal building in the shape of a bird or an aeroplane. If there was some truth in Le Corbusier's famous statement that the house was a machine for living in, then it might be even more true to say that the airport building was a machine for flying in. Passengers had left the ground as soon as they entered the terminal.[3]

In Britain, the great heyday of airport architecture dawned during the early 1930s. Although scheduled passenger services had begun on a regular basis soon after the end of the Great War, the only terminal building of conseuqence until the 1930s was at Croydon, built between 1926 and 1928.[4] Before this, and at the many other landing fields dotted about the country, airport buildings consisted mainly of hangars, sheds and wooden and canvas buildings. Some of the hangars in Britain were brilliant feats of structural design, especially those created to construct and house airships.[5] These were unadorned structures, made for utility not comfort, created by engineers not architects.[6]

Croydon holds a unique place in the history of British aviation. Called the London Terminal Aerodrome, the airport was located approximately ten miles south of London's West End, along Purley Way, then a new arterial road. The site had been used by the Royal Flying Corps since 1915. Two future monarchs learned to fly here. A motley collection of buildings were scattered around the field; the control tower was a hut on stilts with a walkway encircling it. The creation in 1924 of Imperial Airways, the government-subsidised national airline, demanded better facilities at Croydon. So Britain received its first custom-designed air terminal in 1928 (fig. 62).[7]

Considering that it was one of the major and busiest world airports in the inter-war period, alongside Berlin Tempelhof, Paris Le Bourget, New York's Marine Air Terminal (later renamed La Guardia) and Chicago Midway, Croydon's terminal building was architecturally undistinguished. It was designed by the Air Ministry.[8] With the expectation that journeys by flight would soon be as common as rail travel, the obvious model for this new building type was the railway station, for which Croydon could almost have been mistaken if it were not for the control tower on the airfield side.[9] Also, being somewhat in the country, Croydon's terminal was reminiscent of a villa. The style was stripped neo-classicism, with the principal east front articulated by a canopied entrance. The interior, with its large booking and waiting hall, was traditionally furnished. The method of construction was slightly more innovatory: steel frame with concrete block fill-in, rendered with a ground silica cement finish.[10]

Air travel from Croydon was extremely exciting. Passengers making a flight would first register in town at the office of the airline, or its agent, then be driven in coaches to the airport. The luggage, then the passengers themselves were weighed, the scale discreetly seen by the clerk only. Travellers awaiting their flights were kept informed of flying conditions by a large weather map in the central hall which was regularly updated. Embarkation was a walk across the apron to the waiting aeroplane.[11]

62 Croydon Airport, London, 1928. Designed by the Air Ministry. Photograph courtesy of Sutton Borough Council.

For all the thrills which air travel evoked, architectural critics were dissatis-fied by Croydon's inability to express the electrifying atmosphere which should be part of the aeroplane journey, especially when they compared the building to those Modern airport terminals springing up on the Continent which did so much to embody the new spirit of the air. In fact, the whole area of commercial air transportation in Britain during the 1920s had been sluggish, and the ordi-nariness of the terminal at Croydon reflected the nation's and, more specifically, the Government's general lack of interest. In 1927, for example, Germany's avia-tion companies carried 151,000 passengers, while their British counterparts moved only 19,000.[12] Indeed, Germany led the field since, not having been allowed to operate military aircraft after the armistice, it could concentrate on the commercial aspects of air travel. The German government strongly sup-ported towns throughout the country in having their own airports for internal and trans-continental benefits.

At the same time, the 1920s saw the flowering of Modern architecture in Ger-many, and this was reflected in the design of their terminal buildings. Tempel-hof, built between 1926 and 1929 to the designs of the architects Paul and Klaus Engler, was a long low structure, etched in continuous horizontal bands of win-dows. Halle-Leipzig airport, with its curtain-glass restaurant building of 1929, was by Hans Wittwer, partner of the Bauhaus director Hannes Meyer. And

Fuhlsbüttel airport for Hamburg, by Dyrssen and Averhoff in 1928/29, had a much admired curved plan with stepped terraces for viewing the airfield. These airports, and other Continental examples like Amsterdam's Schiphol from 1929, by Berlage's pupil Dirk Roosenburg, were much studied by British architects who by now were beginning to share in the movement to establish a series of local airports around the British Isles.[13]

In Britain, a concerted campaign had been launched in 1928 to place the responsibility for the construction of airports and their buildings with municipal authorities. Initiated by Air Vice-Marshall Sir Sefton Brancker, Director of Civil Aviation, a branch of the Air Ministry, municipalities were encouraged to regard airports as important to their existence as railway stations. One enthusiastic reporter in the *Air Review* envisaged a system of eight thousand airports dotting the country.[14] Sir Alan Cobham, a popular flying figure and pioneering airport consultant, spent the summer of 1929 flying an average of five and a half hours a day in his de Havilland Giant Moth, *The Youth of Britain*, visiting more than one hundred centres to talk to local councillors and residents about establishing aerodromes.[15] Cobham concentrated his efforts on encouraging towns to procure decent landing fields in areas away from tall buildings and to take into account local topographical and climatic conditions.

Brancker was also a leading member of a powerful force of aviation professionals who began to work alongside a small band of architects interested in the new area of airport design. The group was very successful in encouraging the Royal Institute of British Architects to promote airport architecture. They had first met in 1928, simply to judge a RIBA-sponsored student competition to find a design for 'a first-class aerial terminus' to serve London.[16] Substantial prize money of £125 had been offered by the Gloster Aircraft Company and H. H. Martyn & Company Limited. The jury, who visited Croydon as part of their research, comprised no less a figure than Sir Edwin Lutyens, alongside more progressive architects such as C. Cowles Voysey, E. Vincent Harris and Thomas Tait (of Burnet Tait & Lorne). Brancker's flying specialist colleagues included such men as G.E. Woods-Humphrey, managing director of Imperial Airways, and Major R. Mayo, consulting engineer to Imperial.[17] They awarded first prize in the competition between M. Hartland and Donald McMorran, an assistant in Harris's office who went on to a successful architectural career, although not in airport buildings.

Out of this competition jury grew the first most influential instrument of research and public awareness on British airport architecture and planning — the RIBA Aerodromes Committee. Brancker was the chairman for the initial meetings in 1929-30, until his death in the disaster near Beauvais of airship R.101, when it struck the ground and burst into flames. Most of the former jury members sat on this new committee.[18] Its secretary was the energetic young architect John Dower (1900-47), who became the vociferous architectural voice of the group, organising meetings, publishing reports, and making public lecture tours around Britain to speak on airport design. The Aerodromes Committee summed up their field work in a succinct report in 1931 called *Town Planning and Aviation*, in which the group concentrated on the general requirements of civil aerodromes and acknowledged that nearly all of Britain's airport buildings were not worthy to be called architecture, especially when compared to examples like Berlin and Hamburg. Their conclusion was that 'the aeroplane sets a standard which the aerodrome must rival.'[19]

To reinforce their message of the glories that good architecture could offer to 'Britain's pride as a nation', the Committee mounted an exhibition in the RIBA Galleries during April and May 1932 which consisted of photographs and drawings of aerodrome buildings and layouts. With few British examples to offer, most of the exhibits were foreign. The event was considered a success, with an estimated one thousand people attending before it went on a tour of aerodrome clubs and conferences around the country.[20]

So effective was the work of the RIBA Aerodromes Committee, and so influential its members in government circles, that the body was officially dissolved in 1934 and reformed as the Aerodromes Advisory Board, a national organisation outside the sphere of the RIBA under the auspices of the Air Ministry. The main thrust of this new Board was to carry out the Government's programme of encouraging and advising municipalities on the creation of local airports. The Board membership was broader than the RIBA committee, with a greater number of professional institutions represented. As a result, there were fewer architects. Dower, however, remained as Secretary.[21]

One factor leading to fewer architects on the Aerodromes Advisory Board was that the architectural and planning aspects of airports had begun to be taken over by a new breed of professionals who acted as 'aerodrome consultants' to the Board and to any authority or individual seeking direction. At first there had been the possibility of a new professional governing body to be called 'The Institution of Air Port Consultants', with the standard categories of Fellows, Associates and Students. But the Air Ministry felt it more appropriate for the existing organisations, such as the RIBA, Institution of Civil Engineers and the Institution of Mechanical Engineers, to regulate the rules and conduct of their respective members. So by 1935, the Aerodromes Advisory Board had officially sanctioned fourteen independent aerodrome consultants who were designated either as 'aviation consultant' or 'aerodrome engineering consultant', the difference being that the first category was made up of men primarily from a flying backround responsible for safety and site, while those from the second group held professional qualification in engineering and were therefore trained to erect buildings. Out of the total, there was but a single consultant who was a member of the RIBA.[22]

The Aerodromes Advisory Board collapsed before the end of 1935, in some part as a result of its own and the RIBA Aerodromes Committee's achievements. An early success was during the transitional period in December 1933 when the groups' members had overseen the Airports Conference held at the Mansion House in the City of London. Presided over by HRH the Prince of Wales, the conference strongly reinforced the need for local aerodromes. Even if Lt.-Col. Francis Shelmerdine thought one of the most important outcomes of the conference had been the considerable impetus given to the question of wasteful expenditure on aerodrome buildings where only a landing ground was required, such a point illustrated that community leaders and the professional fraternity associated with airports were enthusiastically looking forward to building airport terminals.[23] This conference, followed by their other initiatives, especially the establishment of the aerodrome consultant, gave the Board less of a role particularly as, by 1935, the construction of airports and airport buildings in Britain was well under way.

In 1929, at the same time that Cobham, Brancker and the RIBA were beginning to stir up interest in the nation's need for airports, Britain's first truly innovational airport opened. Heston Air Park, about twelve miles from central London, was a private concern, owned and operated by Messrs. Airwork Ltd. (fig. 63). Starting life as an aerodrome for a members' flying club, it developed into London's second commercial field after Croydon. Heston's architect was Leslie Magnus Austin (1896-1975), who taught architecture at the Royal College of Art and was a member of the Town Planning Institute. Austin's undestanding of planning was evident in his fine layout for the whole site. In plan, which would be evident from the air, the shape was that of an aeroplane. The terminal building (called 'the rest-house', and actually a clubhouse with an integrated control tower) formed the nose of the plane, the wings were long lines of hangars angled slightly back on either side, and the body was the approach road. And stylistically, Modernism had appropriately been commandeered for this new type of building. The terminal was flat-roofed, with external stairs for access to

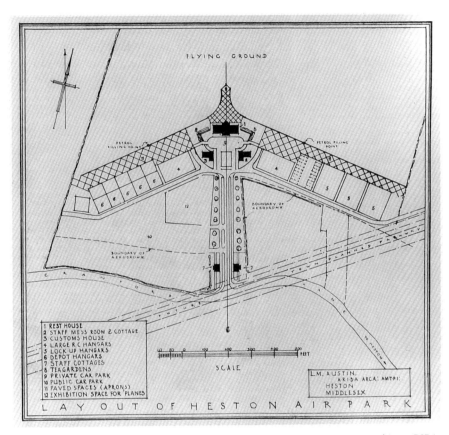

FLYING GROUND

PETROL FILLING POINT

PETROL FILLING POINT

BOUNDARY OF AERODROME

BOUNDARY OF AERODROME

1 REST HOUSE
2 STAFF MESS ROOM & COTTAGE
3 CUSTOMS HOUSE
4 LARGE R C HANGARS
5 LOCK-UP HANGARS
6 DEPOT HANGARS
7 STAFF COTTAGES
8 TEA GARDENS
9 PRIVATE CAR PARK
10 PUBLIC CAR PARK
11 PAVED SPACES (APRONS)
12 EXHIBITION SPACE FOR PLANES

SCALE   FEET

L.M. AUSTIN.
A·R·I·B·A· ARCA: AMT·P·I:
HESTON
MIDDLESEX

L A Y O U T   O F   H E S T O N   A I R   P A R K

63   Heston Air Park, Middlesex. Plan of overall scheme, 1929. Leslie Magnus Austin, architect. RIBA.

viewing terraces, boxy in shape, with metal windows and doors, and white stucco rendering.[24] Heston immediately became the model airport.

Messrs. Airwork was the alliance of Frederick Alan Irving Muntz (1899-1985) and Squadron Leader Sir Nigel St Valery Norman (1897-1943, succeeded as 2nd Baronet 1939). Both men had studied mechanical engineering together at Trinity College, Cambridge. Alan Muntz went on to make important developments to the free piston engine system and to co-found Indian National Airways (1933). But it was the pilot Nigel Norman who was to have the greater impact on airport design when he teamed up with the architect Graham Richards Dawbarn (1894-1976) to form the powerful partnership which created the greatest number and some of the best airport buildings in Britain during the 1930s.[25]

64 Brooklands Aero Club, Weybridge, Surrey, 1932. Graham Dawbarn, architect. Elmbidge County Council, courtesy of English Heritage.

As Heston began to attract various sales and commercial organisations connected with aviation, Norman and Muntz commissioned Dawbarn in late 1929 to further develop the airport. As a result, Dawbarn designed more hangars for the maintenance and garaging of the aeroplanes, as well as offices, showroom buildings, an engine test-house, radio station and even a fine little petrol station. All were extremely fashionable and modern. The showroom for Brian Lewis & Co. Ltd., for example, was co-ordinated in a colour scheme of black, red and silver, with tubular metal furniture and an abstractly designed carpet. The extension to Austin's clubhouse had eight bedrooms, each with en suite bathroom, and carried out in a different colour scheme. The bedroom furniture was built-in, the drawers and doors flush and faced with unstained mahogony plywood. The bar was as chic as any recent West End hotel, with its polished green linoleum top, wrapped in chromium-plated bands and mirrored in the highly reflective white enamelled ceiling and walls.[26] With accommodation for eating and sleeping, Heston was a forerunner of many of today's airports which are smart little villages in themselves.

Similar to Heston was Graham Dawbarn's Brooklands Aero Clubhouse in Weybridge, Surrey, which opened in 1932 (fig. 64).[27] Brooklands, famous for its motor racing track created in 1907, had expanded to include a school of flying set up under the auspices of the founder's widow, Dame Ethel Locke King. Although the clubhouse corresponded in plan with Heston—a tall central tower flanked by single-storey wings—and even superficially appeared stylistically similar, Brooklands shows a greater awareness of the interlocking cubist massing of the Dutch De Stijl architecture of T. van Doesburg and J.J.P. Oud.

In 1931 Norman borrowed a Pussmoth from de Havillands in Toronto, Canada, and with Dawbarn as navigator they flew seven to eight thousand miles around America, inspecting building airport buildings and studying the standards set out by the US Air Commerce Act of 1926. The trip was partly funded by the RIBA Aerodromes Committee (of which Norman was a member) by an award to Dawbarn of the Godwin and Wimperis Bursary. In a busy three weeks of touring, Norman and Dawbarn touched down at between forty to fifty sites, spoke to airport managers and photographed the buildings.[28] By this date, America had experienced an intense period of experimental airport design.[29] The results showed in the numerous and varied airports which the pair surveyed. It was a trip which had a profound influence upon design in Britain.

Nigel Norman and Guy Dawbarn set up practice together as aviation consultants in 1933, with Dawbarn the only approved architect in this new profession. Alan Muntz was a sleeping partner in the first year. Over the next six years, until the outbreak of the War (in which Norman was killed while on active service), the partnership of Norman and Dawbarn built new airports at Birmingham, on the Channel Islands of Guernsey and Jersey, at Perth, Wolverhampton and at Lusaka, then the new capital of Northern Rhodesia. They were the official consultants on many schemes, the most important being Manchester's Ringway airport, Belfast, Hyderabad in India and just before the outbreak of war, on a new City of London International airport. They also prepared dozens of reports on airport sites and aviation routes for various local authorities and national governments around the world.[30] Norman dealt with the mechanics of planning — siting, landing ground, runway layout (he preferred the term 'strips'), lighting, fire protection, signage — and was the lively, outgoing spokesman for the partnership.[31] Dawbarn, a reserved and quiet man, concentrated on the architectural design.

Norman and Dawbarn's works were major contributions to the great building period of pre-war airport design in Britain which burgeoned between 1934 and 1938 as many towns attempted to capture air routes. Wolverhampton's airport at Pendeford was a typical example. First planned in 1934 in anticipation of being a link between London and Liverpool for flights to Germany and the Netherlands, Sir Alan Cobham chose the best site from a list of twenty-five local suggestions.[32] By the autumn of 1937 when Norman and Dawbarn's buildings were completed, Wolverhampton's status had been reduced to an aeroclub, albeit a charming small piece of Modern architecture.[33]

Wolverhampton's position had been usurped by nearby Birmingham which built an airport, opening in 1939, also to the design of Norman and Dawbarn

65 Birmingham Airport, 1939. Graham Dawbarn of Norman & Dawbarn, architects. Photograph
English Heritage.

(fig. 65). It was the partnership's finest work.[34] And if ever a building was meant
to fly, Birmingham's terminal building was it. The only other structure in aviation building history to rival its aerodynamic appearance has been Eero Saarinen's TWA terminal at John F. Kennedy International Airport, New York (1956-
62), which looks like an abstracted eagle poised for flight. At Birmingham,
Norman and Dawbarn played on the more transparent theme for modern aerial
navigation of the terminal building as aeroplane, manifested in both plan and
appearance: the 'cabin' of the terminal was a long concourse bordered on either
side by offices; the 'cockpit' was a rounded five-storey pavilion encapsulating
observation decks, restaurant and control room; and the 'wings' were great balanced cantilevers thrusting over the apron to provide shelter for passengers and
freight. Built of reinforced concrete, the column and beam framework was internally exposed and bush-hammered with a brisk forwardness.

The masterplan of Norman and Dawbarn's other notable and very fine airport, for the Channel Island of Jersey, also deliberately embraced the imagery of
flight (fig. 66). As one commentator observed, the hangar buildings extended

66 Jersey Airport, 1937. Graham Dawbarn of Norman & Dawbarn, architects. Photograph English Heritage.

back from the terminal building, 'in the same mannner as the wings of a swallow in flight.'[35] In plan, the Jersey terminal is like a pair of aeroplane wings of the period, the architects even carefully detailing the front corners at the tips to round and extrude in a similitude that only incoming pilots and conversant passengers would have appreciated. Yet in colour and form, the building was likened to an ocean liner, with the 'clear-cut, workman-like lines usually associated with a ship. Aesthetically this is sound,' reported *The Architect & Building News*, 'since many of the attributes of an airport are identical with those of a seaport.'[36] Modern buildings of the 1930s and naval architecture are commonly paralleled because, as with the Jersey terminal, the stacked modelling is reminiscent of a ship's bridge and the starkness of the building's white render imparts the illusion of a liner afloat at sea. Sited close to the island shore, the maritime qualities of Jersey's terminal were amplified by the addition of promenades, deck chairs and a snack bar for holiday makers who drifted over from the beach as the summer sun waned.

Graham Dawbarn believed that the terminal building was, of all building types, 'a most complicated unit' in terms of planning because its many varied

67 Manchester Ringway Airport, 1938. G. Noel Hill, architect, with Graham Dawbarn. RIBA.

functions had to cater for airline services, passengers, freight and pleasure seek-
ers. With its innumerable entrances and exits, and the landing side as important
as the ground traffic side, Dawbarn considered it as a building type which 'has
no "back".' As such, airports were the most susceptible of all architecture to overall scrutiny. 'The building will be seen on every side from the ground,' commented Dawbarn. 'It will also be seen from every angle from the air.'[37]

Dawbarn's specialised knowledge of airport planning was evident at Manchester's Ringway Airport (fig. 67) where he acted as consultant to Manchester
City Architect G. Noel Hill.[38] Completed in 1938, Ringway took over the functions of Manchester's Barton Airport, which had opened in 1930 — really as a
large hangar with no terminal building — but as it had developed drainage problems it was unsuitable for expansion. Ringway definitely owed more to Hill,
departing from Dawbarn's usual aeroplane plan to present a long structure combining a terminal adjoining the enormous hangar, that gave the appearance of a
grandstand and stable. Hill's refined building was influenced by models of Continental Modernism such as Berlin Tempelhof just as Dawbarn's style relied
upon Art Deco examples he had studied in the United States.[39]

The most beautiful example of a terminal designed for flight was Ramsgate
Municipal Airport (fig. 68), by David Pleydell Bouverie, which was completed
in 1937.[40] One of the most well-known photographic images of 1930s architecture shows the small building appearing to shelter beneath the wing of an aeroplane in a deliberate reflection of the terminal's wing-shape plan. The architectural

68 Ramsgate Municipal Airport, Kent, 1937. David Pleydell Bouverie, architect. Photograph RIBA.

historian Wolfgang Voigt points out the similarity of Bouverie's building to the fantasy wing-only aeroplanes made popular by the 1936 British science-fiction film *Things to Come* which in turn had been based on the H.G. Wells futuristic book *The Shape of Things to Come*.[41]

Also close to the coast, with easy access to the Continent and Channel Isles, is the 1935 airport at Shoreham, Sussex, officially the municipal airport for Brighton, Hove and Worthing (fig. 69). The architect was local, Stavers Hessell Tiltman (1888-1968), better known for his hotels, breweries and public houses. Tiltman's terminal at Shoreham carries more charm than innovation, a circumstance aided by its scenic location on the edge of the plain between the sea and the South Downs.[42] Again, it is a case of the aeroplane plan, with a central control tower, and wings for offices and restaurant; the external end staircases to the roof terrace derived from Hamburg. The influence of American Art Deco is especially strong in Tiltman's design, with fine touches of zigzag metalwork and plastering.

Tiltman had procured the commissions for the terminal buildings at Leeds–Bradford Airport at Yeadon, Yorkshire, and the harbour airport for Belfast, both designed as close variants on Shoreham.[43] But as the War intervened, these projects came to nothing.

Tiltman's and Dawbarn's Modernism was of the soft variety, in the stream of those architects who had graduated with an Arts and Crafts training and were also well grounded in the classical vocabulary of architecture. The work of Le Corbusier, for example, was of less interest to Dawbarn than that of his near-

69 Brighton, Hove & Worthing Municipal Airport, Shoreham, Sussex, 1935. Stavers Hessell Tiltman, architect. Aerial view, *Concrete in Aerodrome Construction*,c.1937, p.12. Author's collection.

contemporaries like the London Underground stations architect Charles Holden. In contrast, Hening and Chitty, the other major British airport architects of the 1930s, belonged to the progressive school of Modernism. Their two principal airport buildings, at Ipswich and Exeter, displayed a forthright simplicity based upon a modular formula created, it was believed, to suit the new machine age.

Dawbarn was always keen to stress that his terminal buildings were designed with expansion in mind, although to have broken his trademark aeroplane plan would have disturbed the ideal. Hening and Chitty incorporated adaptability and future expansion firmly into their designs. 'The flexibility of the construction,' they were fond of pointing out, 'is every bit as important as the fluid plan.'[44] Ipswich[45] and Exeter,[46] which both opened in 1938, are similar in concept and appearance (fig. 70). The architects chose a 15-foot-square grid as the basis for their schemes. The building frames were of steel, the joints designed to take extensions above and alongside. Walls were of brick which could be more easily demolished than if they had been of reinforced concrete. Partitions, in some cases of glazed steel, were semi-movable; had the process been available to them, the architects said they would have used standardised panels. The result of this rigorous strategy were terminal buildings which were asymmetrical in plan, dominated by a repeating square grid evident in the proportions of walls, window patterns, doors and tiles. The beauty of building form was superseded, or at least design-led, by the beauty of what could be perceived as a mechanised

70 Ipswich Municipal Airport, 1938. Hening & Chitty, architects. Photograph RIBA.

aesthetic. In Ipswich and Exeter lay the essence of the architectural movement which was to dominate post-war architecture in the wake of the boost given to standardised units by the demands of wartime production.

Robert Hening (1906-97) and Anthony Chitty (1907-76) had formed their partnership in 1937. Chitty had formerly been in the Tecton office under that most creative of Modernists, Bertold Lubetkin, for whom he had been engaged to assist on the Gorilla House and Penguin Pool at London Zoo. Hening, too, had worked under a leading architect, the Swiss-born American William Lescaze, supervising the erection of the cubist buildings at the progressive school, Dartington Hall in Devon. At Dartington, Hening met Whitney Straight, the son by the first marriage of Dartington's foundress, Dorothy Elmhirst. It was Straight who commissioned Hening and Chitty to build Ipswich and Exeter.

A keen racing-driver and pilot, the energetic Whitney Straight established the Straight Corporation in 1935 to advise municipal authorities on the creation of their aerodromes and then manage them on their behalf. By gathering a group of specialists around him — pilots, aircraft manufacturers and designers, and architects—Straight created a company dedicated to improving a great many aspects of civil aviation in Britain. By 1938, with a staff of 133, who were all offered free flying lessons, he ran an apprentice scheme to train up young technicians, published a highly informative and technical in-house monthly magazine called *Straightaway* and the annual *Straightaway Review*, and developed a general-purpose light aeroplane: the Miles Whitney Straight.[47]

The Straight Corporation was a progression on Norman and Dawbarn's Airwork Limited, and also the National Flying Services Limited (NFS), which had been formed in 1928 by Captain F.E. Guest, a former Air Minister. Guest had tried to achieve the difficult task of creating a network of 22 aerodromes with facilities for flying schools and clubs, alongside one hundred landing sites, with the idea that no locale would be more than fifteen minutes flying time from another. The NFS established a corporate identity with its own livery of black and orange uniforms, cutlery and crockery. But although it did manage a few clubs, the NFS failed in 1934.[48] The Straight Corporation was a greater success, especially in terms of architectural design. Had the War not intervened, Straight would have continued with his impressive patronage of modern architecture.

The Gliding Consultant to the Straight Corporation was Christopher ('Kit') Nicholson (1904-48), a champion glider and an important architect in the early Modern Movement in Great Britain.[49] In 1936, Nicholson completed one of the most widely admired aviation buildings of the period—the London Gliding Club at Dunstable, Bedfordshire (fig. 71). When J.M. Richards reviewed the club in the pages of the *Architectural Review*, he drew upon the commonly perceived image of the unity of technology and aesthetics. 'It is only necessary', he wrote, 'to look at the scientific exactness of design, and to appreciate the formal beauty, of the advanced type of glider to recognise its affinity with the geometrical vocabulary of modern architecture', a proposition given particular emphasis by Dell and Wainwright's seductive photographs accompanying the article.[50]

Nestled at the foot of the Dunstable Downs, to catch the most advantageous wind currents for soaring, the London Gliding Club provides hangar space for up to thirty sailplanes together with club accommodation. With the assistance of his former student, Hugh Casson, Nicholson worked out a system of integrating standard-sized factory components—windows, doors, wall sheetings and light fittings—into a compact plan of modelled grace: a layering of circles, squares and rectangles. The sculptural quality of the architecture was a result of the architect's close aesthetic affinities with his brother, the painter Ben Nicholson—who was then working on his early abstract reliefs—and, in turn, Ben's wife, the sculptor

71   London Gliding Club, Dunstable, Bedfordshire, 1936. Christopher Nicholson, architect. Photograph courtesy of the *Architectural Review.*

Barbara Hepworth. Christopher Nicholson's wife, the designer and painter EQ, created the interior decoration for the club, choosing Aalto stools and painting the bar in deep shades of blue and reddish-brown. Christopher Nicholson's gliding club was the Modern game played at its most advanced level.

While Dunstable was known only to the architectural cognoscenti, the airport at Gatwick in Surrey received public prominence when a large gathering of distinguished guests arrived on 6 June 1936 — many in their private 'planes, others by the novel direct rail link from London's Victoria Station — to take part in the official opening of the terminal bulding (figs. 61 on p. 104, and 72). As part of the celebration, Flight-Lieutenant Gerald Hill descended by parachute and strode across the field to read a poem to Viscount Swinton, the Minister for Air, which included the lines

And Gatwick's Circle to the airman be
The homeward way begun.

The terminal at Gatwick broke radically with all previous designs, making it one of the most innovative and exciting buildings of its type in the world — it was circular.[51]

The aerodrome at Gatwick was owned by Morris Jackaman (1904-80), whose hope it was to serve the London–Paris route in competition with Croydon. Jackaman's interest in aerodromes had started when working with his father, the engineer Alfred Charles Jackaman, when their company designed and built the ferro-concrete hangar at Heston.[52] An accomplished pilot, the younger Jackaman had bought his first aircraft, a de Havilland Moth, at Whiteleys department store in 1927. He soon become part of the flying elite then making such an impact on British civil aviation, alongside for example Nigel Norman, Sir Philip Sassoon and Gordon Selfridge Jr.

The idea for the circular plan came from Morris Jackaman who, with his architects Hoar, Marlow and Lovett, had deliberately set out to avoid the ubiquitous aeroplane formula.[53] Apparently, Jackaman was working late one night, hard pressed to think of an alternative design solution for his airport building, when his father entered the room and told him, 'Oh, for heaven's sake, go to bed. You're just thinking in circles.'[54] Jackaman even applied for a patent on the circular plan, citing the advantages of a large and continuous frontage which did not waste space and was safer for positioning and moving aircraft.

Gatwick's early terminal is a low-lying structure in setback terraces, the control tower at its summit, in a shape which has appropriately lent the building its nickname, the Beehive. At first, Jackaman worked out his circular scheme with the architectural partnership of Harold Frank Hoar and William Francis Benjamin Lovett in a design they called the 'Martello Air Station'. The architects then brought in their friend Alan Fletcher Marlow, who had been with them at the Bartlett School of Architecture, to refine the design and make most of the

72 Gatwick Airport, Surrey, 1936. Nicknamed 'The Beehive', showing (above) the telescopic passage-ways radiating from the terminal and (below) the interior concourse. RIBA.

drawings.[55] Jackaman's family engineering business acted as the building contractors, so it is not surprising that the structure was a creative expression of reinforced concrete and a steel frame, particularly given the building's unusual form.

Internally, the rotunda effect at Gatwick allowed a continuous circular concourse near the inner core, with small shops in the central drum and offices, custom and freight rooms in the two outer concentric circles. The two-storey concourse, and the double switchback staircase leading up to the restaurant on the first floor and down to the 130-foot long subway corridor serving the railway station, were naturally illuminated in the day by large roof lights. Walls and ceilings were distempered in light pink, doors and balconies in green.

At six points the circle is pierced by radiating corridors, three for incoming aeroplanes, three for outgoing. Leading onto the apron from each of the external corridor doors were telescopic arms, extending canopies of steel with canvas coverings which could be slid open along tracks. Thus passengers need never be exposed to the elements, from leaving the railway station, arriving via the underground tunnel, around the terminal, through the covered passageway, to stepping into the aeroplane.

By 1937, the tempo in British airport policy, planning and building had reached a lively and mature pace. The early experiments were bearing fruit: the Government had finally examined a national policy on air transport; the first stage of the country's largest airport building, at Liverpool, was opened; and the architectural profession celebrated their aviation achievements with a high-profile public exhibition.

The Maybury Committee Report of 1937, with its recommendations of a nationwide system of air routes and airports, was the most substantial expression of Government concern for a co-ordinated policy on the country's aviation network. To date, municipalities and private enterprise had generally been left to their own devices. In the light of future defence requirements, the political rumblings on the Continent no doubt spurred the Government into seeing the wisdom of a organised pattern of landing fields and relevant buildings as supplements to the Royal Air Force bases.

Civic pride, mixed with the ambition to maintain a world position as a transport centre, moved Liverpool to build an airport on the edge of town, at Speke, which was expected to complement the city's famous docks — truly an air port (fig. 73). It was even sometimes referred to as 'an air harbour'.[56] A group of members from the Liverpool City Council had paid a visit to Hamburg's airport and come back insisting on a similar design. At Speke, Albert D. Jenkins, the Land

73 Speke Airport, Liverpool, 1937. Albert D. Jenkins with Burnet Tait & Lorne, architects. Photograph courtesy of English Heritage.

Steward and Surveyor to the Liverpool Corporation, working in conjunction with Burnet Tait and Lorne, produced a magnificent amplification of the German counterpart.[57] Like Hamburg, the building is of brick (Hamburg, like England, has a fine tradition of brick architecture), takes a gentle curve in plan with the concave side to the airfield, and is stepped in terraces for sightseeing. In homage to the city's seafaring connections, the great central tower of Speke Airport, rising 70 feet above ground level, is in the shape of an octagonal lighthouse. The adjacent hangar building, also designed by Jenkins, is a small masterpiece in itself, with Art Deco overtones in its decoration.

The feast of fulfilment and potential ambition for British airports came as a highly publicised exhibition entitled 'Airports and Airways' held early in 1937 at the RIBA building in Portland Place.[58] The display mainly took the form of photographs, although a highlight was large models of Jersey and Gatwick airports. There were three themes to the exhibition: aircraft, airports built in Great Britain and abroad, and aerial photographs with special emphasis on British and world cities and their famous buildings. The airport terminal buildings themselves, therefore, were not considered in architectural isolation but perceived as part of the phenomena of flight, amongst the wonder and terrifying beauty of the aeroplane and the magic of viewing the world from the skies above, a revelation previously given only to birds and angels.

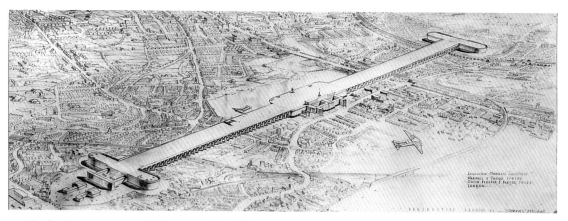

74 Hendon Airport, unexecuted design, c.1938. Marshall & Tweedy, architects. Photograph RIBA

75 (facing page) London Rotary Elevated Airport, unexecuted design, c.1932. Charles Frobisher, engineer. Royal Aeronautical Society.

The airport fostered fantasy worlds which had, and could, come to life. The architects who built airport buildings were often like science fiction writers. Theirs was a vision which frequently outstripped existing technology and built reality. Potent images of the future integration of flying and urbanism coloured the imaginations of many architects. Most striking had been Le Corbusier's illustrations of the aeroplane dwarfed by towering modern blocks and also Fritz Lang's 1926 film *Metropolis,* with flying machines whizzing between futuristic skyscrapers and landing on the top of a tower high above the city. The designer for this German Expressionist scene had been an architect, Erick Kettelhut.

The British shared in this utopian future, especially in what was seen as an inevitable development, the airport located in the heart of London and usually taking the form of a building topped by a landing field. Marshall and Tweedy with Oliver Bernard and Partners produced a scheme for a thin, mile-long building raised on columns, its roof a runway (fig. 74).[59] The top of Paddington Station was considered a potential site for erecting a flat landing ground for autogiros.[60] One very well publicised project was a design by the engineer C.W. Glover, who established a company to build a combined airport and market centre in the goods yard behind King's Cross and St Pancras Station.[61] The airport runways were to be elevated 120 feet above ground level, each one-half mile long and terminating with the peripheral taxiway to give effect of a giant wheel with spokes. The whole was then to be supported on buildings, each serving a different function such as market

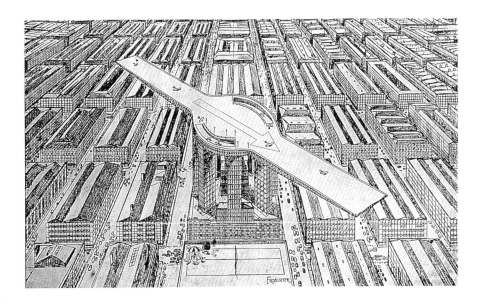

stores, coach station and hotel. The great town planner Sir Raymond Unwin backed this scheme with its advantage of slum clearance in the area.

By far the most imaginative scheme was the London Rotary Elevated Airport, patented in 1932 by the engineer Charles Frobisher (fig. 75). Suggested for either Hyde Park or Regent's Park in the heart of London, the airport was to have consisted of a single enormous runway, 2000 feet long, 300–400 feet wide, and 700 feet above the ground, which would have rotated in the same manner as a swing bridge in order to catch the prevailing winds for take-off and landing. All this was to have sat upon a building at least 50 stories high, housing shops, restaurants, a club, cinema, theatre, and 'car-parking on modern lines of silo-storage'.

The question of a location and plan for a new airport for London vexed architects, planners and critics during the late 1930s. Norman and Dawbarn prouced a scheme for a site near Fairlop, to the north east of the city. But the War intervened, and much to Dawbarn's disappointment the building commission for Heathrow Airport was given to Frederick Gibberd in 1950. A new generation of airports and airport architects had emerged. Post-war terminal buildings were to move towards more homogeneous but nevertheless exciting solutions to the problems of the mass movement of passengers; and this was to be achieved within the context of an international style of architecture which held very few of the inter-war associations of the symbolism of flight and the exciting new powers given to man by the aeroplane.

Acknowledgments: Valerie Andrews; Paul Francis; John King; Jill Lever; Julian Temple; Dr Wolfgang Voigt.

1   Quoted in *Air & Airways*, vol.8 (January 1932), p. 320.

2   The term 'airports' is most often used in this essay although during the period under discussion they were more commonly known in Britain as 'aerodromes' (from the Greek, *aeros* = air, *dromos* = race or course, in other words, the take-off and alighting ground). 'Airport' became more widely used during the 1930s, to distinguish an important field which included a terminal building and had custom facilities. 'Airport' has always been preferred by the Americans.

3   The symbolic parallel between religion and flight was touched upon by the architect and critic Lionel Brett, 4th Viscount Esher, who wrote in an article prefacing a review of the new London Airport designed by Frederick Gibberd, 'For the essence of travel, symbol of our journey through life, is drama, and the role of the architect is to heighten the drama by the way he sets and shifts the scene,' *Architectural Review*, vol.118 (July 1955), p.5.

4   The first civil route was inaugurated on 24 August 1919 with a flight of the Air Transport and Travel Limited from Hounslow airport to Le Bourget, Paris. Flying outside of Britain had been forbidden until 14 July 1919.

5   See Christopher Dean, ed., *Housing the Airship* (London: The Architectural Association, 1989) for a full inventory of air sheds.

6   Engineers were to continue having a prominent voice in airport building design during the inter-war period, notably Henry Angley Lewis-Dale who sat as a member of the RIBA's Aerodromes Committee and wrote papers and books such as 'Flying-Stations: Construction and Maintenance', in *The Institution of Civil Engineers Selected Engineering Papers*, No.17 (London: ICE, 1924) and *Aviation and the Aerodrome: A Treatise on the Problems of Aviation in Relation to the Design and Construction of Aerodromes* (London: 1932).

7   Bob Learmouth, Joanna Nash and Douglas Cluett, *The First Croydon Airport, 1915-1928* (Sutton, Surrey: 1978); Mike Hooks, *Croydon Airport* (Stroud, Gloucestershire: 1997).

8   See *Builder*, vol. 131 (26 November 1926), pp.868-71, 874.

9   Croydon's control tower is of historic importance as 'the first of its kind truly to deserve this name', according to Wolfgang Voigt in 'From the Hippodrome to the Aerodrome, from the Air Station to the Terminal: European Airports, 1909-1945' in *Building for Air Travel: Architecture and Design for Commercial Aviation* (Munich and New York: The Art Institute of Chicago and Prestel-Verlag, 1996), p.40.

10   Croydon closed in 1959. The terminal building still stands.

11   Kenneth Hudson, *Air Travel: A Social History* (Bath: Adams & Dart, 1972), p.22.

12   See John Myerscough, 'Airport Provision in the Inter-War Years', in *Journal of Contemporary History*, vol.20 (1985), for an excellent analysis of policy planning of airports in Britain during the 1920s and 1930s.

13   R.H.S. Mealing, 'The Procedure for the Establishment and Maintenance of Aerodromes', a paper prepared for the 58th annual meeting of the Institution of Municipal and County Engineers, June 1931.

14   *Air Review* (October 1934), pp.84-85.

15   Alan Cobham, 'The Selection of a Municipal Aerodrome' in *The Aeroplane*, vol.37, Air-Park Supplement (30 October 1929), pp.1039-42.

16   *Journal of the RIBA*, vol.35, 3rd series (18 October 1929), p.727. Previous to the announcement of the competition, the RIBA began to arouse interest in airport terminal buildings by publishing a design by P.C.Smith, a second-year student at Cambridge School of Architecture, showing an aeroplane swooping over a monolithic terminal building with a double-barrel vaulted roof, *Journal of the RIBA*, vol.35, 3rd series (13 October 1928), pp.719, 727.

17   Archives and MSS Collection, British Architectural Library, RIBA: 'Board of Architectural Education Committee Minutes', vol.5, pp.123-24, 197-98.

18   *Journal of the RIBA*, vol.36, 3rd series (15 June 1929), p.615; Lutyens, Tait and Cowles Voysey resigned during the 1930-31 session, *Journal of the RIBA*, vol.38, 3rd series (18 April 1931), p.401.

19   *Journal of the RIBA*, vol.38, 3rd series (7 March 1931), pp.296-300; Dower also prepared a report for the RIBA Aerodromes Committee entitled 'Architecture and Town Planning for Civil Aviation' which outlined the possible chapter sections for a book on the subject (Public Records Office: AVIA 2/671) and wrote such articles as 'Architecture of the Airport', *Flight*, vol.29 (30 January 1936), pp.100-03.

20   *Journal of the RIBA*, vol.40, 3rd series (29 April 1933), p.490.

21   *Journal of the RIBA*, vol.41, 3rd series (10 March 1934), p.427; (28 April 1934), pp.627-28.

22   Public Records Office, AVIA 2/537.

23   Public Records Office, AVIA 2/671.

24   *Architects' Journal*, vol.70 (7 August 1929), pp.199-204; *Architect & Building News*, vol.122 (13 Dec. 1929), pp. 726-29. The two hangars at Heston were as much if not more admired than the terminal building. These were designed by Austin and H.F. Murrell, FRIBA. The main hangar was of reinforced concrete with six arched ribs, spanning a floor area of 100 feet by 80 feet, and with extensive folding timber doors that could be operated on a gear and rope system by one person. Except for this hangar, Heston Airport, including all its later additions, was demolished in 1978.

25   'Twenty-five Years of Norman and Dawbarn, 1933 to 1958', p.2. This is a privately printed ehibition catalogue, 26 pages, with a foreword by Graham Dawbarn, 1958. Dawbarn had completed two buildings of interest before Heston; with the great architectural perspectivist Cyril Farey he collaborated on Raffles College, Singapore, which they won in competition in 1924; and Constantine Technical College, Middlesborough, 1925.

26   'Work at Heston Airport', *Architectural Review*, vol.78 (October 1935), pp. 144-46; *Architecture Illustrated*, vol.6 (February 1933), pp.45-49.

27   'The Clubhouse, Brooklands Aerodrome', *Architecture & Building News*, vol.130 (3 June 1932), pp.324-27.

28   In 1932 Dawbarn made a report of this trip, submitted for the Godwin and Wimperis Bursary, entitled 'A Brief Report on the Design and Construction of Civil Airports in the United States of America' (Archives & Mss Collection, British Architectural Library, RIBA).

29   For the best survey of American airport design see David Brodherson, ' "An Airport in Every City": The History of American Airport Design', in Zukowsky, *Building for Air Travel*, pp.66-95.

30   A list of reports is held by the present architectural practice of Norman and Dawbarn.

31   Nigel Norman, *Airport Development* (London: The Royal Aeronautical Society, Aeronautical Reprint no. 69, 1933), being the transcript of a lecture held at the Royal Society of Arts on 21 April 1932; Nigel Norman, 'Aerodrome Design', *Architectural Association Journal*, vol.48 (May 1933), pp. 359-84, being the transcript of his lecture given at the Architectural Association, 1 May 1933, in the presence of the Rt. Hon. Sir Philip Sassoon (Under-Secretary of State for Air), John Dower (Secretary of the RIBA Aerodromes Committee), and Gordon Selfridge Jr. (department store magnate and amateur pilot); Nigel Norman, 'Aerodrome Design', *Journal of The Royal Aeronautical Society*, vol.41 (April 1937), being the transcript of a lecture held at the Royal Society of Arts on 19 November 1936. Concerning runways, or strips, there were none in Britain before the Second World War, as opposed to America where they were the norm: all aircraft landed on grassy fields. This was considered acceptable for a number of reasons: the volume of air traffic was not so high as to require the control imposed by runways, leaving pilots the freedom to take off and land in any direction; and turf in Britain was excellent, whereas in America the soil conditions varied.

32   'The Story of Pendeford', *The Blackcountryman* (Spring 1971), pp.66-69.

33   'Initial Buildings at Wolverhampton Airport', *Architectural Design & Construction*, vol.8 (November 1938), p.447. Wolverhampton Airport was demolished in the early 1980s.

34   'Birmingham Airport', *Architect & Building News*, vol.159 (18 July 1939), pp.187-92; *Building*, vol.14 (August 1939), pp.336-38. Norman and Dawbarn's Birmingham building is now reduced to the status of a cargo building.

35   'Jersey Airport', *Architect & Building News*, vol.153 (14 January 1938), pp.35-40; see also *Architectural Design & Construction*, vol.7 (November 1937), p.506; *Builder*, vol.150 (13 March 1936), pp.532-33, 537.

36   *Ibid.*

37   Graham Dawbarn, 'Building an Airport', *The Aeroplane*, vol.48 (1 May 1935), pp.504-06. The more sinister implications of the ability afforded by the aeroplane to observe in-the-round and over a wide area, was forcefully and poetically described by Le Corbusier in his book *Aircraft* (published only in England, not France, in 1935) which was subtitled 'L'avion accuse' or 'The airplane indicts'. The ugly urban sprawl, he explained, was 'frightening, overwhelming. The airplane eye reveals a spectacle of collapse.'

38   'Ringway Airport, Manchester', *Architects' Journal*, vol.88 (22 December 1938), pp.1026-28; *Architectural Design & Construction*, vol.8 (November 1938), pp. 445-46; *Architectural Review*, vol.85 (February 1939), p.90. G. Noel Hill's Manchester Ringway terminal building was demolished in 1962 and replaced by the present terminal.

39   Dawbarn was also a great admirer and friends with many Danish and Swedish architects. According to his widow, he was 'very impressed by the Danish Broadcasting House', Copenhagen (1938-45) by Vilhem Lauritzen, which inspired Dawbarn's best-known post-war building, the BBC Television Centre, White City, London. (Conversation with Mrs Graham Dawbarn, 16 September 1982, by Peter Rankin).

40 'Ramsgate Municipal Airport', *Architectural Review*, vol.82 (July 1937), pp.3-6; *Architectural Design &* *Construction*, vol.7 (November 1937), pp.509-10. Ramsgate was demolished in the early 1980s. Pleydel Bouverie was a partner for a time with Wells Coates before moving to live in the United States in the year he completed Ramsgate.

41 Voigt, 'European Airports, 1909-1945', in Zukowsky, *Building for Air Travel*, p.47.

42 'Shoreham Airport', *Architects' Journal*, vol.82 (31 October 1935), pp.633-38; *Architectural Design & Construction*, vol.7 (November 1937), p.511; *Architecture Illustrated*, vol.11 (November 1935), pp.135-40; *Builder*, vol.148 (4 January 1935), pp.14-16, 24. Shoreham Airport is still in use, intact except for the intrusion of replacement control room upon the central tower.

43 'Leeds-Bradford Airport', *Architectural Design & Construction*, vol.8 (November 1938), p.449; 'Belfast Harbour Airport', *ibid.*, p.450.

44 Hening and Chitty, 'Notes on the Planning of an Airport', *Architectural Record* (November 1937), pp.18-19.

45 'Ipswich Municipal Airport', *Architect & Building News*, vol.155 (19 August 1938), pp.204-10; Hening and Chitty, 'Design for Expansion', *Flight*, vol.35 (2 February 1939), pp.103-05.

46 'Exeter Municipal Airport', *Architectural Review*, vol.84 (September 1938), pp.95-98; *Architectural Design & Construction*, vol.8 (November 1938), p.451.

47 *Straightaway Review* (1938). With his interest in design, during the year preceding the creation of the Straight Corporation, Whitney Straight had been running Luminium Limited, an aluminium-based design company. In 1935 he had been in negotiations (which were to falter) with Marcel Breuer about the possibility of producing Breuer's 1932 aluminium or tubular-steel furniture. See Christopher Wilk, *Marcel Breuer: Furniture and Interiors* (New York: Museum of Modern Art, 1981), p.127.

48 Terence Boughton, *The Story of the British Light Aeroplane* (London: John Murray, 1963), pp.165-68.

49 Neil Bingham, *Christopher Nicholson* (London: Academy Press, 1996).

50 Quoted in 'Gliding, a Social Activity: The Programme and its Solution: The London Gliding Club, Dunstable', *Architectural Review*, vol.79 (June 1936), pp.254-62; see also *Architects' Journal*, vol.83 (11 June 1936), pp.915-19.

51 'Gatwick Airport', *Architects' Journal*, vol.83 (4 June 1936), pp.868-73; *Architect & Building News*, vol.146 (5 June 1936), pp.271-75 and (12 June 1936), supplement; *Builder*, vol.150 (5 June 1936), pp.1121-23, 1130. The 1936 Gatwick terminal building still stands today, relatively intact, now just one of many of the airport's outbuildings, about one-half mile south of the South Terminal (Yorke Rosenberg & Mardall, 1955-58). Two circular planned airports followed on the Continent: Budadors Airport, Budapest (Borbiro & Klarik, 1937) and Helsinki Airport (Englund & Rosendal, 1938). America followed with the Marine Air Terminal, LaGuardia Airport, New York (Delano & Aldrich, 1937-39), a fine Art Deco building still in service.

52 A.C.A. Jackaman, 'Laying Out and Aerodrome', *The Aeroplane*, vol.37 (30 October 1929), pp.1049-62.

53 Conversation with Alan Marlow, 7 March 1988.

54 As related in John King, *Gatwick: The Evolution of an Airport* (Sussex Archaeological Society, 1986), p.21. See also John King, 'Gatwick's Beehive: A Forgotten Development', *The Thirties Society Journal*, no.2 (1982), pp.25-28.

55 Drawings Collection, British Architectural Library, RIBA: Preliminary design and design by Hoar, Lovett and Marlow (1935-36).

56 T. Stanhope Sprigg, 'Air Harbours of England', *Air & Airways*, vol.8 (June 1931), pp.85-86, in a discussion of an early scheme for Liverpool.

57 *Architectural Design & Construction*, vol.7 (November 1937), pp.507-08; J. Temple and P. Francis, report on 'Civic Airport Buildings, 1927-1939', English Heritage (1994), pp.17-18.

58 RIBA, *Airports and Airways 1937: Catalogue to the Exhibition Arranged by the Royal Institute of British Architects*.

59 Reproduced in David Dean, *The Thirties: Recalling the English Architectural Scene* (London: Trefoil Books, 1983), p.90.

60 *Air & Airways*, vol.8 (May 1931), p.55.

61 *The London Airport and Marketing Centre*, Central Airports Ltd., 1933.

62 *London Rotary Elevated Airport*, n.d.

The British Airport at the Turn of the Last Century

Colin Davies

Speaking at a London conference on airport design in 1997, the architectural critic Brian Hatton remarked that the best way to deal with the problem of airport architecture was to anaesthetize the passengers before departure and wake them up on arrival. For most people time spent at an airport is like time spent in hospital — an unwanted interruption of normal life to be endured rather than enjoyed. This is curious, because it does not seem to apply to other travel interchange experiences such as boarding a ship or a catching a train. Why is it that the architecture associated with the miracle of flight in a jet-propelled machine of awesome beauty should stubbornly refuse to gather around it any of the romance and excitement of the quayside or the railway terminus? Does it perhaps have something to do with the necessary spatial discontinuity between those that are travelling and those that are staying behind — the absence of any goodbye waves from deck rail or carriage window?

If architecture is the ordering of space for the enjoyment of human beings then most airports, and especially British airports, hardly qualify as architecture at all. Heathrow, the busiest airport in the world, is a good example of the apparent inability of architecture to make any human or spatial sense out of the logistic complications of air travel. It is like a functional diagram drawn by a committee which has suffered so much rubbing out, pasting over and ad hoc extension over a period of fifty years that it has lost all coherence.

Of course, some see this complexity as a positive quality. Heathrow is not a building, they say, but a city.[1] It has all the ingredients of a city — workplaces, shops, restaurants, offices, hotels, chapels, everything except permanent housing — and like a city it is a four-dimensional, not a three-dimensional artefact. It must grow and change or die. It is possible to visit Heathrow the way a tourist might visit Venice or Mont St Michel. (These comparisons are not so far-fetched — the central area is an island, surrounded by a flat sea of grass and tarmac and accessible via a causeway in the form of a road tunnel under the north runway.) Yet the actual spatial experience of Heathrow is not in the least bit urban in any commonly recognised sense. It has no centre, no streets, no outdoor public spaces and no prominent monuments, unless you count the control tower, the radar scanner and the half-scale model of Concord at the tunnel gate-

76 Heathrow Terminal 1 Europier, Richard Rogers Partnership. Photograph: John Linden.

way. Look at it with half-closed eyes from inside one of the terminals (if you can find a window), and it vaguely resembles a science fiction city of the future — a collection of strangely faceless buildings, the old ones in orange brick, the new ones in bland curtain walling, connected by tunnels, moving pavements, tubular bridges, multi-storey car parks and roads that rise and fall and interweave.

When Frederick Gibberd drew up the original plan for the development of the airport in 1946, it was necessary to maintain six runways so that piston-engined aircraft could take off and land into the wind — hence the characteristic 'Star of David' plan that is still discernable from the air. Only the two east–west runways are used now, but that original plan still dictates the basic arrangement of the central area. Traffic has increased from one million passengers per year in 1953 to more than fifty-five million passengers per year in 1999; but there has never been a comprehensive redevelopment, only successive waves of piecemeal refurbishment and extension, crowding into the island's fixed boundaries with steadily

77   Heathrow Airport Pier 4A, Nicholas Grimshaw and Partners. Photograph: Jo Reid.

increasing density. Terminals and piers are connected by the built equivalent of lines and loops drawn at different times and in different colours on the original diagram. The process is well illustrated by two recent extensions to Terminal 1. The so-called Europier, designed by by Richard Rogers and Partners (fig. 76) and completed in 1995, is a separate structure, plugged into the main terminal via a walkway.[2] The design of the pier itself makes the most of the limited space available by combining arrivals and departures in a single long room with a curved ceiling and an all-glass wall facing the waiting aeroplanes. Arriving passengers travel along a gallery at the back of the room, enclosed by a frameless glass wall so that they too can share the view out. At the departures level, there are no physical divisions between the waiting areas for each gate, so passengers can use the whole room until their flight is called. The simple, repetitive structure, with its tree-like internal columns (something of an airport cliché copied from Stansted Airport, see below) is designed for economical, modular construction.

78 Heathrow Airport Pier 4A. Photograph: Jo Reid and John Peck.

On the other side of Terminal 1, Pier 4, designed by Nicholas Grimshaw and
Partners and completed in 1993 (figs. 77 and 78), is even more like a bolt-on arma-
ture.[3] The problem was to maintain security barriers between passengers for Belfast,
passengers for the Republic of Ireland and passengers for other cities in Britain, all
on an extremely restricted site at the northern edge of the 'island'. The problem was
solved by an elevated walkway that crosses the normally inviolable land-side/air-
side boundary to a mushroom-like cylindrical lounge on a traffic roundabout and
then hops back to air side to connect with the main pier. It is certainly ingenious,
and the silver tubes of the walkways, like aeroplane fuselages, are entertaining, but
the whole arrangement is really a desperate expedient to shoe horn a few more
square metres of usable space onto an island that is packed to capacity.

Despite these elegant and inventive insertions, the Heathrow central island is
a mess. It still contains a few isolated patches of left-over land amid the tangle of
linear forms, and some of them are even landscaped, but the few small trees have

to fight for space with a jumble of advertising billboards, petrol stations, bus stops, mysterious pieces of mechanical plant and scruffy temporary buildings. But perhaps it doesn't matter. The buildings are not meant to be seen from the outside. Paradoxically, the geometry of take-off and landing makes them difficult to see even from the air. This is a city of interiors and that is where the architectural effort has been concentrated. Once inside one of the three main terminals, the traveller is forced to say goodbye to views, daylight and fresh air until he or she arrives at the gate lounge, where the outlook is dramatically improved by the presence of those beautiful machines. In the meantime, there is nothing to enjoy but the pleasures of consumption. No longer transport buildings with retail facilities attached, from the passenger's point of view these terminals are now more like shopping centres cut in half by security barriers. If the access were easier and the car parks less expensive, then the land-side halves alone would serve very adequately as local shopping centres in their own right.

What can an architecture critic find to say about these interiors? As shopping centres they are not ideal, lacking the quasi-external glazed arcades of their non-airport cousins, and here and there the difficulties of combining shopping and airport functions have forced a certain architectural awkwardness — the extraordinary low ceiling in the check-in area of Heathrow's Terminal 2, for example, or the one-sided shelf of shops in Terminal 3 to which departing passengers are obliged to climb, only to descend again through the passport control channel. But the terminals provide reasonably comfortable, if soporific, environments in which to kill the time before your flight, even if you suspect that the recommended two-hour interval has been imposed mainly to persuade you to spend some money and increase the profits of the retailers and their landlords, the British Airports Authority. Squeezed between the engineering design of the baggage handling areas and the retail design of the shops and restaurants, architectural design is reduced to the choice of cladding systems, suspended ceilings, artificial lighting and floor finishes. For arriving passengers, who are not expected to do much shopping, the environment is even less prepossessing. They are simply ushered through as quickly as possible and dumped in the draughty bus stops or channelled down the moving pavement tunnels to the tube station.

When a major expansion of Heathrow was planned in the 1970s, there was only one possible strategy: abandon the central island and build on land previously designated as an aircraft maintenance area in the south east corner of the site. Here, at last, was an opportunity to devise an up-to-date, self-contained solution to the complex problem of the modern airport. Terminal 4, designed by

79   Hilton Hotel, Heathrow Terminal 4, Michael Manser Practice.

Scott, Brownrigg and Turner and completed in 1986, is effectively a separate airport with its own car park, its own tube station and its own aircraft apron.[4] The
various functions are packed efficiently into a mainly three-storey structure with
arrivals on the ground floor, departures on the top floor and a mezzanine to
absorb the complicated connections between them. On the air side a long,
straight, two-storey pier, completely open on the upper departures level, is a
model of clarity and legibility. On the land side, the access roads are also on two
levels, forming a double forecourt between the terminal and the multi-storey
short-term car park. It is a logical diagram and it is easy to use, but architecturally it is a disappointment. The roof of the check-in concourse, for example,
is supported by heavy lattice trusses that bear down oppressively on the space,
with exposed air conditioning ducts threaded through them. A line of roof glazing over the check-in desks seems only to deepen the gloom. The effect is further
worsened by the decision to paint the structure maroon and clad the walls in dull
grey metal. Fitch and Company were the interior designers. Throughout the
building once again the impression is of architecture failing to master the engineering on the one hand and the retailing on the other.

80   Gatwick South Terminal, YRM. Photograph: Brecht-Einzig Limited.

Terminal 4 has a neighbour that is also worthy of mention: the extraordinary hotel (currently a Hilton) designed by Michael Manser and completed in 1991 (fig. 79).[5] It looks like a small aircraft hangar, or perhaps a taller version of Norman Foster's Sainsbury art gallery at the University of East Anglia. Two linear, five-storey stacks of double-banked hotel rooms form the side walls of the hangar, actually an atrium accommodating the common public areas — entrance lobby, restaurants and bars. Curtain walls of frameless glass draped across the ends complete the enclosure. The simple shed form is given a dynamic impetus by the parallelogram-shaped plan that angles the glass walls towards the approach road at one end and the terminal building at the other. It is a beautifully simple and efficient concept — a machine for spending the night in — but it also has real spatial excitement, views out and plenty of daylight, all the things that are so conspicuously lacking in the terminal buildings. A cheap, utilitarian version of that common airport feature, the metal clad tubular bridge, links the hotel to the terminal across territory otherwise impassable to pedestrians. Even in this relatively uncluttered corner of Heathrow, functional connections are made not by considered spatial transitions but by drawing lines on the diagram.

81, 82 Gatwick North Terminal
YRM.
Photographs: Richard Bryant.

Apart from relatively minor interventions like those by Rogers, Grimshaw and Manser, Heathrow lacks any buildings of real architectural distinction. Sadly the same applies to most of the country's other major airports. At Gatwick, the South Terminal is connected directly to a railway station on the London to Brighton main line, with multi-storey car parks and a hotel on the other side of the tracks. Like the old terminals at Heathrow, the South Terminal has grown incrementally over a period of forty years. The elegant Miesian 1958 building by YRM (fig. 80) has now been completely obliterated by later extensions and refurbishments and by the invasion of the retailers. Inside the terminal a very substantial shopping centre, completely enclosed, with no daylight and called, absurdly, 'The Village', occupies the upper level on the land side. On the air side departing passengers enter a two-storey retail atrium via a grand cascade of steps and escalators, designed by shopping centre specialists Chapman Taylor and Partners. In addition to the three piers attached directly to the terminal building, there is a circular satellite accessible via what is usually described as a 'rapid transit system,' which means a little tram on a raised track.

Another, separate rapid transit link connects the South Terminal and station to the North Terminal, designed by YRM and completed in 1984 (figs. 81 and 82).[6] Like Heathrow Terminal 4, it is self contained, with a double-decker forecourt and its own multi-storey car park. But here the shopping centre on the land side ('The Avenue') gets a level almost all to itself. Passengers and visitors arriving on the rapid transit enter the shopping centre first and then move either up to departures or down to arrivals by escalator. As usual, the shopping centre has no daylight or views, but separating it from the other functions in this way at least permits it to have a character of its own — like an ordinary shopping centre but with more seats than usual. You can almost pretend that you're not in an airport at all. And daylight is not always a benefit. Upstairs in the departures concourse there are square roof lights at regular intervals, but they do little to improve the lighting which seems flat and dull in comparison with the carefully controlled artificial lighting of the shopping centre.

Manchester is Britain's third largest airport. In recent years it has grown on the basis of the success of the London–Manchester shuttle and increased international traffic avoiding the congestion of the London airports. The international terminal, the first phase of which was completed in 1993, is another efficient but dull exercise by Scott Brownrigg and Turner, similar in scale and arrangement to Heathrow Terminal 4 and Gatwick North Terminal.[7] The check-in and land-side departures concourses are generous, high spaces, with glass roofs supported on space frames but, despite the daylight, they seem cavernous rather than airy. Every column and wall is clad in a kind of business suit of sleek metal cladding which imposes a characterless uniformity. Externally the steel-masted suspension structure of the forecourt canopy does little to enliven the clumsy, bulky form of the building.

Manchester does, however, offer at least one structure of real architectural quality: the raised pedestrian walkway, with moving pavements, that links all the buildings together including the railway station, designed by Austin Smith Lord, and a new hotel. Like the Grimshaw and Manser versions at Heathrow, this walkway, designed by Michael Ankett takes the form of a metal tube, elliptical in section, but its simplicity, the refinement of its detailing and the addition of continuous curved glazing makes the long walk from terminal to terminal a real pleasure. For once the line drawn on the diagram is allowed to be a spatial experience, not just a necessary expedient.[8]

The long public debate over London's third airport was finally resolved in 1979 when the government abandoned the plan to locate it on Thames estuary and settled instead for the development of the old military airbase at Stansted in Essex, a forty-minute train journey from the centre of London. Stansted had been used in the 1960s and 1970s as a freight centre with very limited passenger services but there were no terminal buildings of any size or significance. Here at last was the opportunity to build a big airport from scratch on an open site. Norman Foster was commissioned to design it and he attacked the problem with relish.[9] A keen pilot himself, he brought to the task a boyish enthusiasm for the romance as well as the technology of air travel. The new airport would be a celebration of the joy of flight, not a craven retreat into jaded consumerism. His first mental move was to strip away all the logistic, commercial and bureaucratic paraphernalia of the typical modern airport and imagine it in its original, primitive form: a simple, flexible, single-storey structure at the edge of a field. This vision survives triumphantly in the final building (fig. 83). Departures and arrivals share one big room, high enough for all four of its glass walls to be visible over the low structures—shop cabins, check-in desks, security screens, etc.—laid out on its flat, granite-paved floor. Passengers can perceive the full extent of the building the moment they enter it. It is surely this subconciously

83 Stansted Airport, baggage reclaim area, Foster and Partners. Photograph: Dennis Gilbert.

reassuring feature of the space that makes Stansted one of the few international airports people actually enjoy using.

Why had this simple solution never been employed in any previous airport terminal? One answer is that, at 600,000 m³, the space is about four times the normally allowable maximum size for a fire compartment. Foster's were able to argue, however, that the single large volume was actually a positive advantage in the control of smoke, which is the main hazard in any building fire. By doubling the normal ceiling height, a smoke reservoir was created, allowing plenty of time for the building to be evacuated before the fumes reached head height. This is a good example of the way an analytical and scientific, rather than a conventional approach to problem solving can transform the pre-conditions of a design and open up new possibilities. But of course, although the smoke control argument was undoubtedly used to justify the additional height (and cost) to the client, the real reason was to create a lofty, airy space that would lift the spirit.

The roof is a square grid of 121 shallow steel-framed quasi-domes supported by 'trees' at 36 metre centres. It is a roof, and nothing else. It supports no plant, no ductwork, no lighting and no suspended ceilings. This is the secret of its billowing lightness—this and the cluster of triangular roof lights in the crown of each dome, carefully screened by suspended baffles to cut out glare and reflect daylight upwards onto the soffit. Each of the supporting trees has a trunk of four steel columns, and four slender branches braced by tension members bolted to a pyramid on top of the trunk. The clean elegance of the whole superstructure is made possible by the banishing of all plant and services, including the baggage handling equipment, to a concrete framed undercroft that is completely invisible to the building's users. Conditioned air, electrical power and water services are delivered to the main space via the tree trunks, which also support powerful concealed lights shining up into the domes.

This is a space that makes even the best of the concourses at Heathrow, Gatwick and Manchester seem awkward and slovenly. The same care and judgment has been applied to the secondary structures supporting the terminal on the land side—the fan-shaped car park with its covered walkways, and especially the railway station that slides unobtrusively under the forecourt to deposit its passengers right under the first bay of the big roof. The station is no more than a bare concrete canyon but it is made warm and luminous by the simple device of a row of orange floodlights shining on the retaining wall opposite the platform.

On the air side of the terminal, a break occurs in the smooth spatial transition from train or car to aeroplane. Whereas at Heathrow, Gatwick and Manchester the piers that give access to aeroplanes via gate lounges and air-bridges are attached directly to the main terminals, at Stansted they are freestanding buildings connected to the terminal by a rapid transit system. The little shuttle train draws up in front of the big glass wall facing the apron, under an open canopy identical to that over the forecourt on the opposite side. It is like a miniature version of the main railway, but raised up to the floor level of the concourse. From here it quickly dives underground to deposit departing passengers at basement level in the piers. Gate lounges are at the top level of the pier superstructure, with uninterrupted views of the aeroplanes. The freestanding pier arrangement is favoured by airline operators because it eases the movement of aeroplanes on the apron. It also means that the airport can be extended rationally and with the minimum of disruption by simply building more piers. But it has disadvantages from the point of view of the passengers, who must decide when to abandon the duty free shops in the terminal building and make their way to the pier, uncertain what facilities they might find there. The journey on the little train is short

84 Bristol International Airport, YRM. Photograph: Peter Cook/VIEW.

and the relationship between the train and the terminal could not be simpler, but still an element of uncertainty is introduced and the stress level is somewhat increased. That reassuring single space, with land vehicles on one side and aeroplanes on the other, has after all turned out to be an illusion.

Despite this compromise of Foster's original vision, Stansted represented a leap forward in British, and indeed international, airport design. It was the first of a new generation. It introduced a new set of criteria against which all future terminals would be judged, and those criteria — clarity, simplicity, legibility and spatial continuity — were not commercial or operational but architectural. Stansted demonstrated that the airport terminal need not be a bureacratic machine or a shopping grotto, it could be a generous and dignified public building. Many of its most characteristic features — the strict separation of served and servant spaces, the penetration of daylight into the heart of the building, the lightweight 'umbrella' roof unifying the spaces below, the massive tree-like supports, the views out over the surrounding landscape — would be imitated in airport terminals all over the world, from Stuttgart and Hamburg to Kansai and Kuala Lumpur.

85 Luton Airport, Foster and Partners. Photograph: Colin Davies.

The strength and pervasiveness of Stansted's influence is well illustrated by the new passenger terminal at Bristol by veteran airport designers, YRM (fig. 84).[10] The terminal is part of a plan to expand the airport to a capacity of 3 million passengers per annum by 2005. It has a simple, rectangular plan, divided into square bays on a 21.6 metre grid with an eaves height of 10 metres. (The equivalent dimensions at Stansted are 18 metres and 12 metres.) As at Stansted, the roof bays are shallow pyramids with crowning roof lights, supported by columns with tree-like tubular steel branches. The single round columns are concrete, not steel, and they are placed at the corners of every bay, rather than at the centres of alternate bays. Nevertheless, the superficial resemblance to the superstructure of Stansted is very striking. The services strategy is similar too, with air-handling plant accommodated in a basement storey, delivering conditioned air to the main space via free standing service modules incorporating uplighters. External walls, naturally, are all glass. The big difference is that, whereas Stansted is a single high room, Bristol is a more economical two-level terminal, dug into a sloping site. The upper floor, which is at ground level on the air side, forms a balcony overlooking the double-height land-side concourse.

86 Luton Airport. Photograph: Colin Davies.

Ironically, in his latest UK airport scheme, a new terminal for down-market Luton, the holiday makers' airport and home of low-cost operator Easyjet, Norman Foster has abandoned the austere architectural virtues of Stansted in favour of 'brightness and fun' (figs. 85 and 86). Whereas Stansted attempts to keep the retailing and catering firmly under control, subjecting them to a strict architectural discipline, Luton gives in to commercial pressure and goes with the flow. This is a split-level building, with services and baggage handling in a semi-basement at apron level. Departing passengers enter the obligatory double-height concourse at ground level and are immediately greeted by an illuminated wall of advertising over the sixty check-in desks. The rest of the ground floor is packed with shops and cafes in a mainly artificially lit, internalised space—a shopping centre and proud of it. It is only in the departure lounges on the upper level that daylight and outside views reassert themselves. The external envelope too could hardly be more different from Stansted. Dissolving the classical distinction between roof, column and wall, a single curved skin of profiled metal, exactly like an aerofoil wing section with the leading edge facing the apron, wraps around the whole building. Here we can detect the influence of Renzo Piano's gigantic

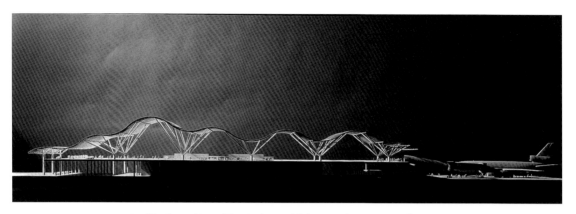

87 Heathrow Airport Terminal 5, model showing the sinuous roof structure, Richard Rogers Partnership. Photograph: Eamonn O'Mahony.

Kansai airport in Japan, though at Luton the pier that gives access to the aeroplanes is at right angles to, rather than in line with, the wing section.

Meanwhile back at Heathrow, proposals to extend the airport with a fifth terminal are well advanced (fig. 87). Everyone agrees that the current state of Heathrow almost amounts to a national scandal, and any curtailment of growth, with a consequent loss of traffic to European rivals like Frankfurt, would be a form of economic masochism. The British Airports Authority held a competition for the design of the new terminal in 1991, with Michael Manser and Renzo Piano on the jury. It was won by the Richard Rogers Partnership. The appointment of the British establishment's favourite modern architect (and Piano's ex-partner) was probably not uninfluenced by BAA's need to present a respectable image to the planning authorities. But Rogers had experience of airport design in the Europier extension to Terminal 1, mentioned above, and in the extensive replanning of Marseilles airport, the largest in France outside Paris.

Despite the current congestion, there is in fact plenty of scope for expansion of Heathrow. About 55 million passengers pass through it every year, but the runways have spare capacity for another 30 million. The limiting factor is the fixed boundaries of that crowded island with its narrow, umbilical tunnel. Terminal 5 will forge a new access link to the M25 motorway at the west end of the site, and will replace the existing sewage works between the main runways.[11] The influence of Stansted on Rogers' design strategy is obvious, though Terminal 5 is much larger and its site more restricted. Like Stansted, it proposes a main terminal building or 'core', with freestanding piers or 'satellites', accessible via an underground rapid transit system, now called a 'people mover'. The core, however, also operates as a pier, with parking spaces for about twelve aeroplanes. It has a light, services-free 'umbrella' roof supported on structural 'trees', and daylight is introduced to the centre of building through strips of roof lights. There are large roof overhangs on both land and air sides, and the walls are all glass, sloping outwards to reduce reflections both of light and of radar.

This is, however, very far from the concept of a single room with arrivals and departures on one level. The site does not allow such expansiveness. In the published designs, the superstructure has three main levels: baggage handling and plant at apron level, arrivals and baggage reclaim on the first floor, and departures on the top floor. Each of these floors is at least a double height and mezzanines are introduced to accommodate offices, shops and ancillary functions. So this is a development of the Stansted prototype and an application of its principles to a larger, multi-level terminal. Every effort is made to maintain legibility and prevent it from degenerating into a collection of separate spaces. The roof is the key, not this time a static, square grid, but a wave form, undulating from land side to air side over the departing passengers on the top level. Each strip of roof lights marks a stage of the journey: entrance concourse, check-in desks, shopping centre and air-side lounges. The wave and its supporting trees form an independent structure enclosing a space which, if too big to be comprehended at a glance, is nevertheless perceptible as a single envelope. The muti-storey structure below — a building within a building — is interrupted by atriums and canyons which bring daylight to the lower levels and reveal the full depth of the building. Departing passengers, for example, can look down into the baggage reclaim hall, and a big central atrium on the land side extends right down to the station platform of the new Paddington–Heathrow rail link below ground level.

The satellites, each with parking spaces for about twenty aeroplanes, are smaller versions of the core terminal. Three storeys high, with departure lounges as usual on the top level, they have the same kind of wavy roof but with two instead of four rows of supporting trees. Here at Heathrow, the freestanding satellite arrangement has added advantages for both the passengers and the airport operator. About 30% of passengers will be transferring to other flights. They will wait in the generous transfer lounges on the arrivals level and will not have to go into the core building at all. These satellites are also bigger than those at Stansted and can accommodate more retail and catering facitilites, which means more convenience for the passengers and more profit for the operators. On the land side of the core terminal, an array of multi-storey car parks, with a hotel and an office block, occupies a triangle of land between the triple-level forecourt and the exit road. The designs show these buildings as a kind of soft landscape which will not distract attention from the main architectural event — the wavy roof of the terminal.

Looking at the plan of the whole airport with the new terminal in place, it is obvious that, unlike the one-off temporary solution of Terminal 4, Terminal 5 is just the first phase of a long-term plan for total redevelopment. More satellites and core terminals will march eastwards in orderly ranks between the parallel runways until they finally invade the island site.

The British Airports Authority controls seven British airports, including Heathrow, Gatwick and Stansted (but not Manchester). Its role as a client is therefore crucial to the architectural future of the British airport. Stansted and Terminal 5 would seem to indicate a spirit of enlightened patronage, but there are worrying signs that in fact architectural quality is relatively low priority for BAA. Stansted was commissioned before the privatisation of the authority (in 1986) and it is almost certain that it would not have been realised in its present form under the new managment. That tall, generous space would have been much harder to justify under a management regime that is now looking for a 30% reduction in construction costs. Norman Foster has not since been employed by BAA, and the appointment of Richard Rogers for Terminal 5 was as much for political as architectural reasons. The overall budget for the new terminal is something less than two-thirds of what is considered normal. It will be, says BAA, a 'shell and core' project, which means that much of the detailed design decision making will be taken out of the hands of the principal architect. Rogers' role will be to wrap an economical, tight-fit enclosure around functional spaces shaped by the more limited vision of interior designers and engineers.

BAA is looking for nothing less than complete transformation of the process of building procurement, design and construction. It seems that the architect's traditional concerns for place-making, cultural context, and the lasting quality of the final product are being marginalised by the drive to improve the short-term efficiency of the construction process. BAA now insists that 50% of the components of a new terminal should be preselected under 'framework agreements' with contractors and suppliers. This may be no more than a common-sense attempt to reduce time and money wasted reinventing the wheel, but it diminishes the influence of the architect and means that buildings like Stansted, in which the smallest details contribute to an integrated architectural whole, will no longer be possible. BAA now sees its buildings as 'branded' products, like chain stores or fast food restaurants — a strategy that seems singularly inappropriate to such a small

88   Southampton Airport, Michael Manser Practice.

collection of sparsely scattered 'outlets'. If this view prevails, then it will surely only reinforce the common perception of the airport as a non-place, devoid of any individual character.[12]

The first airport to be redeveloped under the new management regime was Southampton (fig. 88).[13] A small airport expanding on the basis of flights to the Channel Islands, it is perfectly located next to junction 5 of the M27 with its own station on the main London–Southampton railway line. Designed by Michael Manser, the passenger terminal, though rectangular on plan, has an aeroplane-like cross section. A three-storey 'fuselage' contains customs and security search areas on the ground floor and plant and offices on the upper levels. This is flanked by single-storey land-side and air-side 'lean-tos', roofed by curved, anhedral 'wings' which merge with the roof of the fuselage in a continuous wave-like form. At the junction of wings and fuselage, strips of roof glazing light the concourses below and also allow the top-floor offices a view out. The structure is as ingenious as the plan, especially the way the steel beams of the wing-roofs are connected to the fuselage by means of struts and tension members under the

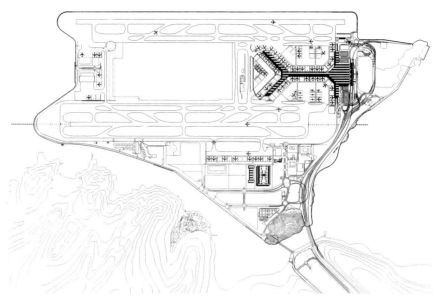

89 Hong Kong International Airport, site plan, Foster and Partners.

roof lights. On the air side the concourse has to be divided into separate arrivals and departures zones, but on the land side it extends from end to end, creating a generous, well lit, upward-expanding space that looks bigger than it is. In an airport as small as this it is possible to make a direct visual connection between the runway and the terminal. A small observation gallery in the 'cockpit' of the fuselage, accessible via a prominent staircase in the land-side concourse, allows non-travellers to see their friends and relatives safely off into the sky. It is thoughtful touches like this that make air travel enjoyable. Internal and external finishes—glass, crinkly aluminium, plywood, and cement particle board with terrazzo floors—are only one price bracket better than industrial, but by devising a unified, economical form, Michael Manser has made the most of the limited BAA budget and the building is a pleasure to use. Only the café in the land-side concourse lets it down. The caterers decided for some reason that a pre-war pub would be an appropriate theme and the resulting stage-set clashes horribly with Manser's efficient enclosure. Perhaps the interior designers were influenced by the fact that it was from this airfield in 1936 that the Supermarine Spitfire made its first flight.

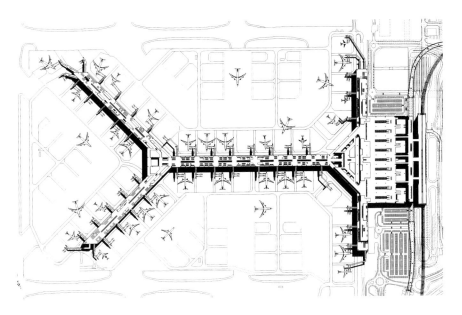

90   Hong Kong International Airport, plan.

Stansted may have been the turning point in British airport design, the moment when the beast that is the modern airport was at last tamed and turned into humane architecture, but it was only the overture. For the full opera we have to leave the British Isles and fly to the recently ex-British colony, Hong Kong, where Foster has designed one of the largest airports in the world and the future transport hub of the whole of East Asia. Until 1992, Chek Lap Kok was just a 100-metre high lump of rock in the sea twenty miles west of Hong Kong. The rock has now been flattened to form an island 6 km by 3.5 km — four times its original area — and the site for the new airport (figs. 89–90). Between the two parallel runways sits a low, undulating Y-shaped passenger terminal building, itself not unlike some impossibly large aeroplane.[14] At the east end of the building stands the Ground Transportation Centre, a larger version of the forecourt and railway station at Stansted, but this time with arriving and departing trains on different levels. This is the terminus of a long, looping line that starts on Hong Kong island, crosses the harbour to Kowloon and then hops from island to island over a series of new bridges, including the world's largest double-decker road and rail suspension bridge. Journey time from city to airport is twenty minutes.

91 Hong Kong International Airport, baggage reclaim hall. Photograph: Colin Davies.

Although in places the terminal is an eight-storey structure, as far as the passengers' experience is concerned it has two main levels: departure level above and arrival level below. This segregation is maintained throughout the building, from the railway station and forecourt right through to the air-bridges that give access to the planes. The building may be enormous — 1.2 kilometres from end to end — but the diagram could not be simpler. Departing passengers enter via bridges across the high, wide canyon of the arrivals hall, to land among the parallel ranks of check-in desks — 288 in all. From here they pass on through the Sky Mart, said to be the biggest airport shopping centre in the world, and step onto the travelators that serve 38 boarding gates ranged along the stem and branches of the Y. If their boarding gate is far distant, they can opt to travel instead on the 'automated people mover' under the building. In the other direction, arriving pasengers pass straight from the air-bridge to travelators on the lower level, which is saved from being a mere tunnel by strips of glass ceiling giving views of the departure level above. Once through passport control, arriving passengers enter a hypostyle hall, with slender round columns on a 12-metre-square grid supporting a troughed concrete slab which incorporates light fittings and curved metal reflecting panels. This bare structural description, though it covers all the main visible features, hardly does justice to what is a truly magnificent space.

92 Hong Kong International Airport, arrival hall. Photograph: Colin Davies.

And this is only the baggage reclaim hall (fig. 91). From here passengers pass on into the arrival hall proper, where space billows upward and daylight floods down (fig, 92). And there, straight ahead on the same level, is the platform for the Hong Kong train.

But I have not yet mentioned the most remarkable feature of this building—its roof. As at Stansted, the secret of the roof lies in the arrangement of the mechanical services, which are tidied away out of sight in the basement. At Stansted, all services, including even the artificial lighting, are delivered to the occupied space via the trunks of the trees that support the roof. At Hong Kong airport there are no trees, only slender concrete columns on a 36-metre grid, and the artificial lighting is mounted at roof level, but the principle is the same. Chilled air is blown into the space above head height through small free-standing towers, called 'binnacles', which also serve as mountings for monitors, clocks, fire hoses and the like. In environmental engineering terms, this creates a layer of relatively comfortable air at concourse level, obviating the need to cool the whole interior volume and therefore saving large amounts of energy. But it also has important architectural implications. It means that the roof is free of intrusive ductwork and machinery. Its only function (almost) is to keep out the rain.

Like the shallow quasi-domes at Stansted, the Hong Kong airport roof is made from triangulated steel frames infilled with perforated metal ceiling panels and incorporating roof lights. The family resemblance is unmistakable. The differences, however, are more important than the similarities. Where the Stansted roof is square, finite, level and static, the Hong Kong roof is directional, linear, undulating and dynamic. Instead of separate domes supported by trees, we have seemingly endless shallow barrel vaults, gently rising and falling over the length and width of the building and supported on columns so widely spaced that they seem only occasional features of the interior. As in all Foster buildings, form is justified functionally. The roof rises and falls for reasons of economy. A high ceiling is appropriate over the arrivals hall, check-in area and multi level shopping centre, but would be wasteful, in both structural and environmental terms, over the narrower spaces occupied by the travelators and gate lounges. The conventional architectural solution to this problem would be to articulate the form, with buildings of different heights connected by circulation tubes or tunnels — the familiar diagrammatic airport plan. Instead, Foster invents a single roof form like a quilted blanket thrown over the building, hovering momentarily on a cushion of air. It is trimmed to fit the plan, narrowing to a single barrel vault over the stem of the Y, but it remains a separate element with its own structural and formal logic. Where the plan changes direction, at the branches of the Y for example, the barrel vaults maintain their constant east-west grain. Again, there is a functional justification for this. Wherever you are in the building you can always look up at the ceiling to orientate yourself. This, combined with panoramic views through the all glass external walls of the sea to the north and the mountains of Lantau Island to the south, make this a remarkably legible building despite its size.

But the best justification of all for the roof form is its utter simplicity. It is, though, a special kind of simplicity, a kind of simplicity that can only be achieved with the help of computers. The roof is made up of 36-metre-square structural shells. Each was assembled from a standard set of steel beams, welded together on site on a special jig then hoisted into position on the concrete columns. The joints between the shells were designed to accommodate large tolerances so that the relationships could be varied to form the gentle undulations of the roof. The shells are all identical, but only outwardly. Because of the undulations, different shells have to withstand different configurations of vertical and lateral forces, and the weights of the steel beams therefore vary. The resulting form may be simple, but there is a hidden complexity. The thousands of three-dimensional structural calculations involved would not have been tackled in a pre-computer age.

Another way to characterise the difference between Stansted and Hong Kong is to say that the former is classical, the latter organic — organic not merely in the sense that it has an animal-like form (some kind of sting-ray skimming along the sea bottom, perhaps) but in the sense that it is a system or network, adapting itself subtly in response to different structural, environmental and functional conditions. The architectural details of the building express this idea clearly, though more perhaps in what is left out than what is included. The emphasis on verticality implied by the structural trees at Stansted — their regular, repetitive nature, and the way that they express their loadbearing function like the columns of a temple — is completely absent at Hong Kong where visually the columns are insignificant and the roof weightless. In any Foster building there is always a relationship between what you see and how it was constructed. Nothing is ever faked. But the translation of construction into form is never purely functional. This is architecture not engineering, and it builds a world, a world based on a paradigm or myth. At Stansted the myth tells of the power and beauty of industrial technology. The structure therefore draws attention to itself, showing off its tectonic qualities. We can see that it is constructed from a kit of factory-made components. Each component — the compression and tension members in the structural trees, for example — has its own distinct character. But at Hong Kong airport these distinctions are played down. The curved tension members that brace the roof shells look more like bones or tendons than booms or struts, and the roof is perceived as an organic whole rather than a constructed assemblage. The design is informed by a new myth, a new way of looking at the world and at technology. The old, expressive, High Tech style, which was an extension of nineteenth-century structural rationalism, has been superseded by a new digital/biological paradigm. If Stansted is the architectural equivalent of the pre-war biplane, Hong Kong is the architectural equivalent of the fly-by-wire jet airliner.

Although the relationship between Foster and Partners and the British Airports Authority had been less than happy on the Stansted project, they nevertheless collaborated very successfully as members of the consortium that built Hong Kong. BAA must surely be envious of a political climate in which the removal all at once of one of the world's major international airports from its old site on the Kai Tak peninsula to a flattened mountain twenty miles away could not only be contemplated but successfully carried out, even through the upheaval and uncertainty of the handover of the colony to China in 1997. How fervently must BAA wish that they could do the same to Heathrow.

1   See Sudjic, Deyan, 'The airport as city,' *SD*, no. 362 (November 1994), pp. 17-22.

2   'Rogers' Heathrow pier opens for business', *Architects' Journal*, vol. 202, no. 22 (7 November 1995), pp.8-9.

3   'Bridge to the sky', *Architecture Today*, no. 40 (July 1993), pp. 42-43.

4   Colin Davies, 'Making a flying start', *Designers' Journal*, no. 21 (October 1996), pp. 19-85.

5   Colin Davies, 'Sterling value', *Architects' Journal*, vol. 193, no. 11 (13 March 1991), pp. 38-45.

6   Brian Waters, 'Fresh flight path for Gatwick', *Building*, vol. 248, no. 7390 (16) (19 April 1985), pp.36-41.

7   John Lloyd, 'New terminal makes light of flying', *Architects' Journal*, vol. 197, no. 20 (19 May 1993), pp.29-42.

8   Deborah Singmaster, 'Manchester Airport's space age, tubular travelator', *Architects' Journal*, vol. 198, no. 19 (17 November 1993), p. 15.

9   Kenneth Powell, *Stansted: Norman Foster and the architecture of flight* (London: Fourth Estate, 1992). Also 'Airports', *Architectural Review* special issue, vol. 189, no. 1131 (May 1991), pp. 36-82.

10   'Bristol fashion: airport terminal by YRM', *Architecture Today*, no. 118 (May 2001), pp. 76-80.

11   Paul Finch, 'The plane leaving Heathrow has been delayed', *Architects' Journal* , vol. 203, no. 25 (27 June 1996), pp. 8-9.

12   Augé Marc, *Non-places: introduction to an anthropology of supermodernity*, transl. John Howe (London: Verso, 1995).

13   Penny McGuire, 'Southerly approach', *Architectural Review*, vol. 197, no. 1176 (February 1995), pp. 81-83, 85, 87.

14   Peter Davey, 'Plane sailing', *Architectural Review*, vol. 204, no. 1219 (September 1998), pp. 50-63, 49-87.

AUTOMOBILES

Architecture for the Motor-Car

David Jeremiah

> Under a spreading chestnut tree
> The village smithy stood;
> Where now there stands a huge garage
> Of concrete, steel and wood.
> The smith no longer swings his sledge,
> He has an easier method found
> Of making £. s. d.[1]

T HE *MOTOR*'S LINES of 1926 would not have amused everyone. After thirty years of motoring on British roads, they were a pertinent reminder of the benefits and dangers of the motor-car. Feared and loved, by the mid-1920s opinion was deeply divided over the manner in which motoring had generated a trade that steadily changed society and landscape.

A New Trade

In the early years of motoring the new services had grown out of engineering workshops, coach and carriage building premises, haulage depots, stables, bicycle repairers and local hardware stores. Garages could be found in converted chapels and theatres and added on to domestic houses. Harrods, for example, entered the motor trade in July 1902, taking over a disused tabernacle in Lancelot Place opposite the store in Brompton Road, for the sale of new and used cars. Whilst many of the new businesses continued to be dependent on such opportunist developments, by the early years of the twentieth century purpose built garages were being constructed and in some instances, such as the French car manufacturer Darracq's new garage and showroom on Oxford Street in 1902, occupied major city-centre sites.

Service was at the core of the new buildings, which had to accommodate machines that were difficult to manoeuvre and demanded regular maintenance and protection. This required a new type of architecture that would blend efficiency with elegance, reassuring the new consumers of the reliability of the motor-car while representing the trade as progressive and innovative. Some of the new building types are easy to categorise, others are less so. From garage to multi-storey car park, filling station to service station, roadside café to road-house, the architecture of the car was aimed at people who were experiencing for the first time the pleasures and responsibilities that came with motoring. Inevitably, many of the buildings associated with the early decades of motoring have been radically altered and in some instances demolished. Even so, it is still possible to identify key stages in the history of motoring architecture and to assess the significant contribution that this building type has made to the development of new forms of commercial design and expression.

At the outset motoring was a fair-weather pursuit, and the early motor-cars needed to be stored for long periods in a protected heated environment, with access to workshops and mechanics. Country houses were able to construct extensive garage-workshop facilities, designed around the servicing of the motor-cars, but there were many other urban households that had neither premises suitable for conversion, nor space to construct a garage. For such motorists, and particularly for those who were touring, by 1905–06 there was a positive flood of new garages. With pleasure, convenience and status defining the culture of motoring, almost every *Autocar* listed the opening of new businesses. Hotels were extending or constructing new garages for their clientele and, as motor manufacturers were entering into new franchise agreements, the existing trade moved into larger buildings and opened new branches in anticipation of future expansion shaped by the demands of the owner–driver. The new garages included 'lock-up' or 'open space' garaging for private motor-cars alongside repair workshops and showrooms. Small-scale repairs could be carried out at city-centre premises, but it was common to find that the main workshops were developed separately.

Up until the early 1920s owning a motor-car was the preserve of the rich, and this was reflected in the type of service provided. Even though motoring at any time of the day was precarious, and at night hazardous, the motorists were provided with a 24-hour garage service. Hire-car facilities, either self- or chauffeur-driven, were usually available, with rest and drying rooms for the local and visiting chauffeurs, and in some instances—such as the Fiat motorhouse in Brighton—provision was extended to include bedrooms. This pattern of development was common across the country, and the origins of Caffyns at Eastbourne provides a good illustration of the characteristics of this new trade.[2] Metamorphosing from ironmongers to gas fitters to electrical engineers, by 1902 Caffyns was occupying a prime site adjacent to the Queens Hotel, just off the promenade. The first suggestion of the potential of a new trade had been raised

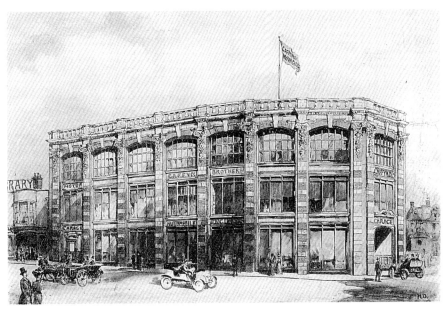

93 Caffyns workshop, garage and showroom, Eastbourne, 1906. J. W. Woolnough.

when the two brothers who were to form the business plan were approached by a hotel visitor looking for somewhere to store a 4-cylinder Renault. They modified their existing premises to accommodate motor-cars, and by March 1905 realised that the future business plan should be based on meeting the needs of the motorist. Land was acquired next to the hotel and a local man, J. W. Woolnough, was commissioned to design a three-storey building that blended workshop with showroom (fig. 93). When the latter was opened in time for the summer season in 1906, Caffyns announced that they had 'pleasure in presenting to the nobility, gentry, and all interested in Motoring a brief account of the splendid facilities they now possess' for storing, supplying and repairing motor-cars.[3] In addition to the hundred-car lock-up and their engineering department, Caffyns offered hire cars with drivers as well as driving lessons. Recognising the importance of the local customer, as well as the visitor, the company also established a coach-building department that would construct the coach-built car to individual specifications.

The first reported professional discussion on 'Motor Houses and Garages' was at the Architectural Association's meeting of 17 October 1906, at which the technical requirements of the private, trade and public garage were considered.[4] In February 1908 the Association returned to the same subject, with a paper presented by C. Harrison Townsend. It was well researched, making reference to developments on the Continent and in the United States of America, and emphasising the practical issues of lighting, heating, ventilation, and the safe storage of petrol. Having drawn attention to this new architecture, it was left to Walter Cave to summarise the current climate.

> We were still in an experimental stage in the matter, and the necessities of the case would, in due time, and when we had settled down to what was wanted, lead to the evolution of a suitable architectural form. An entirely new development like motor-cars must bring in its train a new form in architecture.[5]

For some time the new buildings had little to distinguish them from their commercial neighbours. Many were constructed along the lines of industrial warehouses, and the influence of the large municipal transport depots on scale and style was evident. However, as the trade thought through the relationship of showroom, workshop and parking in one complex, there were sufficient new initiatives to have justified continued attention, but surprisingly the subject disappeared from the architectural debate until the 1920s.

The motor trade had steadily been moving from the back street to the high street, from industrial to commercial centres. This development created increasingly luxurious showroom settings, 'whereas in the olden time one used to enter as likely as not under a clothes lines into back premises where cars and moving machines and broken mangles were mixed up, today enormous glass doors slide back and the car finds itself in some vast hall lit by electric light, and frequently provided with palms and arm chairs'.[6] The formation of the Society of Motor Manufacturers and Traders in July 1902 had been a key event in this development and led to the organisation of what was to be the first of the annual motor shows at Olympia in February 1906. Scotland had its own motor shows,[7] as did some of the regional cities, but it was the growth and standing of the Olympia show, complementing the motor-car manufacturers move into central London, that gave London a distinctive position in the trade. Originating in Long Acre, it was not long before the London motor trade began to move into what were considered to be more aristocratic settings. Rover took up residence in Bond Street, Sunbeam in Princess Street, off Hanover Square, Fiat in Albemarle Street, and Vauxhall in Great Portland Street. Euston Road and Great Portland Street were soon known as the 'centre of motordom'. Regional centres followed similar

94 Caffyns showroom, garage and concert hall, Eastbourne, 1910-11.

patterns: Manchester's motor trade began to establish itself in the central Deansgate area, while Glasgow's began in the similarly convenient St Vincent Street.

Before 1914, the direct influence of the oil companies on the architectural development of motor services had yet to take effect. In 1907–08, however, new premises were designed for the Anglo-American Oil Company at the corner of Queen Anne's Gate and Birdcage Walk in London. Other service industries were also expanding—notably the tyre companies, whose ebullience and confidence was soon testified to by the lavish and exuberant new Michelin Building in Fulham Road, designed by Francois Espinasse and officially opened with great ceremony in January 1911. The Michelin Building was much admired for its tiled motifs and pictorial panels celebrating great motoring achievements with which the company had been associated; but behind the decoration there was a functional building of services and offices. The following May, the Continental Tyre and Rubber Company opened a similarly grand service centre in Thurloe Place, off Brompton Road—which, with its black marble entrance hall and page boys, was thought 'to be more like a private club than a house of business'.[8]

With the growing enthusiasm for motoring, buildings for local trade became similarly assertive. Caffyns new garage and showroom in Meads Road, Eastbourne, of 1911 (fig. 94), not only occupied a prime site between the Town Hall and the county cricket ground but also included a first floor concert hall that could be used for dances and receptions; a card room, that could act as a lounge and refreshment annex; and a supper room.[9] It was at this time that W. R. Morris opened his first High Street garage in Holywell Street, Oxford. Designed by local architects Tollit and Lee, it was explicitly intended for the sale, storing, hiring and repairing of cars. Another well-publicised development of the same year was Tom Norton's 'Automobile Palace' at Llandrindod Wells, finished in a glazed classicism and with its shallow curved frontage broken by rampant lions on the roofline. Exploiting a sloping corner site, the Automobile Palace allowed direct access to the first floor workshops and garaging from the rear of the building.[10] By 1914, the Claud Hamilton Garage at Kelvinbridge in Glasgow, with its 90 lock-ups and 150 open spaces, was thought to be the largest garage in Britain.[11]

The arrival of the multi-storey car park was an event of great significance. In 1903 the London Motor Garage Co. Ltd. had established a showroom, workshop and garage parking at 33–37 Wardour Street, but three years later this development was eclipsed by the Mitchell Motor Garage constructed to meet the needs of London's theatreland (fig. 95). It was set out on five floors, moving cars by lifts and turntables. Pre-dating commuting by motor-car, day-time parking, between 8.00 AM and 6.00 PM, was half-price, during which time three of the floors were used as showrooms. The illustration is a free interpretation of the garage that was accessed down side streets off Wardour Street and Dean Street, with a shop reception on Wardour Street.[12] A good introduction to the range of its services is provided in *Motor Roads to London*, published by the company. Its third edition of 1912 explained that

> The establishment includes, in addition to the repair shops, separate departments for painting, coachbuilding, the sale of accessories, vulcanising and tyre-repairing, the sale of second-hand cars, the hiring of high-class laudaulettes and touring cars, and a storage department where cars, each in its separate lockup, can be stored away for any period.

> American and Continental visitors are specially catered for, and the management is always at the service of clients for advice in the arrangement of tours and all matters relating to touring.[13]

West End parking, or 'garaging' as it was often called, continued to attract attention and just before the First World War a further garage was constructed in Wardour Street; and early in 1919 the coach building company Salmon & Sons

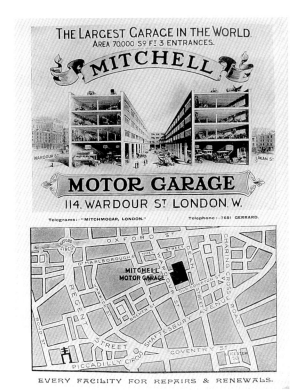

THE LARGEST GARAGE IN THE WORLD.
AREA 70,000 SQ FT 3 ENTRANCES.

MITCHELL

MOTOR GARAGE

114. WARDOUR ST LONDON. W.

Telegrams:—"MITCHMOGAR, LONDON."   Telephone:—7681 GERRARD.

EVERY FACILITY FOR REPAIRS & RENEWALS.

95 Mitchell Motor Garage as advertised in the Catalogue of the 5th International Motor Exhibition, London, 1906.

completed a three-storey garage in Castle Street, just off Long Acre.[14] These were pragmatic schemes, and it was an account in the *Illustrated London News* of 18 October 1919 that gave Britain its first visual impression of the potential scale of the new architecture for the motor-car. With a full-page illustration of an American proposal for an eighteen-storey circular 'Sky-Scraper Park', able to hold seven hundred cars, the possibilities of the multi-storey ramped driveway garage were graphically explored.

Underlying all of these developments was a concern to improve the efficiency of a service trade, and no initiative was more important than the eventual introduction of the petrol pump. Of the rituals associated with the journey, filling up with petrol was of primary importance, and up until the First World War anyone planning a major trip or following a little used route was likely to carry extra petrol cans. Despite the increasing numbers and expectations of motorists, suppliers were thinly spread across the country, concentrated on the large urban or established tourist centres and the buying of petrol, particularly of the right quality, continued to be a cause for anxiety. The first hint of change came with the appearance of the kerbside petrol-pump on a British high street, erected in 1915 outside the premises of Legge and Chamier's, Shrewsbury, by the American pump manufacturers S.F. Bowser & Co.[15] Further expansion was very limited, and then brought to a halt by the Great War.

After 1918 there was in Britain a general reluctance to follow the American example, partly because of the obvious threat that pumps posed to the existing trade outlets and partly out of suspicions concerning the accuracy and reliability of the new pumps themselves. But the fears and opposition were steadily overcome as first Bowser's promoted its new petrol pump at the 1919 Olympia Motor Show and then, early in 1920, Pratt's launched a publicity campaign to promote new pumps manufactured by Gilbert & Barker.[16]

Trade and public reservations notwithstanding, this was to prove a defining moment in the development of the architecture for the car. Apart from designing buildings capable of accommodating the motor-car, architects now had to come to terms with positioning the petrol pump as a central part of the design. Pumps were monumental in scale, and when fitted with a globe were well over ten feet high. Housing the pumping mechanisms and, at the same time, able to withstand the weather, pump forms were invariably functional and, when painted in company colours, their impact on the architectural and environmental surroundings was dramatic. For the first time architects were being asked to design around an industrial product. Some accepted the challenge with great imagination; others never missed an opportunity to attack it.

New Landmarks

With motoring no longer confined to the very rich, new motorists were taking to the road in increasing numbers. As the middle classes were encouraged to enjoy the pleasures and freedom associated with 'going for a drive', the trade spilled out on to the high streets and village greens, and then proceeded to fill in the gaps between cities, towns and villages. While some of these motor services continued to be provided by speculative adaptations, elsewhere new architectural forms were emerging as the trade adjusted to the introduction of the petrol-pump and the growing demands of the owner–driver.

Although the installation of kerbside pumps gained momentum after 1918, no-one had been prepared to invest in an American-style roadside filling station.[17] The breakthrough came in 1919 with the decision by the Automobile Association[18] to open ten filling stations across the country for the exclusive use

96 Pratt's Petrol Filling Station, Battersea Bridge, London, 1921.

97 Pioneer Filling Station, as pictured on the front cover of *Light Car & Cyclecar*, 27 April 1923.

of its members. Set back from the road, the prefabricated wooden structures of the AA's stations—reminiscent of a colonial hut or small sports pavilion—housed a Bowser petrol pump and a 500-gallon tank. There were no repair facilities, but there was a telephone. The first one was opened on 2 March 1920 at Aldermaston, and by the following September four others were in service.

Even more significant than the AA's petrol stations was Pratt's enterprising decision of 1921 to open a number of filling stations in different parts of London. The first design, sited at the south end of Battersea Bridge, was based around a curved concrete double road, with the pumps on a central island and concrete surround walls and kiosk all finished in white Portland cement. This constituted Britain's first urban petrol-filling station (fig. 96).

Towards the end of 1921, the Pioneer Filling Station was opened on the London to Portsmouth road between Putney and Kingston. Following the AA model, it was a simple timber structure with canopy extending over two Pratt pumps. A building, rather than architecture, nevertheless it was further confirmation that the filling station was becoming a permanent part of the British landscape (fig. 97). When Shell eventually decided that it could no longer ignore these developments and launched its own petrol pump in December 1921, it unleashed a pattern of competition that for a time resulted in an uncontrolled installation of kerbside facilities.[19]

In this fertile climate, the important decision to build an integral garage, showroom and forecourt almost went unnoticed. Recognised at least by the motoring journals, the Blue Bird Motor Co. Filling Station (fig. 98) on the King's Road in London's Chelsea signalled the new direction in which the trade was moving. Its filling-station forecourt was opened in March 1923 and a garage showroom, designed by Robert Sharp, was added in 1924. The showrooms were incorporated into two flanking blocks, each with three floors of domestic flats; in between were the garage and workshops, which could also be accessed from the side road. There were private lock-ups, lounges, a refreshment room, a hire service of Rolls-Royce cars, and, with the first floor suspended from the roof, an open-plan space for garage and workshops. It was the model for the future.[20]

While much of the general architectural debate during the 1920s inevitably focused on the style and aesthetics of filling stations, the trade tended to be more interested in the layout of the forecourt. As attention turned to the provision of a speedy and efficient service, the problem arose as to whether it was more effective to place the petrol pumps in a long line, or to cluster or stagger their arrangement. In the end, the choice was substantially influenced by the access and con-

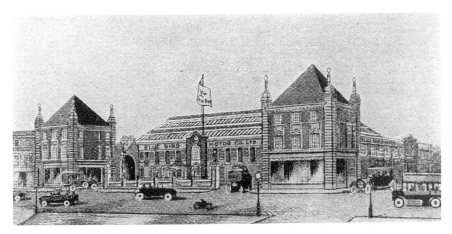

98   Blue Bird Motor Co., Service Station, Robert Sharp, as illustrated in March 1924.

figuration of each site and a growing awareness of the need to provide some form of cover for the motorist while being served with petrol. A linear arrangement of petrol pumps was by far the most common choice, although there were some interesting alternatives. For example, in April 1922 General Auto Limited of Shepherd's Bush arranged six pumps around a central service kiosk with a pitched roof providing protection from bad weather.

By the mid-1920s, the planning implications of the expanding motor trade were increasingly obvious. The parking of motors cars in streets and garages was becoming a major issue, and the spread of petrol filling stations was in many instances greeted with alarm.[21] Motoring came to be seen by many architects and planners as a threat to the countryside and a danger to the fabric of city life. Along with suburbia and ribbon development, the petrol pump and filling station acquired a special notoriety in the interwar years. This unsavoury reputation was aggravated by the fact that this new service industry began to occupy sites previously thought to be unprofitable;[22] more significantly, the spread of motor servicing provided the first major instance of American culture impacting on the towns and villages of Britain.

Against this often hostile background the motor trade made consistent efforts to achieve a harmony between the new buildings and their surroundings. Urban developments were usually dressed up with classical details, while the picturesque 'Old English' was the preferred style for the rural setting. Thus a 1926 garage and filling station at Farningham in Kent by Gervase Bailey was modelled as a sixteenth-century Tudor gate house, while a small, timber-framed 'Tudor cottage' filling-station at Colyford in East Devon of 1928 provided a covered area for the services, a small shop and cloakrooms. Indeed a rash of thatched services appeared in the late 1920s and early 1930s, including much-praised examples at Cranford in Middlesex, Kennford in Devon and Eashing in Surrey. Amongst the classical styled garages that attracted attention were the white glazed Central Garage in Wade Street, Leeds, by P. E. Snowden of 1925, with its murals of motoring scenes in the showrooms, and the Travers Garage in New Market Street, Newcastle-upon-Tyne, by Cacket and Burns Dick of 1924–25, with its four floors, ground-floor showrooms and basement workshops. Architectural house styles were also being imitated as companies opened up regional and national networks. For example, from the late 1920s Watson & Co of Liverpool employed a 'classical moderne' style in their garages at Liverpool, Birkenhead, Colwyn Bay and on the Embankment in London, all designed by D. A. Beveridge.[23]

The 1920s also saw the motor trade embrace new heights of architectural grandeur. The 1921 Wolseley building in Piccadilly by W. Curtis Green, with its commercial classicism and extravagant finish, set a standard pursued by many of Wolseley's rivals. The aesthetic treatment of its street frontage was rewarded with the RIBA bronze medal, and Green's vision of a motoring Elysium incorporated Roman Doric columns lacquered in plain red, which divided the showroom into nine squares (each of which was to be occupied by a car), doors and screens decorated in gold and either a red or black lacquer, and marble pavements — all of which was set off by the plain stone of the walls and white plastered ceiling.[24]

In the autumn of 1926, Citroen opened its new showrooms in Devonshire House, Piccadilly — next door to Rootes. Constructed as a replica of Napoleon's tomb in the Invalides, with a balustraded balcony and rotunda, the showroom stretched through three floors.[25] When Fords adapted 88 Regent Street to a showroom in 1930, one reviewer thought it to have 'an atmosphere which may be that of Florida';[26] the upper part of the two-storey showroom was judged 'a study in silver and gold, the gold mosaic of the piers merging into the green as they fan toward the ceiling, which is composed of eighty-one coffered panels, the whole being covered with silver metal leaf.'[27] Decorated with similar flamboyance was the Voss Motor Car Co. garage and showroom in Liverpool. Occupying the whole of the ground floor of the eleven-storied India Building, and designed by Herbert J. Rowse in 1924–26, it showed how the trade could exploit inner city sites. The building comprised five hundred office suites, a café, restaurants, hair-dressing saloons, and swimming and Turkish baths; the garage was linked to the offices by telephone; and the showroom itself was decked out in yellow and black, with recessed lights and brass fitments in splendid art-deco detail.[28]

Hotels also began to introduce motor services for their guests, with the early petrol pumps discreetly hidden in courtyards, and purpose-built basement or ground-floor garages catering for every need. A well-publicised garage extension of 1924 for the Station Hotel, York, claimed to be 'fully equipped for the convenience of the tourist, whose cars can be thoroughly overhauled and examined'.[29] There was a recognition of the importance of the 'motel' concept currently being developed in Los Angeles and at France's new 'Halte-Relais Hotel' variant, launched at the 1925 Paris Arts Decoratif Exhibition. Designed for the motorist needing one or two nights' stay, the latter comprised all the necessary services for the private vehicle. Yet it was not until the early 1930s that Britain could boast any comparable facilities. Instead, Britons appeared to prefer the growing number of 'hedgerow' refreshment stalls — wayside bungalow tea-rooms with a petrol-pump at the garden gate and cheap accommodation for the commercial trade.[30]

In British city centres parking was by the mid-1920s creating increasing problems. Nevertheless, public unease over the growing demand was outweighed by the clamour for larger facilities providing greater speed in parking than was offered by the established lift systems. American developments had continued to attract interest, particularly those using the d'Humy Motoramp system, which allowed four- and six-storey garages to be accessed by ramps. 'You jump in and drive out, without waiting perhaps five minutes or more till the lift is free.'[31] In 1923 the concession for building this system in Britain was acquired by the London-based architect Walter Gibbings, who had an extensive practice designing industrial buildings for the motor trade, including the Dunlop works at Birmingham. Using the site of an old workhouse in London's Poland Street, in February 1923 Gibbings announced his plans for the first ramped multi-storey car park in Britain. An entirely utilitarian structure, it was initially planned to take five hundred cars, with the prospect of expansion to take up to a thousand. Opened two years later, it followed the principles of the early garages, being equipped with petrol pumps, tyre fitting facilities and a workshop for minor repairs as well as waiting rooms, cloakrooms and a lounge. Its centrally located ramps, with the separate access and exit routes, revolutionised the movement of parking cars.

For those in favour of accommodating the motor-car in city centres, going underground was also considered to be a serious alternative. In the spring of 1925, the Automobile Association put its authority behind a three-dimensional model illustrating the manner in which an underground car park could be constructed

99 Macy's Garage, Balderton Street, London, Wimperis and Simpson, 1926.

under Leicester Square.[32] Although it was believed to be possible without any loss of the garden amenities, the proposal was unrealised. Instead, it was Hastings in Sussex which built the first British single-floor underground promenade car park, in 1931.[33] Suitably impressed, Blackpool devised a similar scheme for an underground promenade car park that would have stretched for more than half a mile, and considered building a pier that would accommodate two thousand cars. Neither scheme was built, but the intention underlined the importance of parking as a planning issue.

The first multi-storey garage to be opened specifically for the shopper was Macy's Garage in Balderton Street, London. Designed by Wimperis and Simpson and completed in 1926, it was recognised as a distinctive piece of architecture. Classical in form and detail, its grand colonnaded entrance also provided cover and the framework for a line of Hammond petrol pumps (fig. 99). Owing much to the examples provided by railway stations, with its simple pilasters and egg-and-tongue architrave, it was considered to be 'designed in a decorous urban manner',[34] and sufficiently distinguished to be included in the 1927 RIBA 'Exhibition of Modern Architecture'. Arranged on four floors, with a ramp to the first floor and lifts to the other three, it offered free parking for shoppers at the adjacent Selfridge's store of 1908, along with repair and service facilities, dining and rest rooms, and a room for chauffeurs.[35] Intent on opening service stations and multi-storey garage facilities in and around London, the newly formed company Lex Garages chose to develop a company style using classical forms encased in glazed terracotta blocks and surmounted by an austere dome.[36] This format was used in two garages of 1928 in St John's Wood, opposite Lords Cricket Ground, and Robert Sharp's Little Pulteney Street development in the heart of Soho. On a long narrow site, using a ramped system set out on five floors, Sharp's car park was able to accommodate up to a thousand cars. Including the usual range of service rooms and petrol pumps, it also boasted a restaurant and theatre ticket office.

The RIBA's 1928 competition for a 'Motor Garage in the Theatre Area of London' prompted designs of limited originality but at least drew attention to the importance of this type of facility. For the winner, Thomas Spencer, the competition provided the opportunity to develop two essays for the *Architects' Journal*. In the first, of 15 October 1930, Spencer set out his proposal for a ring of underground car parks to be built round central London, leaving the motorists to complete their journeys by public transport. His second essay, of 14 January 1931, was a well-argued and copiously illustrated account of 'The Modern City Garage' in which he acknowledged that a lift system offered important economies of space but ultimately judged in favour of the ramp.

In the meantime, the campaign for the ideal garage had been reinforced by the Petroleum (Consolidation) Act of 1928, which at last had provided local authorities with increased powers to control the design of buildings and to prohibit new filling stations in areas of historical or scenic importance. This led to the appointment of the Petroleum Filling Stations Committee which, in its report of May 1929, directed attention to the colour of the pumps, signage, advertising, illumination, and the overall screening of the sites. Aesthetics were now a prime consideration. The *Daily Express*, in conjunction with the National Garden Guild, organised a competition to find the ideal petrol station, while the RIBA held one to find the best garage sign.[37] The RIBA, however, remained largely unimpressed with the architectural development of motor servicing. In its 1929 International Exhibition of Modern Commercial Architecture of 1929, the small section on transport architecture devoted little attention to buildings for the motor-car, other than a sample of garages from France and Germany.

It was not until two years later, in April 1931, that the RIBA began to address the broader concerns of motor facilities. The catalogue for its travelling exhibition of photographs on *The Architecture of Modern Transport* declared that:

> It is imperative that we keep a hold on future developments by every means in our power, for unlike the railway, road transport is almost ubiquitous. Garages, parking spaces and filling stations catch the eye at every turn, and it scarcely needs any further warnings than the many awful examples already existing, to convey the consequences of a lack of proper design.[38]

Overall, the 1931 exhibition provided a well-informed selection of British garages and related services, with British classical, art deco and picturesque examples set alongside modernist Continental ones. While filling stations were accepted as tolerable, the petrol pump remained an object of abuse, and the popular professional conclusion was that Britain lagged behind its Continental neighbours in nearly every branch of the architecture of transport.[39]

New Forms—New Services

Harangued by the government, the press and the professions, it was little wonder that the motor trade turned eagerly to modernism. The association of the Modern Movement with motoring architecture had begun with Wallis, Gilbert & Partners' design of 1930–31 for the Daimler Hire Company Garage in Herbrand Street, London (fig. 100).[40] By 1933 the motor trade had begun to believe that, through a combination of concrete and modernism, it could develop its own architectural style. Representing the trade's avowed 'new ideas and ideals',[41] this was an architectural expression which could be identified with the popular obsession with speed and the emergence of the streamlined motor-car. The resulting architectural solutions were further enhanced by the opportunity to exploit the improvements in plate glass, steel, new building materials such as vitrolite, and the ideal of going 'all electric'.

Shell Mex and B.P. Ltd had aligned itself with modernism with the design by Stanley Hall, Easton and Robertson for its exhibition stand at the 1933 Motor Show. In an advertisement of September 1933, Bowser's, the petrol-pump manufacturer, offered an all-inclusive service for designing and equipping the 'Typical Filling Station' in the modern style. Bowser's design was based on the concept of

100 Daimler Hire Company Garage, Herbrand Street, London; Wallis, Gilbert & Partners, 1930–31.

a small modern house, reinforcing the idea that the filling station was providing a service for the modern family (fig. 101). In reality, of course, modernism was also an architecture of facades which could helpfully mask the large workshops while presenting an image of modernity for the passing motorists. This neat fusion of interests was evident in Cameron Kirby's Modern Movement service stations of the early 1930s for Stewart & Ardern's at Ilford, Catford and Staines. Streamlined towers were a popular feature for designers such as Kirby. Yet it was the cantilevered canopy for petrol pumps that established the idea that the motoring public was getting 'As near the garage of to-morrow as the garage of to-day can be.'[42]

Given the ever-increasing expansion of the trade, it is difficult to provide a meaningful overview of the range of design work, and this introduction only provides a brief indication of some of the more imaginative design solutions of the 1930s.[43] Basil Spence's design of 1933 for Southern Motors in Causewayside, Edinburgh (see fig. 3 on p. 3), with its inventive cantilevered forecourt supporting first floor offices, was a unique solution for an infill development. It made no pretence at harmonising with its adjoining neighbours, and the structural fins piercing the façade, portrayed in Spence's sketch as a blaze of light, were

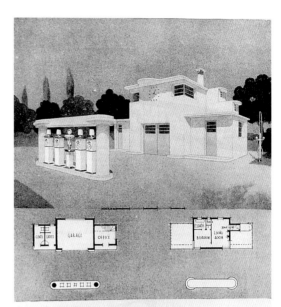

A TYPICAL FILLING STATION
DESIGNED AND FULLY EQUIPPED BY
S.F. BOWSER & CO (LONDON) LTD.,
ST. ANN'S HILL. WANDSWORTH, S.W. 18.

101 Filling Station, Advertisement,
September 1933.

You may consult us — without obligation — regarding your particular requirements, not only in connection with filling station equipment, but also from an ARCHITECTURAL STANDPOINT. Our Architects' services are at your disposal.   Phone. BATtersea 1652-3-4

designed to convey the fun and excitement of motoring even for the mundane tasks of filling up with petrol and checking the oil and tyre pressures. Even more exuberant was Harry Weedon's 1936 modernist design for a circular filling station with snack bar.[44] Distinguished by a pylon with a globe and picked out in neon lighting, it occupied a major intersection on the recently modernised Birmingham to Coventry road at Sheldon (fig. 102). Just as dramatic was Henley's Service Station on the Great West Road in Brentford, by Wallis, Gilbert and Partners of 1936–37, with its streamlined central tower and cantilevered canopy running the length of the showrooms and covering a line of twenty 'Wayne' petrol pumps, grouped in fives. The more functional Airport Garage at Hounslow, by Roper, Son and Chapman of 1937, with showrooms and garage built on a curve and an extended forecourt covered by a glass canopy supported on metal stanchions, brought new insight into the possible configuration of the forecourt. At the same time the better-known Golly's Garage in Cromwell Road, Earls Court, by Seymour, Orman & Adie,[45] was an outstanding design which

102   Collier Filling Station, Sheldon, Birmingham, 1936, Harry Wheedon.

overcame the problems of a restricted site to harmonise signage and commercial requirements within a domestic scale. Here the island of eight pumps was protected by a cantilevered concrete canopy, inset with glasscrete lights, which extended over the greasing bay and provided a sensitive linear divide between the green terracotta slabs of the ground floor and multicoloured brick of the first floor. Jackson's Garage in Bon Accord Street, Aberdeen, of 1937, by A. G. R. Mackenzie, was an outstanding example of a large scale development in a domestic neighbourhood and one that deserves wider recognition. Seen locally as 'Futuristic Architecture', the result owed just as much to the success with which its rear façade sensitively maintained the symmetry and style of the early nineteenth-century domestic architecture of Bon Accord Square.[46]

Of the filling stations incorporated into inner city developments in the 1930s, none came grander than the 1933 petrol-filling station on an island site at the Eastgate end of the new Headrow thoroughfare in the centre of Leeds. The street was already dominated by the large and pompous Town Hall and Museum/ Library, and the civic authorities awarded the commission to the master of the Imperial Baroque, Sir Reginald Blomfield. The latter then proceeded to design a filling station in the shape of an eighteenth-century English market cross, constructed of brick and Portland stone with a copper dome. The petrol pumps were located in three of the archways allowing access from either side, thus providing 'ultra rapid service of petrol and oil by electrically operated Bowser petrol pumps'.[47] But, having gone to such lengths to sustain an architectural harmony

103 Garage, Showroom & Ice-rink, Bournemouth, 1931, Seal & Hardy.

across the redevelopment scheme, within a matter of years the filling station was overshadowed by the monumental, modernist Quarry Hill flats.

As the motor-car trade moved towards providing an increasingly comprehensive service, there was a growing trend towards the construction of large industrial buildings designed to provide such facilities. One such example was the garage for Tate of Leeds of 1936, by Victor Bain and Allan Johnson, whose impressively simple lines dominated the New York Road.[48] The reinforced concrete structure, with its façade of brick and its two corner bays finished in terracotta, had five floors of showrooms, workshops and offices, and a basement that was primarily for the repair of commercial vehicles but which also housed the petrol pumps. The range of the new services were to be matched by speed of service. When Kennings opened its new Sheffield garage in 1937, it claimed to be able to wash, oil, grease and polish a car in eight minutes, with other servicing carried out in the same 'modern speedy manner'.[49]

City-centre parking produced some interesting solutions. Two designs for garage and showrooms of 1931–32, by Seal & Hardy, commandeered prime central sites in Bournemouth overlooking the bay. Designed as much for the new tourists as the local population, the first development was a redevelopment of an

104 Olympia Garage, Maclise Road, London, 1937, Joseph Emberton.

existing garage, redesigned to incorporate an ice-rink, distinguished by the first-floor window openings with ziggurat outlines edged with neon strips (fig. 103). The second, a year later, was a six-floor ramped garage for nine hundred cars, with restrained moderne facades at front and back in yellow glazed tiles.[50] Although the ramped arrangement was now accepted as the most efficient solution, Robert Sharp's 1931–32 design for Moon's Garage on Kensington Road, intended for nearby Olympia and with showrooms and filling station, used three lifts to serve five floors of parking for four hundred cars and a service workshop on the top floor. It was a steel-framed building, finished in Dorking brick and indistinguishable from the commercial architecture much favoured in London. Perhaps not surprisingly it was considered to be 'the best-looking garage in London'.[51] For his own Olympia garage of 1937, Joseph Emberton used ramped mezzanine floors, capable of accommodating more than a thousand cars. Successfully fitting into a long narrow site on the Maclise Road end of the exhibition buildings, the structure introduced a style of commercial building popularised in the post-war reconstruction programme (fig. 104). This and other new developments provided twenty-four hour service and high quality cloak-room facilities. The 1934 Cumberland Garage and Car Park in Bryanston Street,

Marble Arch, by Sir Owen Williams for the new Cumberland Hotel did so, as did the 1935 Scottish Motor Traction Salerooms and Service Station in Central Glasgow's crisp modernist style. The latter claimed it could provide 'changing rooms, baths, etc., to save the business man the inconvenience of going home when he wishes to dine in town'.[52]

Such new buildings were all the outcome of private investment. Yet the problems of traffic in town and city centres remained the responsibility of municipal authorities—a subject that generated much discussion but little direct action. Blackpool's 1935 scheme to resolve its town centre parking needs was recognised as one of the earliest moves by a local authority towards developing an integrated transport facility. When considering the building of a new bus station, Blackpool Corporation decided to incorporate a four-storey car park above the open-plan bus station, on a site adjacent to the railway station and the recently constructed market. Designed by the Borough Engineer, the simple mass of the car park, with its art deco detailing and seven decorative panels featuring old and new transport executed in cream terracotta, was accentuated by the open colonnade of structural supports for the bus station.[53]

Incorporating garages into large-scale urban developments remained a popular choice. The monumental 1934 redevelopment scheme for flats and offices on the south side of Berkeley Square, London, by Wimperis, Simpson and Guthrie included Stewart and Ardern's 'Morris House' showroom. On a suburban scale, but singularly distinctive, was Stewart and Ardern's showroom and filling station which formed part of the new developments surrounding North Harrow Station of 1933–34, masterminded by W. Hender Winder. Situated at a major road intersection, at the end of a long parade of shops and flats, the Harrow design was dominated by a brick tower of civic dimensions which included a flat and a drive-through archway for the petrol pumps. An equally imaginative design was the Seaford Motor Company's comprehensive development of its High Street site in 1936. This embraced flats and showrooms, and its forecourt gave access to a large workshop hidden behind a curved façade, which followed the side road from the front to the rear of the building. With Val Meyer and Watson-Hart's designs for Russell Court, Woburn Place, and Fountain House in Park Lane this type of approach reached epic proportions. Containing eight and nine floors of flats respectively, each block had showrooms, parking space, and a service station run by Moon's Garages. Considering the antagonism towards the filling station, it was an extraordinary piece of innovative thinking, the Park Lane development designed to provide 'the first and only garage and sales service in the World's most exclusive thoroughfare'.[54] Similarly impressive was the 1938 Eton Garage at Chalk Farm by Toms and Partners. It was a multi-floor garage for three hundred cars, with a row of shops, a showroom and petrol filling station, built adjoining the underground station in a form and style that imaginatively sustained the architectural unity of a scheme for three residential blocks of flats.

It was the roadhouses which brought a distinctly new form of architecture to the British landscape: buildings for people on the move. It is not always clear what distinguished the roadhouse from the hotel or inn, and often the distinction seemed to have much more to do with marketing concerns than design issues. Most were built for the weekend-away motorists, seeking an interlude from suburban life. The emphasis was thus on elegant leisure. Some had bedrooms, but others were simply in the form of a country club. Ballrooms, bars and cocktail bars, large restaurants and sun lounges were common features. Many had some form of games facility, with the open-air swimming pool becoming particularly popular. In 1933, *Autocar* listed thirty such roadhouses within reach of London. Some were conversions of existing inns, and Tudor–Jacobean revivals were heavily in demand, but by the mid-1930s a significant proportion were being executed in modernist guise.

The Knight Roadhouses of the early 1930s were the first to be developed as a chain, catering more for travellers than for evening and weekend entertainment. Modernist in style, 'combining the charm of modern domestic architecture, with the service of a modern hotel',[55] they were similar in plan without being identical. The first was constructed three miles south of Coventry at Ryton-on-Dunsmore, and others were built at Hinckley, Nottingham, Wansford and Leicester.[56] For the pleasure-seekers, one of the most ambitious schemes was the 1933 modernist 'Showboat' at Maidenhead by D. C. Wadhwa & E. Norman Bailey. It was equipped with a swimming-pool, restaurant, ballroom, tea and sun-bathing terraces, club-room and bar, offering the English motorist an experience comparable to that of a Riviera holiday. With similar aspirations, but much greater architectural coherence and expression, was the 1936 modernist Maybury roadhouse in Corstorphine, Edinburgh, by Patterson and Broom (fig. 105).[57] Two roadhouses of the same year—The Comet on Barnet By-Pass by E. B. Musman and the Finchale Abbey roadhouse at Durham, by Percy L. Browne and Son—are particularly good examples, with comprehensive ranges of facilities and stylistic interpretation. There was an austere modernism about the functional rectilinear quality of brick-faced and steel-framed Finchale Abbey, while at the Comet—with its large, curved windows extending out from a central

105   Maybury Roadhouse, Corstorphine, Edinburgh, 1936, Patterson & Broom.

rectangular block—the architectural expression is not dissimilar.[58] Whatever their style, the most noticeable feature of the overall plan of the roadhouses was that they were surrounded by car parks. Forty years earlier, the demand of the motorist had been for garages to protect the car. Now, with the improved technology and changing designs of the motor-car, exposed parking space was considered sufficient.

Despite the quality of many of these developments, the RIBA remained sceptical that things had got better. Its 1939 exhibition, *Road Architecture*, was a manifesto which presented 'a visual summary of the chief road evils to-day, of the causes of those evils, and of the means by which they might be removed.' Inspired by Sir Charles Bressey's 1938 report on London's highways, the exhibition primarily concerned itself with the need for a national plan for traffic and road systems, 'a system that should be a unity, an organised whole, a great machine'.[59] Consequently, although examples of good and bad architectural practice formed the core of the exhibition, the primary thesis was directed towards matters of environment rather than architecture. Reinforcing the position taken in earlier debates, it put forward the argument that the architect as planner could save the city and the countryside by overcoming the conflict between roads and buildings. The objective was to formulate a National Plan that would lead to 'increased health, free movement, amenity and happiness'.[60] Largely ignoring British architecture and dismissing most of its new road systems, models of good practice were illustrated with European examples and the American Free-Flow systems.[61]

Against the background of this debate, it is Erich Mendelsohn's design for a site in central Blackpool that provides a suitable conclusion to this brief introduction to forty years of architectural design for the car. Published in 1939, the proposed plan was for a hotel and multi-storey garage, joined by a mezzanine with public restaurant, and incorporating a new street that created a central traffic square. The whole scheme was unified at street level with twenty-three new shops.[62] With planning curtailed by the onset of the Second World War, it was never to be built. However, it remains a significant illustration of the continuing desire to find new ways of accommodating the motor-car within an urban setting, and in concept and style it anticipated much of the thinking behind the city-centre schemes of the post-war reconstruction.

Motoring had brought about new trades and industries. It had revitalised rural life and had changed the conventions of travel and leisure. The architecture of roadside services was a shocking reminder of how much social and cultural change had taken place. In terms of architectural design, the importance of the emerging profession of industrial design was yet to be fully appreciated, and there was still a need to develop a clearer response to the American-inspired concept of the 'drive-in' and 'drive-thru' culture of motoring.[63] In a debate that had become increasingly preoccupied with problems of ribbon development, traffic flow and city-centre congestion, attention had turned away from the 'artistic' architectural concerns to questions regarding the 'amenity' values of new road systems.[64] As motoring for the millions became a reality, the question for the future was how architecture could engage in the broader planning issues of designing for the motor-car.

1   *The Motor*, 26 January 1926.
2   Caffyns—along with a range of similar companies from this period, such as Henley's, Mann Egerton, Kennings, and Hollingdrake—deserve more detailed study for their influence on twentieth-century industrial, and commercial architecture. Partnerships between motor agents and manufacturers also resulted in some important architectural developments, a notable example being that of Stewart & Ardern and Morris, an association formed in 1912.
3   Caffyn Bros, Publicity brochure, Eastbourne, 1906.

4   *Builder*, 27 October 1906, p. 403.

5   *Builder*, 15 February 1908, p. 182.

6   *Autocar*, 1 April 1911, p. 439.

7   At first there had been competing shows between Edinburgh and Glasgow, but from 1908 it was ratio-nalised into one organised as the Scottish Motor Traders Show.

8   *Automotor Journal*, 22 April 1911, p. 429

9   The rear part of the building was damaged in the Second World War, and when rebuilt a petrol forecourt was introduced, which has since been converted to showrooms.

10   Tom Norton had two other garages, at the railway station and the Hotel Metropole.

11   *Scottish Country Life*, August 1914, p. 418. Up until 1905 Hamilton's had been listed as Electrical Engineers; 1906 added Motor-car Engineers.

12   The garage is still in use as a car park.

13   Mitchell Motor Works, *Motor Roads to London* (3rd ed., London: 1912), Introduction.

14   Garage parking was expensive. Rates were different for the size of car. Quoted for the hour, prices ranged from 2 to 3 shillings for six hours. Terms could also be arranged for the week or year.

15   See David Jeremiah, 'Filling Up: The British Experience, 1896-1940', *Journal of Design History*, 1995, vol. 8, no. 2, p. 97-116.

16   Pratt's was the trade name of the Anglo-American Oil Co., in 1924 the name was changed to Pratts, and then in 1935 it became Esso.

17   *Motor*, October 1918, published an image of the American Filling Station.

18   The Automobile Association had been founded in October 1905 in response to the punitive action of police speed traps, and over the years it had steadily increased the services for its members.

19   Shell had been formed in 1897, introducing its scalloped shell trademark in 1904. Shell collaborated with Vickers to produce its own pump, which was launched at Hale in Cheshire.

20   Now converted into restaurant, bar and quality supermarket.

21   Ever since the Advertisements Regulation Act of 1907 had been framed to bring the spread of advertising boards under control, legislation had been linked to the expanding motor trade. Sensitive to the growing criticism, in 1923 the Commercial Motor Manufacturers gave space for a Town-Planning Exhibition to be shown at its trade exhibition at Olympia, but while the motor trade continued to make great efforts to counter the criticisms, the architectural profession remained sceptical of its commitment to good design. At the forefront of the critics was the Design and Industries Association. Lobbying government and industry it mounted a range of campaigns through publications, articles and exhibitions that used the photographic record to contrast the good and the bad of the garage and service station. See *Architectural Review*, December 1929; *Face of the Land, DIA Yearbook, 1929-30* (London, 1930).

22   See 'Filling That Corner Site', *Motor Commerce*, June 1927, pp. 64-67.

23   By the mid-1920s some garage developments were being referenced as 'Service Stations'. There was no particular incident that prompted this description, but it would seem that where the workshop remained at the centre there was a continuing preference to refer to the facility as a garage, with service station more likely to be used when the filling station had the dominant position in relation to the garage and showroom. Location also had some influence, with service station more often used when the site was on an arterial road, serving through traffic.

24   By 1929 the building had been taken over by Barclays Bank, and there was a feeling that perhaps its style had always been more appropriate to banking, althoug it is currently in the process of being turned into a restaurant.

25   *Motor Commerce*, 9 October 1926, p. 360.

26   *Building*, May 1930, p. 227.

27   *Architectural Review*, June 1930, p. 335.

28   Other developments incorporated commercial and recreational facilities. For example, the Jones Motor House, opened in 1926 in the Morningside district of Edinburgh, had showrooms on the ground floor and a first floor 'Plaza salon de Danse' and café catering for high teas and weddings. In March 1975 the dance hall was closed and the building was subsequently demolished, to be replaced by a supermarket.

29   *The British Builder*, February 1925, p. 286.

30 For example, there was 'The Firs' on London Road, St Albans, a Georgian house, converted c.1926, that provided a petrol station, a dining room for lorry drivers and chauffeurs, and sleeping accommodation.

31 *Motor*, 13 October 1920, p. 483

32 Leicester Square was currently served by a garage, opened in the adjacent Whitcomb Street in April 1923.

33 Still in use.

34 *Architect & Building News*, 24 February 1928, p. 308.

35 In May 1927 the garage was taken over by Car Mart Ltd., that used the ground floor as a showroom, the middle two floors as a public garage, and the top floor as a fully equipped service station. Four years later, Ford formed Dagenham Motors to handle the distribution of its vehicles in London and took over the garage as a wholesale distribution and service centre, turning the third floor into a large showroom. It is currently a rental department for Avis.

36 Following on from the successful development of the Voss Motor Company in Liverpool, Mr Voss was the prime mover in setting up Lex Garages Ltd.

37 In 1928 the Royal Society of Arts had organised an industrial design competition for a petrol-filling station to be built at the intersection of two roads; it is also worth noting the *Architectural Review*'s campaign against the 'Wicked Garage Proprietor', *Architectural Review*, March 1929, p. 140. A City Garage competition was held in conjunction with the Manchester Building Exhibition of 1931, and six years later a competition for a Garage in a large city was run in association with the Birmingham Building Trades Exhibition.

38 *The Architecture of Modern Transport*, pamphlet, RIBA (London: 1931).

39 A series of articles by H. Robertson & F. R. Yerbury reinforced this position, see: 'Motor Garages in Paris', *Architect & Building News*, 14 September 1928; 'The Imaginative Modern', *Architect & Building News*, 26 July 1929; 'A New Conception of Display', *Architect & Building News*, 25 April 1930; 'Parisian Motor Showrooms', *Architect & Building News*, 10 July 1931.

40 It has recently been converted into office accommodation.

41 *Motor Commerce*, November 1933, p. 58. The Daimler garage used the same ramp for both the up and down movement of traffic. More demanding on space than systems based on the d'Humy model, it also increased risks of collision. However, in this case, as the garage was primarily a company garage with the private driver restricted to the basement with its separate entrance, it was felt that the dangers were minimal. Designed to allow for further floors to be added, the building remained unaltered.

42 See Cresta Garage, 1934, Worthing, by A. J. Seal; advertisement, *Worthing Directory*, 1935.

43 At a time when there was no fixed idea on lay-out, the architect G. Alan Fortescue produced a model for a unit system that could be extended vertically and horizontally, accommodating workshops, showrooms and filling station. Shown at the 1933 Olympia Motor Show, it was suggested that a swimming pool, a tea garden or a badminton court could be added at little extra cost. Fortescue had designed a garage at Brondesbury, 1930, and was to design a Motor Showroom, Rickmansworth, 1937, and Inwards Garage, Ruislip, 1938. Other service stations of note include: 1933, Pippbrook Filling Station, Dorking, by Imrie and Angell; 1936, Showrooms, Filling Station and Garage, Southampton, by Eric E. Brown for Wadhams; 1936, Garage for Shaw & Kilburn Ltd., Park Royal, London by E. Howard & Partners; 1938, Oscroft Service Station, Castle Boulevard, Nottingham, by Reginald W Cooper. In 1935 Caffyns decided to go modern, from a crop of new developments the 1936 East Grinstead design by Peter D. Stonham & Son was the most interesting, although now much altered.

44 Now demolished.

45 Now demolished, it had been identified as a good example of garage architecture by the RIBA 'Road Architecture' Exhibition of 1939.

46 Jacksons had moved on to the site in 1922, and during 1936 acquired the adjacent properties to make room for the new building. No longer a garage, the showrooms have been converted into a Yates Wine Lodge.

47 *Motor Commerce*, September 1933, p. 57. The filling station was owned by Appleyard of Leeds, Ltd.

48 Isolated by the new road structure, the building is now a business storage centre.

49 By then Kennings Ltd were operating a chain of garages across four counties, and were entering a new phase of expansion. The Sheffield garage has been converted into business units and cinema.

50   Unfortunately, the front façade was destroyed during its conversion into a hotel.

51   *The Architect & Building News*, 12 August 1932, p. 189. Building now demolished.

52   *SMT Magazine*, November 1935, p. 96. Building now demolished.

53   It was not finished until early 1939. Lex Garages approached the corporation with a view to leasing the whole space, but by then there was a growing awareness that parking fees could become an important source of municipal revenue. The whole building is now hidden behind a clumsy metal cladding.

54   *Autocar*, 8 April 1938. p. 17.

55   *The Architect & Building News*, 4 November 1932, p. 142.

56   Ten other sites were under consideration, but so far I have been unable to locate any information on their development.

57   Recently carefully restored as a casino. Not all applications for new roadhouses were approved by local magistrates; interesting to note that in October 1937 Dundee were unsympathetic to a proposal for a roadhouse on modern lines for the working man, with food and temperance refreshment at prices within his reach.

58   Others of note include the 1934 Roadhouse at Leigh on Sea by Laurence J. Selby, and the 1937-38 Chez Laurie Roadhouse on London Margate Coastal Road (two miles from Herne Bay) by W. Michael Bishop. Not strictly roadhouses, but built with the motorist in mind and worth noting, are the 1931-32 Berkeley Arms Hotel in Cranford, Middlesex by E. B. Musman in French Chateau style; the 1937 Abbey Hotel on the North Circular Road, Wembley, by Henry Oliver; the Roundhouse at Beacontree by A. W. Blomfield; and the 1938 Prospect Inn, on the London–Ramsgate Road at Minster, Kent, by Oliver Hill. The 1933 timber-framed roadhouse 'Laughing Water', by Clough Williams-Ellis, which juts out over the lake at Cobham Hall, Kent, provided nothing more than a restaurant.

59   *Road Architecture*, RIBA Catalogue (London: 1939), p. 6. Exhibition opened 1 March 1939.

60   *Ibid.*, p. 16.

61   The catalogue cited the modernist service station at Staines, Golly's Garage in Kensington, Wheedon's Filling Station at Sheldon, and the Comet at Barnet.

62   *Architectural Design and Construction*, August 1939, p. 279.

63   See J. A. Mackle, 'Traffic Conditions in America', *Motor*, 13 October 1920, p. 481-83.

64   These were issues that were picked up in the Ministry of Transport 1946 report, 'Design and Layout of Roads in Built-Up Areas', as architecture for the motor-car continued to be dominated by systems and schemes.

From Chaos to Control: The Architecture of the Bus and Coach Station in Inter-war Britain

Julian Holder

One of these days, someone in authority will wake up to the fact that the motor-coach is a normal means of transit. That will be when there is a regular half-hour aeroplane service between London and Manchester, and when the railways have decided to rebuild King's Cross.[1]

WHATEVER THE ACCURACY of these predictions of 1930 the opinions of 'the man on top of the Clapham omnibus' have long been taken as an embodiment of average public opinion and, if true, demonstrate that road passenger transport was to be the dominant form of public transport, wherever it was located, for much of the twentieth century. A consequence of this dramatic growth was the creation of two ubiquitous new twentieth-century building types — the bus station and the coach station. Although created for essentially similar types of vehicle the bus station and the coach station have a different history due to the conflict between public and private ownership during the inter-war period. This was a conflict put most starkly by the Labour politician, and sometime Minister of Transport, Herbert Morrison when he wrote that 'the phrase-mongers, who even to-day urge a policy of free competition in transport, are living, intellectually, in a world that is long since dead. Conservative politicians may praise competition; Conservative capitalists are killing it.'[2]

The local authority bus station acted as the central public arena for the picking-up and setting-down of passengers within a prescribed, and increasingly regulated, local authority area. Standing at both the end and the beginning of a series of staged stops on pre-defined routes, with services working to a set timetable, at its best the bus station could both embody and project civic ideals on a grand scale. The dynamic spatial relationship it maintained with its district defined the psychological geography and boundaries of towns and cities throughout the country. These boundaries were often illustrated in cartographic form by maps showing areas of operation put on display in the bus station. At worst, which was most cases, the bus station was little more than a town square with some shelters, or a kerb-side designated as a stop by custom and practice and rendered tawdry by advertising.[3] When American travel consultant Walter Jackson visited Britain on a working holiday he was struck by the 'astonishing absence of sheltered loadings as well as of centralised joint stations.'[4]

Although the bus station could also receive privately operated long-distance and express coaches this extra provision was only granted by the local authority to the coach company on a commercial basis. The result was that the private coach operators usually combined with other long-distance operators to create their own coach-station on the edge of town or, given the seasonal nature of much of their business, find cheaper alternatives, usually a kerbside. When Walter Jackson and his wife left Sheffield for Birmingham 'the station turned out to be just another of those open kerbs with nothing more than a post sign. A tiny sweetshop was the booking office.'[5] The private coach companies relied more on the comfort and speed of their vehicles to secure custom than their passenger facilities.

These prosaic points are worth making at the outset of this essay if the differences between the bus and coach station, together with the technological, economic, social, and political pressures which created this new building type are to be fully appreciated. Each also developed its own culture which extended beyond the confines of either buildings or vehicles to give a distinct 'structure of feeling' to everyday life for millions of ordinary citizens. These two separate branches of the passenger transport industry only came about during the interwar period as a result of significant changes in the nature of British society and the developing notion of socialised industries. The reflection of these changes in the industry created what became known as 'the road movement' and, by 1930, had been enshrined in the Road Traffic Act.[6]

The omnibus, first used as an aristocratic form of transport in seventeenth-century Paris, was, once harnessed to the automotive power of the petrol engine, developed as a means of mass-public transport in the late nineteenth and early twentieth century.[7] Initially operating as an extension to municipal tram operations, and railway stations, its freedom of movement allowed both the new suburbs of Edwardian Britain to remain connected to the existing urban transport system of tram and railway without the considerable cost of extending the lines, and for tourism to be developed beyond the tentacles of the railway line.[8]

However these early motor-omnibuses were mechanically unreliable, and, in terms of their braking efficiency, potentially dangerous as many a newspaper headline suggested to the public. The poor physical condition of Britain's roads, and especially its narrow 'hump-backed' country bridges, contributed their own set of problems to the early 'road movement.' Additionally, with no adequate legal regulation of passenger vehicles, so-called 'pirates' (the unlicensed operators with small vehicles who dangerously raced ahead of municipal trams to steal their passengers) gave the industry a poor reputation. If small enough to avoid being classed as 'heavy motor vehicles', charabancs and small coaches were exempt from the 12 m.p.h. speed limit—in operation until 1928 when it rose to 20 m.p.h. Although some private operators worked as carriers under license to local authorities, the development of bus and coach travel was thus held back until after the First World War due to its poor record of safety, reliability, and the physical state of the roads. True, Eastbourne Corporation established a fleet of omnibuses as early as 1903, and in 1906 the General Manager of the Sheffield Municipal Transport system was recommending to his local authority that there should be no new tram lines laid and 'any experiment in the near future should be made by means of motor omnibus.' However this was a recommendation not enacted until 1913.

Only following the First World War, and the creation of a Ministry of Transport in 1919, did a number of factors combine to allow the more rapid development of bus and coach travel, and the argument for stations began to be made. During the forcing-house of war, improvements in engine design and brake technology had been so rapid that capital investment in buses became a happier prospect for local authorities, many of whom established their own construction facilities on the back of their expertise in the construction and maintenance of trams. This greater confidence in the vehicle itself was now coupled with increased confidence in the quality of staff. The end of the First World War released many men into the civilian workforce with newly found mechanical skills who were able to both act as drivers and work in maintenance garages. The ambitious 'Homes fit for heroes' housing campaign of the immediate post-war years created just the kind of new suburban estates in need of a bus service, whilst an equally ambitious road-building programme, also conceived partly as a form of unemployment relief, ensured a smoother and safer quality of ride for the new suburban passengers. Earlier road construction, which had largely been designed with prominently sloping sides to ensure surface water and debris fell to the gutters, caused many vehicles to overturn. Indeed the 'Adverse camber' and 'Hump-backed bridge' signs, created by the Ministry of Transport, remained a prominent warning on many of Britain's older roads well into the twentieth century. Finally, and most persuasively, the lower cost of oil in post-war Britain as a result of the increasing development of oilfields in America and the Far East made bus and coach operation more economically viable.

Yet, although it was now overcoming the practical impediments to its wider adoption, the bus also had to overcome less tangible impediments in the shape of class discrimination as, despite its French aristocratic origins, it was associated with a lower social strata of society. The extent, and nature of this prejudice, and also its presumed overthrow, can be judged by a contemporary observation that 'Omnibuses are everybody's vehicle, and the days have long gone by when people of distinction were almost ashamed to be seen riding in one, and ladies blushed at the thought.'[9]

With the Ministry of Transport unifying a whole messy panoply of earlier government departments, with improved safety and reliability, cheaper fuel, and the gradual social acceptance of the omnibus by a wider public than ever before, its development during the period between 1918 and 1930 was more assured though still slower than might have been expected. For many local authorities the bus was still viewed as a newcomer which threatened its heavy investment in the tram system. It was a vehicle to be feared, or at best patronised, rather than fully embraced. The gradual change over from tram to bus is physically embodied in many new tram depots of the period which now incorporated bus maintenance garages. In 1928 Liverpool Corporation opened a large new central tramway depot covering a site of 9 acres on Edge Lane. Designed in a grand neo-Georgian manner, as one reviewer pointed out 'the gradual adoption of motor omnibuses for the purpose of extending the tramway services has required an efficient separate department for the repair and maintenance of omnibuses.'[10]

Even where the bus was fully embraced it was still seen very much as an extension of existing tram services rather than the more flexible, economic, and quick means of transport it truly was. Beyond the scepticism, or reluctance, of many local authorities to switch from tram to bus, or to use the trolleybus as a compromise solution, it must be remembered that the powerful rail companies — especially once rationalised into the four major companies of the Southern, the LMS, the LNER and the GWR in 1923 — also lobbied hard to maintain their share of the travelling public's purse.[11]

Once local authority adoption of motor buses was decided upon, usually as a result of losing revenue to the 'pirates' and the demands of an expanding local population, the choice was simple: either to convert the existing facilities, or build anew. This was no simple choice as conversion also carried with it the legal obligation to lift all the existing tram track and reinstate the road.

Shortly after the end of the First World War, and eager to build on the 'Civic gospel' proclaimed so influentially by Joseph Chamberlain and other politicians

106   Barnstaple Bus Station, designed by the Borough Surveyor, E.Y. Saunders (1922).

before the First World War, a few local authorities were quick to provide passenger facilities for the bus. In 1922 the new Barnstaple Corporation Bus Station (fig. 106), designed by the Borough Surveyor E.Y. Saunders, was opened on one of the most historic sites of the town, the former Great Quay. It was from here that five of Barnstaple's six ships which formed part of Sir Francis Drake's fleet against the Spanish Armada set sail in 1588. The new single-storey bus station was designed to complement the adjacent Merchant's Exchange of 1709 so the whole group formed an attractive backdrop to the river and an appropriate symbol of civic power continuing the traditions of the English mastery of the seas.

Similarly when Rotherham came to provide a new bus terminus in 1933 (following the road-widening schemes which were necessary even for successful tram operations), it grasped the opportunity for a similar scheme of civic improvement. Situated below Rotherham's medieval parish church the Borough Surveyor designed a bus shelter in an appropriate late Gothic Revival style adjacent to a large cafe in 'Modernised Tudor' designed by J. Mansell Jenkins.[12] Such opportunities for private enterprise to fulfil, at least partially, the necessity for providing passenger facilities in the form of large catering premises was a convenient way to forestall the provision of purpose-designed stations, which had to include such facilities, by less enthusiastic local authorities. The balance of public and private provision was uneven throughout the country and reflected the political composition of the local authority as much as the financial influence of local, and regional, business. With few successful schemes to emulate, public expectation was low and the blurring of the public and private spheres perpetuated such low expectation. Other schemes, overly ambitious, were only partially realised. One such was the large municipal bus station in Piccadilly, Manchester. Here the Manchester Corporation architect, G. Noel Hill, designed illuminated shelters laid out in long platforms which were to have been the approach to a magnificent new combined City Art Gallery and Public Library, designed by Barry Weber in Beaux-Art style and set in formal gardens. As with many local authorities the historic significance of the town square, sanctioned by centuries of use as a central meeting place, made it the obvious choice as well as a sign of a local authority determined to 'move with the times.' The usual attempt to provide a modicum of comfort for passengers was the more functional approach as taken at Gateshead and Durham. Here no amount of extra ornament, or vaguely Art Deco motifs, could disguise the adoption of the workaday Victorian railway station canopy (fig. 107).

Within the grandiose architectural schemes of local authorities such as Liverpool, Manchester, or Walsall, lay two main precedents: the tram depot as a large walled enclosure for garage and maintenance, and the railway station for its system of covered platforms. Such a precedent was not only efficient but, as a reviewer of a suburban London coach station in 1930 noted, it also implied efficiency for 'as a piece of ordered design [it] compares very favourably with any one of our railway terminal stations.'[13] However it was this convenient legacy which, in terms of the architectural debates of the 1930s, needed to be thrown out and the bus and coach station re-thought from first principles if it were to achieve its own archetypal form. As one of the few designers of a station which came close to this Modernist ideal, G. W. Jackson, argued 'Stations must be stations and not glorified garages.'[14] Yet the railway station legacy and Beaux-Art pretensions of Edwardian civic culture made the easy alliance with modernity achieved by the airport a faint possibility. Only in the earlier visions of a future industrial city by French architect and urbanist Tony Garnier was the motor bus afforded anything like the appropriate dignity of a modernist setting before 1930.

107 Durham Bus Station, clearly displaying the heritage of the Victorian railway station.

The one bus station which stood well above the others of the period in its attempt to find an appropriate architectural form was Derby (fig. 108). Both as an example of Modernist ideology and as an expression of municipal ambition, it was the finest of its age and set the pattern for future developments. As the obituary of its designer noted in 1959, 'The design of the Bus Station was then quite revolutionary and, even now, has not really been bettered.'[15] As a progressive local authority Derby was implementing an ambitious re-development scheme along its riverside, and in 1929 pressed for a special Act of Parliament to create its new station.[16] Designed by the Derby Borough Corporation's new Chief Architect, C.H. Aslin, in consultation with the Royal Fine Art Commission, and opened in October 1933 after two years of planning it was the final element of a scheme which included new council offices, police headquarters and covered market.[17] The plan aimed to create one central station for all buses and coaches, whether public or private, and paid as much attention to planning as it did to design. On opening, it eliminated the need to use any of the twelve separate pick-up stops in the city centre, and the station also became the only authorised stand for excursions and private operators from outside the borough boundaries. Despite unhappiness at the scale of charges imposed on private operators for use of the station the Trent Motor Traction Company wisely took a lease on one of the three platforms for its own exclusive use, vacated their own station in Albert Street, and were accordingly able to influence the final design. When, by 1936, the Trent Motor Traction Company had absorbed all its smaller independent rivals it was also able to operate its buses from the third platform and thus take the lion's share of the station.

Derby ably demonstrates the largely unregulated growth of bus transport during the inter-war period that necessitated such an ambitious scheme. In 1914 only eighteen local authorities had run buses. By 1928 this number had increased to ninety. These figures do not take account of the number of independent operators plying for the public's trade, often at the expense of the local authority, and neither does it take account of the impact, especially during busy periods, of the numbers of long-distance, express, and private hire coach operators coming into a town. The result of this increasing activity was the growing problem of congestion in towns such that a Royal Commission on Transport was established in 1928 to report to Parliament on what steps should be taken. The publication of the report sounded the death knell of the tram with its finding that 'Our considered view is that tramways, if not an obsolete form of transport, are at all events in a state of obsolescence, and cause much unnecessary congestion and considerable unnecessary danger to the public.'[18] It also argued that rationalisation, as achieved by the re-organisation of the railway companies in 1923, was now desirable amongst the bus and coach companies. Many saw this as a prelude to nationalisation.

To understand this finding it is necessary to look at the development of the private coach operator in the years leading up to the Road Traffic Act of 1930. No less than the earlier history of the bus, the coach also suffered from a bad public image with the suggestion of 'vulgar and low-class patrons.' 'If a modern motor coach could speak,' an article of 1931 argued, 'it would have some rebellious things to say. Like a docile elephant provoked to anger, it would trumpet forth its rage at the unfair treatment it has received. For always the motor coach seems to be referred to in terms of abuse.'[19] This abuse centred on a number of aspects of private coach travel which distinguished it from the bus. Apart from what was seen as their role in the general despoilation of the countryside, coaches which had reached their destination, if on an excursion, needed to be parked for much of the day before the return journey thus creating congestion. If operating

108 Derby Bus Station, designed by C.H. Aslin (1933).

express services from the suburbs, or from town to town, coach pick-up points were often little more than a road-side kerb outside a ticket office which also caused congestion on both road and pavement. Occasionally an under-used part of a railway goods yard could also double as a coach station and even pub car parks, or delivery yards, were popular stands. As a promotional brochure of the 1930s argued, 'these embarking points have no degree of permanency to inspire public confidence, and leave an impression as of some more or less temporary service essentially haphazard in operation, especially when contrasted with the railway station and even with the aerodrome.'[20] Additionally as the shortest distance between two points was always taken by the express coaches many towns were treated merely as through routes. This increased the congestion caused by those coaches which were either parked-up, or waiting at kerbsides.

The positive image of the private coach company was built upon its reliability, comfort, and ability to compete with the railway companies in providing express services from one town to another. As the architectural critic Frederick E. Towndrow wrote on the new generation of diesel-engined coaches in 1932 'There is no denying that the latest ones are beautiful and excellently appointed.'[21] However its buildings, at least initially, were not seen as reinforcing these qualities in the public's mind. The sudden rail strikes of the inter-war period, beginning with that of 26 September until 6 October 1919, which left both commuters and tourists stranded, was the making of the private coach companies—if their employees were prepared to run the gauntlet of union pickets in order to get passengers to their destinations. But whereas the bus service had come to represent municipal values and a civic culture, the coach operators were seen as contributing to congestion, illegality, and public nuisance. Notable exceptions were such operators as the Trelawney Motor Services of Penzance. Their garage, designed in 1921 by local practice Cowell, Drewitt, and Wheatley in the same somewhat tame and casual classicism as Barnstaple Bus Station nonetheless gave a respectability to the new endeavour with its classical facade.[22]

Initially these private operators were, typically, ex-military personnel 'demobilised' at the end of the First World War. They used their newly found mechanical skills, together with the wide availability of surplus military vehicles or cheaply imported Ford Model-T's, to 're-mobilise' and operate charabancs for the increasingly popular day trips. These could then be supplemented by operating as 'pirates' on local authority routes where, as new council estates grew, supply could not keep pace with demand. Additional sources of revenue included party bookings and foreign visits, those to the battlefields and cemeteries of Flanders being particularly popular after the First World War. An advertisement in the *Barnsley Chronicle* in 1919 announced 'The Beechfield Motor Company, having replaced their luxurious Dennis car-a-banc which was commandeered by the Government in 1914, are now open for booking parties for long or short tours.'[23]

Typical of such operators was Monty Moreton Ltd. of Nuneaton. A father and son business they decided to leave the collieries during the Depression following the First World War and bought a Ford one-ton chassis in Market Bosworth in 1923. 'At first the business was based in Jodrell Street, Nuneaton, near the abbey, and the first services made full use of the adaptability of the Dixie body. With the vehicle equipped as a fourteen-seat bus, miners were first taken to local collieries: that completed, workers (mainly girls) were carried to work in Hinkley; and lastly the body was swapped in less than half an hour for a lorry body and the vehicle did duty on goods during the middle of the day. In the evening the process was reversed.'[24]

This account gives a good idea of the scale of operations of those who formed the bulk of the business in the 1920s. Further examples abound such as Stephen

Hayter, 'Like many other pioneers who constitute the 'small men' of the bus industry today, Mr. S. Hayter, proprietor of the Yellow Bus Service, Stoughton, near Guildford, started by driving his own bus on a new local route . . . in 1921.'[25] From these small beginnings Stephen Hayter's business prospered and in the 1930s he commissioned a prepossessing streamlined facade to the Yellow Bus Garage. Gradually most small independent operators were bought up or amalgamated with rival concerns. The case of the Bassett Bus Company of Gorseinon, South Wales, is an interesting case in point. It was formed in 1917 and issued with a license by Swansea Corporation and the Swansea Rural District Council to run services between Gorseinon and Swansea 'with one reservation that no passengers should be taken on or set down within the borough of Swansea except at the terminus.'[26] Within a year it was receiving offers to be taken over from the larger South Wales Omnibus Company. Despite competition, and thanks partly to local loyalty, Bassetts kept going and from their initial fleet of a few charabancs they and a staff of six in 1917 rose to own thirty-six buses and a number of coaches, with a staff of over one hundred in 1935 when they eventually sold out to the newly formed United Welsh Company.

When the newly established Traffic Commissioners, created by the passing of the Road Traffic Act in 1930, issued their first annual report in 1931 its statistics were the first attempt to give an accurate national picture of such small operators. Of a total of 6434 operators, 2760 owned only one vehicle, those owning two numbered 1336, whilst the relative success of companies such as Bassetts can be judged by the fact that they would have fallen into a category owning between 25 to 49 vehicles and numbered only 80.[27]

The building requirements of many such operators, at least initially, was little more than a garage in which to house and service their vehicle with little thought being given to the efficiency of the design, the use of the building for promotional purposes, or passenger comfort. In Bassetts case as they expanded they moved from their original garage, which could then be used as a repair depot, to larger new premises. Operators such as Trelawney Motors of Penzance and the Burnell Brothers of Cheddar had started early when passenger facilities were hardly an issue. In 1905 Burnell Brothers used a twelve-seat charabanc to take visitors from the railway station to Cheddar Gorge for a twopenny fare. By 1922 they had grown to a fleet of seven, trading under the name of 'Lorna Doone' coaches, to provide excursions between the Gorge and the nearby resort of Weston-Super-Mare for holiday makers. Their new garage premises in Cheddar, and especially the associated advertising, was precisely the type of 'blot on the landscape' against which the indignation of the Council for the Preservation of Rural England, and the 'Cautionary Guides' published by the Design and Industries Association, was directed.[28] What was aesthetically acceptable in the town was far from acceptable in the country. However with the growth of tourism, and especially the popularity of the day-trips to such destinations as Cheddar Gorge and Weston-Super-Mare, such 'outrages' were destined to increase.

In 1928 the large Bristol Tramways and Carriage Company's Beach Garage and Omnibus Station was opened in Weston-Super-Mare. Designed by their own staff architect, H.A. Penney, it presented one of the better frontages of its day in its use of pre-cast stone which, claimed the *Tramway and Railway World*, 'has the effect of white marble' and, for once, a well-proportioned classical design.[29] It adopted what became the standard layout for a combined station and garage of a large, sometimes top-lit, garage behind a more 'architectural' front for waiting rooms, offices, etc. for public view. The frontage stretched for 180 feet and as an exercise in facadism Weston-Super-Mare is bettered only by the 1933 bus garage of United Automobile Services in Newcastle-upon-Tyne.

By the early 1930s, and fuelled by the competition with the railway companies, long-distance coach travel increased markedly. So did the associated problems. In Winchester twenty thousand public service vehicles were reported to pass through the city every year. This resulted in the City Engineers Office creating a new municipal coach station in 1934. It was located in the former Hyde Lodge Estate which was set in five acres of land: a small mansion was converted to the waiting facilities whilst the open platforms were laid out in the estate gardens and traffic controlled from a central control tower open to the elements.[30] What is most notable about Winchester, and most similar coach stations, was its position on the periphery of the town, such was the determination of local authorities to tackle the problem of traffic congestion in town, and even village, centres.

The model for such edge of town conversions was the coach station of Black and White Motorways, Cheltenham (fig. 109), often referred to as the 'Charing Cross of the coach network' and frequently credited with being the first coach station in the country. It was the creation of George Reading, whose operation began in 1926 with just three coaches and by 1931 had grown to sixty-six coaches.[31] Foreseeing the coming problems of increasingly restrictive legislation and understanding the benefits of co-operation with his rivals Reading's work at Cheltenham was widely reported and in 1931 it was felt that the station's 'facilities both for operation and for the public comfort and convenience sufficiently rare as to call for special notice.'[32] Created out of a converted former three-storey

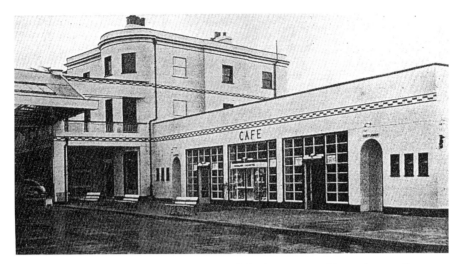

109   Black & White Motors, Cheltenham, the so-called 'Charing Cross of the coach network'.

Georgian house, the most impressive feature of the Cheltenham station was the integrated approach it took to its corporate image.[33] Not only was the house converted to offer a booking hall, snack bar, waiting room, cloak room, cafes, and offices (for a clerical staff of fifty) but the whole conversion was united by the controlled application of a black-and-white chequer-board colour scheme from the exterior painting, to the inlay of the cafe furniture, floor coverings, china, waitress costumes and driver and porters uniforms, and the coaches themselves. As the *Tramway and Railway World* noted 'There is psychological insight in this plan, as no one who passes through the coach station can forget the favourable impressions created by the decorative scheme so closely linked with the name of the company.'[34]

As the nerve centre of one of the largest long-distance operators in the country Cheltenham welcomed passengers changing services from as far as Paignton and Bournemouth in the south, to Nottingham and Derby in the north, Swansea and Aberystwyth in the west, to London in the east. It is clear to see in this vigorously applied corporate identity the pervasiveness of new American ideas of marketing. There is certainly no doubt that private operators looked to the more famous transatlantic cousins, such as the Greyhound Lines and the Sante Fe Trailways, for models.[35] Neither can there be much doubt that it was a successful undertaking. A description of its inspection facilities reads more like a contemporary Formula One Grand Prix pit stop than what we tend to think of as coach servicing 'Directly a coach has disembarked its passengers it is driven over a pit when it is dealt with by a squad of eight men, whose duties are as follows: (1) engine, water hoses, controls, wires and tappets, (2) oil and water refill, (3) road springs and brakes, gear box and back axle levels, (4) petrol refill, (5) batteries (always topped) and electrical fitting, (6) wheel nuts, (7) interior cleaning and disinfecting and (8) windows, exteriors. No driver is permitted to drive away unless 'O.K.' and the date is chalked on the windscreen.'[36]

In 1934 the operators journal *Bus and Coach* claimed that 'One of the landmarks in the road passenger industry when it is viewed from the future will be the year 1934 by reason of the institution of what has become known as the Cheltenham Scheme.'[37] This was an ambitious scheme of rationalisation to reduce costs and increase the efficiency of the long-distance coach services operated by six major companies.[38] It was also a scheme that had been foreseen by the architect G.W. Jackson in 1931, echoing the arguments of the Traffic Commissioners, when he wrote that 'stations for the joint use of a number of companies must in due course be provided.'[39]

The increasing volume of traffic at Cheltenham resulted in the construction of a larger all-night cafe block which became patronised not merely by those waiting for a connecting service but local theatre-goers and other visitors. They would use the station's car park and other facilities as a civic amenity, further blurring the distinctions between public and private provision. The cafe also housed Black and White's own Publicity Workshop 'where two men spend all their time designing show cards, posters, etc., and making mechanical models and other publicity devices for window displays at booking offices.' A visitor in 1934 found that 'It was almost like being in Gamages or Bassett Lowkes at Christmas time.'[40]

The congestion problems which beset popular tourist destinations throughout the country were doubly true of London where large numbers of coach services effectively treated Victoria Embankment, Oxford Circus, and other convenient roads as passenger stations. In the Annual Report of the London and Home Counties Traffic Advisory Committee of 1930 it was reported that 'The influx of large numbers of motor-coaches into the Metropolis is a matter which is causing some disquietude. We anticipate that the increasing employment of this type of vehicle will render it necessary at an early date to take steps to ensure that motor-coaches during their period of waiting in the Metropolis, shall be accommodated off the public highway.' Yet as Herbert Morrison noted 'The elements of the London passenger transport problem are not fundamentally different from those of the more serious and complicated national problem.'[41]

Those private operators in London who were either large enough, or concerned enough, to provide stations usually found themselves relegated by the local authority to undesirable locations on the edge of town from where, once again, the passengers would have to continue their journey by some other means. Orange Luxury Coaches established a coach station at Effra Road, Brixton in 1927 which, in 1932, reported handling 300,000 passengers.[42] Yet given the seasonal nature of coach trips, during the winter months it closed to become an amusement arcade. Similarly Kings Cross Coaching Station was located just on the fringe of the central 'banned zone' but had sufficient demand to have been designed to accommodate forty-eight coaches loading simultaneously.

Although both these buildings of the late 1920s were purpose-designed, the normal pattern for the private company with limited resources was the adaptation of some existing building. Both George Ewer and Co. Ltd (operators of the Grey-Green Coach Service) on Stamford Hill and the M.T. Company on New Cross Road did just this though, as *Bus and Coach* magazine correctly reported 'From the outward appearance of the headquarters of George Ewer & Co., Ltd., … it may well be thought that these premises were used only for garaging vehicles and carrying out running repairs.'[43] With an increasingly aggressive attitude on the part of government, especially in the pronouncements of Herbert Morrison, and the threat of legislation (perhaps even nationalisation) hanging over the heads of the private operators, they were reluctant to take such bold steps as commissioning purpose-built facilities in the early 1930s unless they had to.

One way in which coach companies tried to get around being the unwelcome guests at established tourist sites was to create their own. The growth of travel in inter-war Britain was stimulated not merely by an increasing awareness, and easy access to, visitor attractions such as cathedrals and country houses, together with the promotion of rambling, but actively promoted by the companies themselves.[44] At Loggerheads, near Mold, the Crosville Company created their own visitor attraction by buying the attractive Colomendy Hall and estate of some 70 acres. This was re-landscaped to create pleasure grounds with a teahouse and afforded the opportunity for extensive rambling in the surrounding countryside, though, as *Bus and Coach* acknowledged, it had already become 'a recognised venue in the earlier days of the "chara" before the vehicle attained the dignity of "coach".'[45] Part of this appeal lay in the presence of the public house on the road through Loggerheads. When Crosville bought the estate to be in line with contemporary developments it renamed it the 'Loggerheads Road House.' This was a mere marketing ploy since the purpose-built road houses of the

110 Dreamlands Coach Station, Margate, designed by C.F.S. Palmer.

period were often designed specifically to accommodate coach-parties with large restaurants and catering facilities and were even known to incorporate bus shelters in their design. Elsewhere attractions such as the amusement park at Dreamlands, Margate, boasted its own Moderne coach station, or grand shelter, by C.F.S. Palmer to handle its burgeoning visitor numbers (fig. 110).[46]

The increasing chaos of passenger transport was finally arrested by the 1930 Road Traffic Act. Apart from those issues already mentioned, and the increase of the speed limit to the dizzying heights of 30 m.p.h., this Act created for the first time a set of national standards and a regulatory system which took licensing out of the hands of the local authority. It divided the country into thirteen Traffic Areas each presided over by its own Traffic Commissioner and staff. At Traffic Courts the Commissioner issued licences for routes, fares, staff, and vehicles. They could also take appeals, often from the increasingly threatened railway companies who nonetheless were major investors in coach companies throughout the inter-war period. Whilst the Traffic Commissioners had no specific powers to insist on the provision of bus stations such facilities could be a consideration in the decision on whether or not to grant, or renew, licenses. Most importantly they could insist on the use of a specific station by an operator they issued a license to, as part of the authorised route.[47]

However this did not always favour the local authorities as might be supposed and more often than not local politics had their part to play in the creation of new bus and coach stations. 'The question of bus stations,' Ernest Godbold noted in 1935, 'provides an all too easy opportunity for local authorities and private enterprise to quarrel.'[48] In Lowestoft the local authority had determined to build a new municipal bus station despite the objections of the Eastern Counties Company who had already secured a site themselves. The Council went ahead with the construction at a cost of £1,500, and then required, via the Traffic Commissioner, that Eastern Counties used the new station at an annual cost of £250. An appeal to the Traffic Commissioners found in favour of the site chosen by Eastern Counties as more suitable, and even a subsequent appeal to the Minister of Transport upheld their decision. 'Lowestoft Corporation is now the proud possessor of a bus station which is not likely to be used very much' reported the operators journal in 1937.[49]

Elsewhere the cost of bringing a case could often stop the plans for a new station dead in its tracks. In 1938, as the General Manager of Crosville Motors later recalled, 'Crewe Corporation promoted a bill which amongst other things would provide a bus station in a situation not far from the Square. In other words it looked as if we would have to pay handsomely for what we were then getting for nothing. And so we lodged a petition.'[50] Rather than contemplate the expense involved in fighting this opposition, and the possibility of a costly second reading, the Corporation subsequently withdrew the clause relating to the bus station. In Morecambe the local authority had spent two years fighting the Ribble Bus Company in just such a case and success could never be assured.

Both these examples illustrate the 'easy opportunity for local authorities and private enterprise to quarrel' and the pitfalls which could occur. They also demonstrate the success of the station at Derby in anticipating the Road Traffic Act on so many points. Not far behind the success of Derby was the new Bournemouth Bus and Coach station (fig.111) designed by Jackson and Greenen. When it opened in 1931 it was heralded, with some justification, as 'the finest in the country' where 'Passers-by stop and stare at it, watching the buses and coaches zooming in and out like bees about a hive.'[51]

The novelty of this particular hive was that it was designed as two separate

111　Bournemouth Bus and Coach Station (1931), designed by Jackson and Greenen.

stations, one on top of the other. The top floor was reserved for the operation of the Hampshire and Dorset Bus Company, whilst the bottom was the coach station for the 'Royal Blue' coaches of the Elliott Brothers.[52] Built of reinforced concrete on an awkward trapezoid-shaped site the vehicles made their entrances and exits from this dramatic building by separate concrete ramps at the blunted apex of the building, the central ramp for the buses being flanked by two ramps for the semi-sunken coach station. Once inside, the vehicles circled a central waiting hall. As a model of co-operation it was precisely the type of endeavour the Traffic Commissioners were trying to bring about in an attempt to end the large number of separate stations and pick-up points in a town, often the result of take-overs during the 1920s. As a new image for a new building type, together with the later example of Lancaster Bus Station, it succeeded where many others failed to present a new image for a new building type.[53]

Despite the lack of compulsory powers the Traffic Commissioners, through their licensing role and comment in its Annual Reports, had very effective coercive powers to increase the provision of stations and bring them into line with the

112 Eastern Counties Bus Station, Norwich.

kind of advanced stations created at Derby, Bournemouth, and Lancaster. In this respect the most effective aspect of the Act was section 91(1) which laid down conditions in cases where vehicles could stop for longer than it was necessary to pick up and set down passengers. Initially, as the case of Crewe illustrates, there was strong resistance and resentment towards the Commissioners from many of the private operators who had previously been largely free to play one small local authority against another, knowing that the worst that could happen was that it might face a modest fine. Now the more draconian licensing powers insisted that private operators sat up and listened. The government's decisive action in establishing the London Passenger Transport Board in 1933 turned many into unwilling converts. In a distinct change of tone for a trade journal James H. Bordass of the Yorkshire Electric Tramways Ltd. wrote an article in *Bus and Coach* in 1934 entitled 'We want more bus stations . . . and the Traffic Commissioners can help us to get them.' Illustrated by pictures of Derby, Bournemouth, and Victoria, and looking to airport facilities as a model, it found heavily in favour of stations and only questioned who should provide them. Resistance eventually seems to have turned to positive enthusiasm as the larger operators became still larger and used their economic power to create facilities which either put their competitors out of business or drew them in. The Eastern Counties Company were a particularly avaricious concern who, having eventually bought up even the smallest pockets of competition in East Anglia found that they had bought routes they found it hard to run at a profit, but were now obliged to do so by the Traffic Commissioners. The Eastern Area Traffic Commissioner was similarly aggressive in his remarks about the desirability of improving passenger facilities in the region, with the effect that Eastern Counties provided some of the best stations of the period at Norwich (fig. 112), Chelmsford, and elsewhere.[54]

Showing a heavy debt to the urbane Modernism of Holland and the work of W. Dudok, this new generation of super-stations were imposing in their sheer mass. As the architectural critic Julian Leathart noted of Eastern Counties new station at Norwich in 1936, the architect's 'task of welding the independent units of this building into coherency has been met with considerable measure of success.'[55] Taking a further cue from the development of the architecture of the airfield, the Norwich coach station incorporated a projecting observation tower not unlike that found for the control of aircraft. The following year the new Eastern National Station in Chelmsford showed the same detail but it was reported that 'The company's experience has been that the public have been quick to memorise which bus leaves which bay, though the inspector on duty at the station announces all departures. It has not been found necessary to bring into use the control tower which projects from the second storey of the office block, and the broadcasting equipment for which it was destined has not yet been installed.'[56]

In an editorial which opened 'With almost every week bringing news of a project for the erection of a new bus station', *Bus and Coach* of May 1936 argued for the central role of the bus station in the town: 'It is not merely a question of using the station as a bus terminal, but of using it as a focal point of the town; the station should be regarded as part of the town itself, and of direct value to the inhabitants, particularly the tradespeople.'[57] Such an argument, echoing the position of the Traffic Commissioners (and, coincidentally, the Mayor of Norwich in his opening speech as reported elsewhere in its pages) was bringing the bus and coach into the centre of towns rather than keeping them to the edges and side streets. This was a significant change in thinking. It was also to become a means of combating the arguments in favour of nationalisation which were developing. The Road Traffic Act had not been the end of the assault on the passenger transport industry. With the creation of the London Passenger Transport Board in 1933 private operators had been given an even clearer signal to put their houses in order. In effect they went one better by using their property not merely as a demonstration of their commitment to providing a good service but as a means of

113   London Terminal Coach Station, Clapham Road, London (1930), designed by E.W. Wallis.

insurance against nationalisation. 'There is,' the same editorial concluded, 'in our view, one very important consideration to be borne in mind: it is the lesson learnt from the compulsory acquisition of London undertakings by the Board under the London Passenger Transport Act of 1933, that bricks and mortar are worth more than profits in the case of compulsory acquisition.' The sober stylistic similarity between the stations built by the United Counties and Eastern Counties companies and the suburban stations of the Green Line (which now formed part of the London Passenger Transport Board) may be due more to private operators wishing to present the same image of public service as epitomised by the London Passenger Transport Board than to any notion of following architectural fashion.

When the *Architects' Journal* reviewed the new London Terminal Coach Station on Clapham Road (fig. 113) in 1930 it announced 'Here is a sign of the times: one of the first motor coach termini to be erected in London.'[58] Designed by Edward W. Wallis, the 635-feet-long enclosed station was capable of dealing with 400 coaches per day and with parking space for 250 and was but the centre piece of a larger re-development of flats, shops and cafes in a version of classicism it would be more appropriate to call 'impoverished' rather than 'stripped.' Where the *Architects' Journal* saw it as a 'sign of the times', *Building* was more scathing when it claimed that 'for a modern problem, this has hardly been expressed in a modern way. We still cling tenaciously to rusticated piers and the corruption of pilasters.'[59] Nonetheless, in a telling reference to the experience of contemporary rail travel, *Building* claimed 'It is at least free of enamelled tin advertising plates, which bespatter those dirty portals of civilisation, King's Cross, Paddington, and Liverpool Street.' Although aimed specifically at the independent operator in search of a convenient London location it soon had a significant rival in the shape of the newly formed Green Line Coach Station in Soho.

In July 1930 the London General Omnibus Company, the East Surrey Traction Company, of Reigate, and the Autocar, of Tunbridge Wells, were merged to form the Green Line Coach Company.[60] The LGOC, formed in 1913, and in effect granted a monopoly by the London Traffic Act of 1924, had already opened in 1928 'a new departure in the form of a covered omnibus station serving as a starting point and terminus for a considerable number of road passenger services in the London traffic area.'[61] This station, at Richmond Road, Kingston-on-Thames, replaced the long-standing arrangement between the 'General' and the Southern Railway Company to use the courtyard of Victoria Railway Station. Its new location was still close to Southern's Kingston station and to the trams of the London United Tramways Company. Referring to the rapid improvement in engine design during the 1920s, the *Tramway and Railway World* reported that its site adjacent to the Kingston garage had the further advantage of making facilities 'available in the event of that rare occurrence nowadays — a breakdown of an omnibus.' The LGOC had been battling with private operators for some considerable time. During the holiday period, and at a time when private operators into London were increasing at the rate of almost twenty coaches a week, there were more than one hundred country routes into London and the LGOC had begun experimenting with fast express routes to combat this suburban competition The results were encouraging enough to elicit the hope that 'London has at last been given express communication with the Home Counties equal to anything that can be found in the provinces.'[62] Within two months of the creation of Green Line the new company announced its intention to create a new central coach station for London.

On Christmas day 1930 Green Line opened a startling new building in Poland Street, London (fig. 114). Classed as a temporary structure it's fashionably frivolous Art Deco, or perhaps more accurately Jazz Moderne, style may well have been

114   Poland Street Station, London, for Green Line Coaches (1930).

informed by the fear of a brief working life in view of the forthcoming 1930 Road
Traffic Act. Designed by Gordon Jeeves the station was designed to cope with up
to six coaches operating from it simultaneously, or could provide shelter for up to
nine. To the front were waiting rooms and the inspectors' booking and inquiry
office, to the rear the enclosed loading platform and a drivers' refreshment room.

Within two months of opening it was reported that there was a coach entering or leaving the station every five minutes during busy periods and that this was
evidence enough that its central location suited not only the thirteen services
which were using its facilities but that 'the arrangement suits the convenience of
the public.' This was not a terminus in the strict sense of the word, a final destination for the services, but rather a central loading point for services which ran
across the city. The convenience of then having to walk, perhaps with luggage, to
Oxford Street to travel onwards might need to be questioned. Clearly for the suburban London commuter such a central enclosed facility was a boon: it solved the
situation described as still being common as late as 1933 where 'passengers find
themselves dropped at one side of a large town with the prospect of crossing it to

secure a connection to their destination. They are possibly dropped in a side street chosen because it is a traffic backwater. The place to which they must go is equally a "backwater". At neither point is accurate information available, and the long-distance journey involving a change of vehicle is quite often a species of exploration on the part of the passenger.'[63]

At pains to stress their superiority over the elderly rail and tram networks, the choice of style by Green Line is clearly important in its connotations of modernity rather than tradition, newness as opposed to age. Green Line, especially once it became part of the London Passenger Transport Board in 1933, used its buildings both to provide comfortable surroundings and as part of its corporate identity and as an amenity for the town. As the *Tramway and Railway World* noted 'the station is an attractive and novel building' and 'at night its flood-lighted exterior and brilliantly illuminated interior are an acquisition to the locality.'[64] In the opinion of the *Architect* and *Building News* 'it is the prototype of the medium-sized motor-coach station such as will almost certainly be built in all the smaller towns of England within the next few years'[65].

Despite this confident prediction, the Poland Street Coach Station had few imitators. Most of the subsequent stations and garages for the Green Line Company were designed to a dignified, and standardised design by Wallis Gilbert and Partners (fig. 115). As part of the wider policy of 'patient progress' initiated by Frank Pick at the London Passenger Transport Board, and in harmony with the ideals of the Design and Industries Association, Green Line received considerable accolades for the sensitive way in which they sited their buildings in the greenery of the home counties. Of particular note was their headquarters at Reigate where the favoured brick modernism of Dudok seems to elide with a more romantic English Arts and Crafts tradition in keeping with Surrey.[66] Yet it was this same practice who designed what is probably the best known inter-war coach station — Victoria. More than a coach station Victoria, the creation of the London and Coastal Coach Company, was a large commercial property undertaking comprising not merely a covered coach station for up to eighty vehicles but, above it, three storeys of lettable office space and a restaurant large enough to double as a dance hall. This ambition to invest in property, to acquire 'bricks and mortar' — or in this case reinforced concrete — allowed Wallis Gilbert and Partners to design an impressive building which, as one critic commented 'In their horizontal-isimus, I take it that they wished to suggest the swift horizontal movement of the motor coach.'[67] It also represented a further stage in the development of the coach station, and one to be repeated later at Blackpool, Swansea, and elsewhere

115 Windsor Bus Garage, designed by Wallis, Gilbert and Partners.

of large commercial undertakings in which a covered coach station was but one element of an ambitious building. Steady letting income provided by the offices would go some way to offset the seasonal fluctuations of the coaching industry.

Where the design of the combined garages and stations for the Green Line, and the London Passenger Transport Board, had been praised for their sensitivity to Home Counties topography, a sensitivity which was evident in the choice of traditional materials rather than the more Moderne forms, Victoria represented the kind of Jazz Moderne style the practice had developed in the startling series of daylight factories they designed for sites throughout the country but mostly associated with the Hoover and Firestone factories and their like along London's Great West Road.[68] 'If this indeed, is concrete, then let us have more of it' wrote *Building* magazine in its eulogy of the main entrance of Victoria Coach Station (fig. 116), 'it is quite the most interesting piece of work of its kind I have ever seen.'[69] 'I hardly know whether it is meant to be modern or just exciting' wrote the architectural critic Frederick Towndrow on the opening of the station in 1932.[70] London and Coastal Coaches Ltd. was a combine, or marketing company,

116   Victoria Coach Station, London, by Wallis, Gilbert and Partners.

of nine coach companies operating into London who 'pooled' their receipts to mutual advantage. As such it was but a purpose-designed version of such experiments which had begun in the 1920s in the north of England and reached their nadir in the operation of the Cheltenham scheme.

By the late 1930s both the local authority bus station and the private coach-station had come of age. They had developed from initial kerbside operations at the end of the tram or railway line, to operating from well-planned, central and attractive facilities in the centre of town, such as were to be found at Derby, Lancaster, Northampton, Norwich, and Bournemouth. The chief impediment to the local authority station was the slow death of the tram and the opposition of the powerful commercial interests represented chiefly by the railway companies.

The influence of the Road Traffic Act of 1930 had been to allow a more equitable treatment of both public and private operators to the benefit of the public. It also, as many of the examples above demonstrate, encouraged a more unified and integrated passenger transport service for the public. Where such co-operation was not forthcoming the government continued to pursue a policy of speaking softly whilst its Traffic Commissioners carried a big stick—that stick was the threat of nationalisation. Where such a threat failed to achieve co-operation the private operators took a longer view and invested in property. Ultimately buildings are constructed on land which has a commercial value and the private coach companies began to invest in land and to build ambitious facilities on it, not merely as a means of improving the efficiency of their service but as a form of insurance against nationalisation. By ensuring that compensation for compulsory purchase would be an expensive and damaging option for the government they seemed to have won the day. From the early 1930s it was increasingly realised that 'In the possible event of the nationalisation of transport, or even on the formation of transport boards, bus stations and similar property have a definite value more easily assessed than goodwill and profit-earning capacity.'[71]

I am indebted to a great many people and institutions for help with this essay and they are listed here in no particular order but each receive my gratitude and thanks knowing the part they played. Bob Ashton at the Sandtoft Transport Museum, Sharon Brown at the Museum of Liverpool Life, Clare Foley at the Derby Museum and Art Gallery, Andrew Foster, Elain Harwood, Clare Hartwell, Kenneth Holder, Joe Kerr, Paul Roach, Roger Hall, Michael Plunket, Steve Parissien, Joan Skinner, the late Michael Stratton, George Turnball at Greater Manchester Museum of Transport, and the staff of the Manchester Central Reference Library, London Transport Museum, Birmingham Museum of Transport, National Tramways Museum, Royal Commission on the Historic Monuments of England, Royal Institute of British Architects Library, Local Studies Libraries of Weston-Super-Mare, Sheffield, Walsall, Plymouth, Newcastle-upon-Tyne, Taunton, Lancaster, Rotherham, Barnsley, East and West Sussex, Guildford, Trafford, Bristol, Essex, Norwich, Cheltenham, Bournemouth, North Devon Athenaeum, Barnstable, and the many enthusiasts who have generously shared their expertise with me. Most importantly I must, as ever, thank Alison, Holly and Jacob who, though they sometimes enjoyed the 'outings,' only wish I'd stop doing it.

1   *Building* (February 1930), p.82.
2   Herbert Morrison, *Socialisation and Transport; the organisation of socialised industries with particular reference to the London Passenger Transport Bill* (London: 1933), p.24. Morrison was Minister of Transport 1929–31.
3   The disfigurement of Britain by advertising was a constant argument of the so-called 'good design' lobby epitomized by figures such as Harry Peach, Clough Williams-Ellis, W.R.Lethaby and the Design and Industries Association. For the broad environmental and cultural outlines of this debate see John Sheail, *Rural conservation in inter-war Britain* (Oxford: 1981), and Stefan Szczelkun, *The conspiracy of good taste: William Morris, Cecil Sharp, Clough Williams-Ellis* (London: 1993). The arguments of Clough Williams-Ellis and his supporters were articulated in two of his works of the period, *England and the octopus* (Portmeirion: 1928) and a collections of essays edited by him, *Britain and the Beast* (London: 1937). On a particularly successful campaign fought by the Design and Industries Association to remove advertising by the Shell Corporation see Pat Kirkham, *Harry Peach, Dryad and the D.I.A.* (London: 1986).
4   Walter Jackson, 'A bus man's holiday in England and Wales', *Bus and Coach* (November 1938), p.430.
5   *Ibid.*, p.431. An interesting complement to Jackson's holiday is supplied by the architectural critic Frederick Towndrow in 1932 when he wrote in *Building* (April 1932), p.176. 'Last autumn I took a tour through England and Scotland by motor-coach; not a conducted tour, but a casual happy-go-lucky one, in which I went to any place I chose. And it always was there.'
6   The Act was brought in by the Labour administration of 1929–31 taking advice from a series Royal Commissions established in the 1920s following the establishment of the first Ministry of Transport in 1919. On this key piece of legislation see 'The restriction of road passenger transport in the 30's; a critique', in Derek H. Aldcroft, *Studies in British transport history 1870-1970* (London: 1974), pp.187-207; and David Kaye, *The British Bus scene in the 1930's* (London: 1980).

7   See John Hibbs, *The history of British bus services* (London: second revised edition, 1989), and for developments prior to the introduction of the petrol-engine see M.J. Freeman and D.H. Aldcroft, eds., *Transport in Victorian Britain* (Manchester: 1988), especially Chapter 4, 'Urban transport' by T.C. Barker.

8   The Great Western Railway was particularly quick to make use of the motor-coach to supplement and extend its train service and by 1904 had over seventy vehicles in operation.

9   Quoted in J. Joyce, *The story of passenger transport in Britain* (Shepperton: 1967), p.142. It is curious in this context to note the view of Margaret Thatcher that a young man who found himself travelling on a bus by the age of 30 should consider himself a failure.

10   A great tramway depot in Liverpool, *The Tramway and Railway World* (15 March 1928), p.133. The Edge Lane Depot clearly fits into the Georgian aesthetic being strongly promoted by the Liverpool School of Civic Design under Charles Reilly at the time. See Joseph Sharples, *Charles Reilly and the Liverpool School of Architecture* (Liverpool: 1996).

11   It is interesting to note that whilst the opportunity to compete with road transport was not granted to rail companies by the government until 1928 most of the countries of continental Europe never encouraged such competition at all but continued to protect their national railway companies. As a reviewer of the London Terminal Coach Station in *Building* (February 1930) noted 'the motor-coach business hardly seems to have developed at all in the continental countries, and yet the trains are not so crowded.' See generally T.R. Gourvish, *British Railways; a business history* (Cambridge: 1986).

12   *The Rotherham Advertiser* (18 March 1933), p.12.

13   *Building* (February 1930), p.82.

14   'Road stations', *Bus and Coach* (1931), p.141. This is one of the few articles to deal specifically with the design of the bus station; see also J.C. Fistere, 'Bus terminal construction', *Architectural Forum (*December 1930), pp.781-84, F.O.Baddiley, 'The Design and construction of omnibus garages', *Royal Institute of British Architects Journal* (21 December 1935), pp.177-88, and G.C. Campbell-Taylor, 'Planning and running a bus station', *Bus and Coach* (June 1936), pp.198-200. On the whole the architectural magazines of the day were more impressed by the design of garages then stations, partly for the ever more daring roof spans being created. Examples illustrated during the period include the Hampshire and Dorset Motor Services Garage, Poole (*Brick Builder*, September 1929, p.15); Southdown Motor Services Ltd. Garage, Portslade (*Bus and Coach*, vol.2, 1930, p.164); Western National garage, Plymouth (*Brick Builder*, September 1932, p.35). Amongst the more architecturally noteworthy were the Leicester omnibus garage by W.H. & H.G. Riley (*Architects Journal*, 17 July 1929, pp. 97-99; *Brick Builder*, September 1929, pp.45-46; *Transport World*, 15 March 1934, pp.154-55) and the important garage at Wythenshawe, Manchester, by G. Noel Hill an early example of concrete shell construction, and at the time the largest in the country with a roof span of 180 feet, based on a Swedish example (*Bus and Coach*, March 1940, pp.48-50)

14   *The Derbyshire Advertiser*, 25 April 1959. As revealed at the 'Destination Anywhere' conference, held at the Paul Mellon Centre, London, March 2000 its influence seems to have spread beyond its own genre to be re-cast as a railway station by the LMS at Hoylake. The LMS Chief Engineers Office was based in Derby from 1935. See V.R. Anderson and G.K. Fox, *A pictorial record of L.M.S. architecture* (Oxford: 1981). See also, Maxwell Craven, *Derby; an Illustrated history* (Derby: 1988).

16   Philip Wards, 'Traffic problems produce a £31,000 municipal station', *Bus and Coach* (November 1933), pp.414-17.

17   Aslin went on to become the County Architect of Hertfordshire County Council which, after the Second World War, pioneered the use of prefabrication in the provision of an ambitious school building programme. See Andrew Saint, *Towards a social architecture; the role of school-building in post-war England* (London: 1987)

18   *Royal Commission on Transport. Final Report. The co-ordination and development of transport.* (Command paper 3751), (London: 1931), p.163.

19   'Coach and omnibus station, Bournemouth', *Building* (May 1931), p.233.

20   British Steelwork Association, *Motor-coach stations* (London: British Steelwork Association, n.d.), p.3.

21   *Building* (April 1932), p.177.

22   I am grateful to Mike Nesbit of Penwith Borough Council, Penzance, for help in identifying this building.

23   *The Barnsley Chronicle* (27 December 1919). In the *Royal Institute of British Architects Journal* during 1919

Sir Frank Bains wrote on 'War factories and sheds; their construction and adaptation to future needs.' It seems more than likely that some former military buildings were converted to charabanc garages as part of the peace dividend.

24 K.L.Turns, 'Private bus operations: a note on Monty Moreton Ltd.', *Transport History*, vol. 3, no.3 (1970), p.295.

25 L.D.Kitchin, 'Efficiency without tears', *Bus and Coach* (July 1938), p. 249.

26 Thomas Massey and W.E.Minchinton, 'A note on the motor bus services in the Gorseinon area of South Wales, 1917-35', *Transport History*, vol.1, no.1 (1968), p.72. This condition attached to the granting of the license was typical of the way local authorities tried to curb the worst excesses of kerbside operation.

27 *First Annual Reports of the Traffic Commissioners 1931-32* (London: H.M.S.O., 1932), p.5. See also, 'After six years of the licensing system', *Bus and Coach* (January 1930), pp.30-32, and generally, D.L.Munby, *Inland transport statistics; Great Britain 1900-70* (Oxford: 1978).

28 Burnell's premises are illustrated in *Commercial Motor* (28 March 1922), p.175. S.P.B. Mais, 'The plain man looks at England' in *Britain and the beast* (London: 1937) paid particular attention to the despoliation of the Cheddar Gorge by tourism, an example of which is discussed in Alan Powers, 'In search of the Caveman restaurant', *The Thirties Society Journal*, no.5 (1985), pp.18-23.

29 Bristol Tramways and Carriage Company's Beach Garage and Omnibus station at Weston-Super-Mare, *The Tramway and Railway World* (15 March 1928), p. 154.

30 Winchester municipal coach station, *The Transport World* (8 November 1934).

31 The Oxford Bus Preservation Syndicate, *Black and White; a pictorial reminiscence 1926-76* (Oxford: 1976).

32 'Cheltenham as a motor coach centre', *The Tramway and Railway World* (15 October 1931), p.237.

33 For a useful discussion of corporate identity in a transport undertaking see Adrian Forty, *Objects of desire; design and society, 1750-1980* (London: 1986).

34 'Cheltenham as a motor coach centre', *op. cit.*, p.238.

35 The New York Terminal of Greyhound Lines, designed by Thomas W. Lamb, was illustrated in *Architectural Forum* (December 1930), *The Architectural Record* (September 1935), p.149-151, and *Bus and Coach* (October 1937). *Bus and Coach*, amongst others, regularly reported the latest new terminals in the USA, such as Kansas (*Architectural Forum*, December 1930), Newark (*Bus and Coach*, December 1934). Miami (*Bus and Coach*, February 1938), Indianapolis (*Bus and Coach*, December 1938).

36 C.F. Hayward, 'A nerve centre of long-distance co-ordination', *Bus and Coach* (December 1934).

37 *Ibid*, p. 348.

38 The core of this group were Black and White, Midland Red, Royal Blue, Greyhound, and United Counties who collectively traded under the title of Associated Motorways. Other 'contact' services who participated in the scheme included Southdown, Ribble, Western National, Southern National, etc.

39 'Road stations', *Bus and Coach* (April 1931), p. 141.

40 C.F. Hayward, 'A nerve centre of long-distance co-ordination', *op. cit.*, p.440.

41 Morrison, *Socialisation and Transport*, p.vii.

42 'Suburban coach stations have arrived', *Bus and Coach*, vol.4 (1932), p. 187.

43 Similarly Walter Jackson found that he was discharged at Birmingham into 'what is apparently a garage.' *Bus and Coach* (November 1938), p.431. Other notable conversions included the glass-domed former Industrial Hall in Edinburgh, and in Hereford, a former prison.

44 See Adrian Tinniswood, *A history of country house visiting; five centuries of tourism and taste* (London: 1989), and Peter Mandler, *The fall and rise of the stately home* (London: 1997) and more generally Ian Ousby, *The Englishman's England; taste, travel and the rise of tourism* (Cambridge: 1990).

45 R.C.Anderson, *A history of Crosville Motor Services* (Newton Abbot: 1981), W.J. Crosland-Taylor, *Crosville; the sowing and the harvest* (new revised edition, Transport publishing, 1987). *Bus and Coach* (August 1936), p.279 noted that 'A growing number of former patrons is establishing week-end cottages in the district.'

46 *The Architect and Building News* (15 June 1934), pp. 311-16. The topic of bus shelters is an important topic in its own right with notable designs by the Arts and Crafts architects C.F.A. Voysey, Randall Wells, and good council designs found in Leicester, Birmingham and elsewhere. Such buildings in miniature could be a problem as when the Walsall County Court found that a poorly sited shelter constituted a public nui-

sance and ordered it to be removed (*Bus and Coach*, January 1937, p.3.) For a good contemporary survey of public houses of the period see Basil Oliver, *The renaissance of the English public house* (London: 1947).

47 See T.C. Baker and C.I. Savage, *An economic history of transport in Britain* (London: 1970) and D.H. Aldcroft, *British transport since 1914; an economic history* (London: 1975).

48 *Bus and Coach* (January 1935), p. 35.

49 *Bus and Coach* (April 1937), p. 124.

50 W.J. Crosland-Taylor, *Crosville; the sowing and the harvest*, p. 170.

51 E.E. Godbold, 'Two road stations in one', *Bus and Coach* (April 1931), p. 136. On the idea of buildings as beehives see Juan Antonio Ramirez, *The Beehive metaphor; from Gaudi to Le Corbusier* (London: 2000)

52 R.C. Anderson and G. Frankis, *History of Royal Blue Express Services* (Newton Abbot: 1971).

53 On Lancaster see *Transport World* (1939).

54 Similarly United Counties adopted this manner, with rounded corners, for its series of stations built during the 1930s, see L.D. Kitchin, 'Bus stations of 1936', *Bus and Coach* (May 1936), pp.150-53, and P.M.A. Thomas, 'Modernising maintenance', *Bus and Coach* (May 1939), pp.158-61.In 1938 Walter Jackson praised the United Counties station at Northampton alongside Derby.

55 J.R.Leathart, 'Current architecture', *Building*, vol. 2 (1936), p.288.

56 *Bus and Coach* (October 1937), p. 363.

57 *Bus and Coach* (May 1936), p. 148.

58 *Architects Journal* (22 January 1930), p. 173. It is noticeable that not until after the Road Traffic Act of 1930 did architectural magazines pay much, if any, attention to road transport buildings. In 1931 the Royal Institute of British Architects held an exhibition entitled 'The architecture of modern transport in London' when most of its examples were foreign.

59 *Building* (February 1930), p. 82.

60 K. Warren, *Fifty years of the Green Line* (London: 1980), D.W.K. Jones and B.J. Davis, *Green Line 1930-80* (London: 1980), *'Bell Street,' East Surrey* (St. Albans: 1974), T.C. Barker, *A history of London Transport* (London: 1974).

61 'An outer London omnibus station', *The Tramway and Railway World* (13 December 1928), p.362.

62 'New coach station for London', *The Tramway and Railway World* (18 September 1930), p. 155.

63 *Bus and Coach* (January 1934), p. 28.

64 'A London station for Green Line coaches', *The Tramway and Railway World* (12 February 1931), p. 102.

65 *The Architect and Building News* (22 May 1931), p. 258. The building was also reviewed in *Architecture Illustrated* (April 1931), and *Building* (February 1931).

66 See, generally, 'Progress of Green Line coaches', *Transport World* (15 September 1938), pp.133-35. Green Line stations and garages were enthusiastically covered by the architectural press. See, for example, *Architects Journal* (30 November 1933); the *Royal Institute of British Architects Journal* (26 January 1935); *Architecture Illustrated* (August 1935); *Architect and Building News* (25 October 1935); *Builder* (27 December 1935);.Wallis Gilbert and partrners also designed new premises for the Maidstone and District Motor Services Ltd., in Sheerness 'on the most modern lines' in 1933, *The Tramway and Railway World* (9 March 1933), p.143.On Frank Pick see Christian Barman, *The man who built London Transport; a biography of Frank Pick* (Newton Abbot: 1979), and Nikolaus Pevsner, *Studies in art, architecture, and design.* vol. 2 *Victorian and after* (London: 1968).

67 *Building* (April 1932), p.176. The building was also reviewed in *The Tramway and Railway World* (11 February 1932 and 14 April 1932). See also Frank Woodworth, *Victoria Coach Station; the first fifty years* (Rochester: 1982). Blackpool's new station is reviewed in *Bus and Coach* (June 1939), and Swansea's in *Bus and Coach* (October 1940).

68 Joan Skinner, *Form and fancy; factories and factory buildings by Wallis, Gilbert & partners, 1916-1939* (Liverpool: 1997). Skinner's book also contains a useful discussion of the misuse of the term Art Deco in relation to inter-war architecture.

69 *Building* (April 1932), p.177.

70 *Ibid.*, p.177.

71 *Bus and Coach* (February 1937).

The Motorway Service Station

David Lawrence

IN THE HISTORY of road transport buildings, perhaps none has been more mis-understood and abused than the motorway service area. As points of embarkation and departure, we accept that we will spend time at railway stations and airports. But in our own cars, the desire is to get where we are going as soon as possible, and the motorway service area is more a distress stop than a place to be detained. Motorways are the trunk routes of the road network, unavoidable conduits along which millions of us travel for work or leisure. This means that the built manifestation of the service area is an architecture encountered by the many rather than the elite; the associations we make with these buildings refer not to the architecture but to the experience of their interiors. They are not memorable like the spaces of the great train sheds and airports, the modern classicism of Charles Holden's tube stations, or the dynamic voids of the Jubilee Line extension stations. Instead, they are memorable for the quality of food and service available within them.

Development of British motorways came during a period of extensive national regeneration and accelerated social change. Steady employment, reasonable wages, and individual mobility enabled the rapid liberation of the working classes, and fuelled their desire and ability to consume. This growth in mass consumption contributed to the dream of a society in which all classes could be equal. As a metaphor for modernity and progress, speedy travel became accessible to the masses through the cheap family saloon. As a significant agent of equality, the motor-car would need to be sustained by appropriate venues. Architecture too had a role in the expression of progress and technology. New constructions such as the Humber Bridge and Post Office (now Telecom) Tower were modern wonders and attracted their own tourists.

Roadside service

The British filling station had begun as an assembly of petrol pumps thrown up at the roadside, with a nearby building adapted for its new use. Gradually the fuel dispensers were relocated to a pull-in off the road, organised as a forecourt and service station. This was provided with purpose-built structures for cash handling, some equipment sales, and for vehicle maintenance. Refreshments were few, travellers resorting to coaching inns, hotels and roadhouses. Cafés and dormitories were available to truck drivers.

Italy, Germany and North America had shown the benefits for industry, commerce and communications to be gained from building express motor roads. British plans had been passed around since the first decade of the twentieth century, but two wars and several governments had seen to it that nothing was done. Only in the late 1950s, when post-war reconstruction and decentralisation increased the need for new fast freight and passenger links, was the issue of a national transport network addressed with serious intent. With railways out of political favour, motor transport was seen as the key to making these connections. Motorways would relieve the 'A'-class roads and divert overspill traffic from subsidiary routes. Preston by-pass—the first section of British motorway—opened in December 1958. The seventy-five mile first section of the M1 London–Birmingham motorway followed this fragment in November 1959.

In line with policy on express roads abroad, the argument was put forward by Government that motorways contributed to economy and road safety, as they limited the traffic using existing roads and reduced the fuel consumption of journeys off the motorway. Stopping on the motorway itself was prohibited except in an emergency, so off-road rest areas had to be offered. To feed the motorised masses, it was no longer sufficient for rest stops to be an ad-hoc assembly of transport café, filling station and breakdown recovery service; comprehensively planned facilities were needed. Here was the potential for design that could respond to the entirely artificial landscape of the motorway itself. But the government had no clear idea about what scale or type of service should be offered and looked to Europe and North America for examples.

The United States started building its limited-access Interstate Highways in 1956. On these roads, rest areas consisted of parking areas with basic toilet facilities. More sophisticated amenities were provided on State Turnpikes or toll roads. Five bridge restaurants were built on the United States' Illinois Tristate and Northwest Tollway system, in 1959, and one had already come into use in Oklahoma. Visiting British Minister of Transport Ernest Marples admired these installations and put them forward as a pattern for future service area developments in Britain. It was believed that people were thrilled by the spectacle of speeding vehicles, and anything the designer could do to bring customers into proximity with the road was encouraged.[1]

Service areas on the Italian *autostrade* were run by private concerns such as food producers and caterers, in partnership with oil companies. A special society was established by the Italian Government to approve building designs and arrange essential services for the sites, which were spaced at 20- to 25-mile intervals. In common with the turnpike bridges, several Italian service area buildings straddled the highway, looking like futuristic cruise ships with masts and flags, and heavily stylised window details.

In contrast to early British operations the German autobahn *raststätten* (rest places) were usually operated by local firms using trained staff. They were commonly a more restrained affair, styled on the lines of a small restaurant, in some cases with an hotel attached.

As consultant engineer to the Ministry of Transport, Sir Owen Williams determined sites for motorway services. Promoters of motorway construction both here and abroad held the belief that the new highways would open up the countryside; Ministry policy was to site service areas 'in places where the motorway passed through pleasant rural scenery, so that their potential users might find them attractive and restful'.[2] In fact, with no accurate data on the stopping and eating behaviour of motorists, the decision on locations was basic.

The distance between service areas was set at between twelve and fifteen miles, with every other site to be developed at first and the remaining sites to be brought into use when traffic levels were sufficient to warrant it. Space for service areas was included in the main motorway land takes, and held in reserve for future development. Purchased out of public funds, the sites were of the minimum acreage considered necessary, and this accounted for the approximately round shape of the original plots. No consideration was given to a layout that might be appropriate for services, and the rigidity of planning was further underlined by the absolute fixing of the boundary through provision of a perimeter road. Development along the motorway itself was not permitted, and access was limited, so service areas were expected to operate as self-contained entities in isolated locations. Basic utilities were run up to the site edge; the Ministry undertook only to complete simple landscaping and erect a footbridge. Every other element of the service area had to be built and paid for by the operator.

The government advertised for tenders on site leases; interested parties had to commit themselves to a certain sum for the buildings, a 50-year lease calculated according to the Ministry's expenditure in buying and preparing the site, and a rental based on a percentage of gross turnover. Government revenues would rise in line with operators' profits (and for a time exceeded them). Tenders were in two parts: a financial offer and a scheme for buildings. Regulation of site construction and operation was precise and took no account of commercial needs, a conflict that would affect the industry for many years. Signs and notices were limited to the control of traffic exiting the highway, filtering through the site and returning to the road. No advertising of any sort was permitted. A twenty-four-hour catering service had to be provided. No alcohol could be sold and the sale of goods was limited to tobacco, confectionery and a few gifts.

Starting out

The British motorway service station industry began with some very different schemes. Two service area sites were planned for the first section of MI: Newport Pagnell and Watford Gap. Blue Boar, whose name became synonymous with mediocre motorway catering, was originally to take on both sites. With a segregation determined by the Ministry of Transport, Newport Pagnell would be exclusively for cars and Watford Gap for lorries. In the end Blue Boar settled for Watford Gap and hotelier/caterer Fortes got Newport Pagnell. Watford Gap opened on the same day as motorway MI — 2 November 1959. Its construction was subject to brick shortages and the cafés were not in use until late 1960. In the meantime Blue Boar had to purchase some garden sheds from which to sell sandwiches. Having already built some filling stations for Blue Boar, Harry W. Weedon and Partners designed the site. In contrast to the practice's cinema work of the 1930s, Watford Gap was little more than a series of functional blocks without architectural merit. Motorway services were sufficiently novel to attract some interest: one of the architects for Watford Gap appeared on television to explain how the service station worked.

Newport Pagnell (opened 15 August 1960, fig. 117) was let to Forte and Co., who commissioned Sydney Clough, Son and Partners for the design. Forte's eagerly grasped a new opportunity for expansion of their catering activities on a national scale: within a year they would announce plans for a chain of motels with restaurants and filling stations. For economy and rapid construction,

117   Newport Pagnell, M1, seen in 1968. Photograph: Russ Craig.

Newport Pagnell was prefabricated using a proprietary building system and consisted of two single-storey catering buildings and a covered way built around the
concrete bridge raft provided by the Ministry of Transport. Designers planning
double-sided sites (upon which the government insisted) had the difficulty of
determining an overall treatment that included bisection by the motorway. At
Watford Gap the issue was avoided by having separate, duplicated buildings;
Newport Pagnell suggests a comparison with the railway station: a building for
each direction of traffic, with a connecting footbridge.

      Neither of the projects was received favourably by the architectural press,
and one magazine commissioned Leonard Manasseh to design a model service
station scheme. Clearly based on American diner practice, Manasseh's proposal
included an effective traffic circulation arrangement, use of appropriate local
materials where possible, and efficient planning of kitchen and dining areas. The
practice was not selected to design any service areas, but the value of this model
seems to have been confirmed when a government report published some seven
years later reiterated several of its key points.[3]

The Ministry held a number of competitions to secure the architectural designs. After accomplishing the first full-scale service station at Newport Pagnell, Sydney Clough, Son and Partners designed the Farthing Corner (M2) and Knutsford (M6) sites for Top Rank Motor Inns, an off-shoot of the J. Arthur Rank media and entertainment organisation. Rank styled their services as 'Motorports'. Opened in 1963, both these schemes were of the bridge type. Farthing Corner perhaps emphasises the fascination with passing traffic: pavilions on either side of the motorway linked by an open-air terrace to be used for dining in good weather. With the designers minds set firmly on dreams of the Continent (this was the fast road to Dover) and sunny holidays, no account seems to have been taken of the discomfort to customers caused by traffic noise, pollution or inclement weather.

Fortes added two more sites at Keele and Charnock Richard (fig. 118), both on M6, in 1963. In these projects the operator tried to learn from the experience of overcrowding at Newport Pagnell. Buildings were bigger, more streamlined, but still made of prefabricated parts, this time using the once ubiquitous 'Vic Hallam' system of steel frames with wood and coloured glass spandrels. With the remote locations of these sites, water tanks were a necessity, and were here expressed as distinct forms attached to the bridges. Architect Terence Verity brought his experience as chief art director at Associated British Cinemas to bear on the interiors, installing bright coffee bar colour schemes of pale blue, pink, yellow and gold.

As more motorways were started, several companies moved in to compete for their share of the catering trade. Ross Group diversified from fishing and frozen food production when they opened what was then the most northerly service area on M1 at Leicester Forest East in 1966. Designed by Brian Leather at Howard V. Lobb and Partners,[4] this would be the last of the bridge restaurants. It was also the most elegant in design—a single streamlined form over the highway, with sheer glass staircase enclosures and cantilevered balconies at either end, and a free-standing tower that served as chimney enclosure and landmark. Leicester Forest East was aesthetically the closest of the bridge buildings to their American antecedents. Dining facilities included a restaurant service, with fresh fish from Ross's own trawler fleets, in an environment styled by Conran Design Group. A clue to the restricted space available within the bridge was the siting of transport cafés some distance away in the car parks. Was this also a segregation of 'clean' and 'dirty' customers?

118 Charnock Richard, M6, seen in 1968. Photograph: Russ Craig.

The problem of elevated service stations

Bridge buildings were most suitable when the majority of the site was flat. Construction and operation costs were greater due to the extra storey, and the stairs deterred or prevented some individuals from reaching the eating areas. Kitchens were duplicated, incurring further expense, although one set of catering facilities could be closed whilst maintaining the twenty-four hour service in the other. Based on a fixed raft, this arrangement did not provide well for future extension. By its very nature the bridge would be costly to expand widthways, and there was a limit to the possible width before the bridge reached the Ministry's definition of a tunnel, a feature not permitted on British motorways unless a necessity of topography. Any addition to the bridge at either end was also more distant from the kitchens, increasing staff time.

119 Forton M6, 1965.
Collection: David Lawrence.

Bridge restaurants made no allowance for an escape from the motorway; the user remained in the environment of vehicles and the super-human scale of the road. As advertisements they were failures too: by the time drivers saw the bridge it was too late to turn off.

Top Rank actively sought out innovative design for their motorway services, and was responsible for what are perhaps the most iconic buildings of the genre. Large all-purpose practice T. P. Bennett and Partners worked for Rank, and to a relatively generous budget, on the 'Motorports' at Forton and Hilton Park (both on M6). Planning of Forton commenced in 1963, and Hilton Park the following year; Forton came into use in 1965. At Forton, which was within reasonable driving distance of Preston and the main north-west seaside resort of Blackpool, the operator and architects capitalised on projected high traffic levels by adding to the expected amenities a 65-foot high observation tower with restaurant (fig. 119). Towers were a popular symbol of progressive architecture during this

120 Aust, M4, 1966. Photograph: Ian Hodgson.

period, and constructed in many cities. The design is reminiscent of an airport control tower, thereby making positive associations with the most exclusive form of mass transport.

As a variant on the tower, Hilton Park had a projecting deck restaurant on the northbound side, oversailing the lower floors and footbridge. Inside the building, the grand atmosphere was emphasised by the inclusion of a sizeable staircase, and two passenger lifts. Building materials were aimed at durability, and in common use for public buildings of the period: hard engineering bricks, in-situ concrete, and terrazzo floors. Hilton Park was completed in 1967. Operator Top Rank had based their financial calculations on government traffic forecasts that failed to materialise due to road diversions, and the service area remained closed to motorists until 1970. Even after several years' use, neither Forton nor Hilton Park had repaid its investment.

Having captured some of the main north–south motorway trade, Top Rank turned their attention to the growing fragments of M4 and successfully competed for the prestigious site at Aust (now called Severn View, M48) close to the first Severn bridge (fig. 120). A series of designs (including among them work by the Archigram group) had already been rejected in an attempt to raise the aesthetic standards of new service area projects. Russell, Hodgson and Leigh had been involved in hotel development for Rank, and had a wide background in furniture design through the work of partner Gordon Russell. They won the second competition. Set at the river's edge and overlooking the bridge, Aust was accessed from a long slip road up from M4. This was the first single-sided site — so no bridge building needed — and Top Rank requested one monolithic block to contain all services except the fuel forecourt. In plan, the building was based on two conjoined polygons, elevated as faceted walls so that views of the Severn Bridge and river were available in all directions. Nine hundred diners could be fed at once in three catering areas within the building, where an array of kitchens and food stores was hidden from view by placing the building in a depression of the ground. Architect Ian Hodgson cited the work of Marcel Breuer in New England as influencing his choice of western red cedar siding for the Aust project. Lower walls were made of local stone from across the Severn. The large scale of Aust made it inflexible in the face of changing catering practice, and almost the whole ground floor had been abandoned within a few years once pre-cooked food deliveries were introduced. With the second crossing of the River Severn taking M4 away from Aust, few customers call at the services, and present operators Moto have disposed of the building, opening a small outlet closer to the motorway.

In the latter half of the 1960s, the impact of a burgeoning leisure industry made itself felt on the operation of motorway service areas. Architects working in retail and entertainment brought an imagination to design of amenities that was much needed if motorists were to be distracted from the road even briefly. In its ambitious development and exuberant promotion by Mecca Leisure Group, Trowell (1967, fig. 121) on MI seems to have exemplified ideas of glamour and fantasy that recurred during the decade. Mecca's empire included ballrooms, ice rinks, restaurants and bars. Motorway catering looked like being a good prospect, especially as Mecca felt the existing operators were not giving it their best efforts. Kett and Neve, the architects for Trowell, noted that Mecca had little idea of what a service area should look like externally, and were also forced to comply with the standard 'bridge and two sides' format. They determined to realise their own idea of motor architecture with a streamlined building of glass and steel made distinctive by somewhat mannered monitor roof lights and glazing details. This was all very well, but the client wanted commercial interiors.

Taking French restaurants and the Disney style of customer service as models, Mecca styled Trowell as a 'Village', based on the theme of local folk hero Robin Hood. Kett and Neve were required to abandon their contemporary interior

121   Trowell, MI, 1967. Photograph: Russ Craig.

design and refinish the restaurants in a pastiche mediaeval style. This was accomplished by the installation of murals depicting Hood and his group, and heavy wooden furniture and fabric valancing fixed to ceilings. Trowell proved to be very popular with customers, but Mecca was not happy with high rents paid to the government. After the 'Village' was sold to Granada in October 1977, it was rapidly refurbished in a functional low-maintenance style.[6]

Closest yet to the metropolis, Granada's Heston aimed at capturing trade bound for Heathrow Airport or fuelling up for the long haul west. Designed by James A. Roberts, architect for the radical redevelopment of Birmingham and Liverpool in the 1960s,[5] Heston introduced to British motorways the feature of a staggered layout, with two amenity buildings spaced some distance apart along the motorway without any physical connection between the sides. Roberts experienced difficulties persuading Granada that his two-storey, glass-fronted design was appropriate, and Heston was built to a much reduced specification. Compromise is ever present in architecture, and designers do not always like to see their vision of a future building diminished by others, but here Granada may have

122   London Gateway (formerly Scratchwood), M1, seen in 1999 after substantial alteration.
Photograph: David Lawrence.

been reasonable in letting business sense overrule the desire to be flamboyant. The catering service was privileged over the aesthetics of the architecture, and profits were good. Both sides of the service area have since been entirely redeveloped. Fortes noted the success of Granada's Heston, and saw to it that motorway services ended the 1960s with a glamorous flourish in the shape of Scratchwood (fig. 122), London's first truly urban service area.[7] Scratchwood was an important opportunity for Fortes to advertise the presence of their services further up the motorway. Garnett Cloughley Blakemore and Associates, architects of several boutiques in London's King's Road including the 'Chelsea Drugstore' restaurant/boutique immortalised in a song by the Rolling Stones, designed the single catering building. Inspired by sunnier and more sophisticated places than Hendon, the architects employed a colonnade of marble and granite coated concrete columns (this owes much to a structural feature developed by Skidmore Owings and Merrell), to set off the smoky brown glass windows. Planning was innovative, with one kitchen for the three serveries. *Architects' Journal* feted Scratchwood for its 'anti-motorway philosophy . . . [it] deliberately turns its back on traffic. It is intended as a haven of tranquillity, a soothing influence on frayed nerves, and a refuge from the stresses and irritations of motorway driving.[8]

Poor service, inflexible architecture

Motorways became an accepted part of travel, and the ever-increasing traffic levels made them an experience to be endured rather than relished. In the provision of service, motorists were a target audience for commercial activity. Competition for catering sites had been so intense that operators offered to pay rents far higher than were realistic, calculating their returns on Government traffic flow forecasts even before the new roads had been finished. To recover profits, caterers aimed to provide their services as economically as possible, within the basic framework of government specifications. The first service areas were unable to cope with so much traffic: 'no one had thought enough about an age of day-trippers who would want scenic enjoyment, ease of travel, food, shopping and travel information as part of the whole motorway package'.[9] Problems affecting service area design were many: changing population figures, increased speed of travel through better vehicle design, land use change, travel behaviour, eating habits and catering methods.

As a result of widespread criticism aimed at service areas by the media, the Minister of Transport Barbara Castle commissioned a detailed study of the industry from University College London (UCL). This was largely undertaken by Bev Nutt. Delivered in February 1967, the research was aimed at increasing the understanding of factors influencing the profitability and quality of British service areas, and looked at service area design, operation and use in England, Germany, Italy and the United States. With no central framework for appraising planning or design, and no control over the financial offer by the operator which would effectively determine the success or failure of the tender package, designers of service area buildings were hardly encouraged. The report claimed that the symbolic form of the link or bridge was inappropriate: there was no statistical evidence whatsoever that 'eye catching' developments, sited over or immediately adjacent to the motorway to act as advertisements for the operators, attracted any more trade than single-sided developments.

The report noted that the different categories of catering demanded — from transport café to waitress service restaurant — were likely to change as eating habits and lifestyles altered: any building in which these demarcations were fixed was liable to become obsolete. Even though the commitment to a fifty-year site lease implied fixed developments, the study argued that designers should consider less permanent construction. Flexible planning was needed which did not rely solely on the Ministry's traffic prediction statistics — suggesting this was the first evidence of a move away from thinking in terms of a purely economical approach to service area design. The report outlined a scheme that could be utilised for future sites, consisting of one main amenity building of low-cost materials that could be easily extended, a footbridge, and a basic shelter/toilet structure on the less heavily trafficked side of the motorway.[10]

Beyond 1970

Of the few designers working in the service area business, some knew each other personally, and others had common links through operators and design organisations. The UCL recommendation for the production of more flexible and utilitarian buildings for service stations, coincided with a sense among motorway caterers that the first series of developments had been more costly than the profits justified. Operators also became aware of the need to maintain business through better facilities.

But buildings are advertisements, whether they are to convey service, opulence, or refer to some kind of culture like the fast-food restaurant. Most operators relied upon the architects to advise them of what was appropriate, and continued to build service stations that drew on various themes in styling. Some were more successful than others. With a useful motorway system becoming a reality in the early 1970s, there were fresh opportunities to compete for new sites. Esso was the first of the oil companies to speculate on service area development, seeing them as a way of increasing fuel sales (as traffic moved away from A-roads and on to the motorways) and as practical links for travellers between a growing chain of overnight stops. Working alongside the oil firms was another generation of architects, with a desire to produce good quality buildings quickly. Through Bev Nutt, architects Castle Park Dean Hook had been involved with the UCL research and, together with Challen Floyd Slaski Todd (architects of the 'Roundabout' filling station on Western Avenue), the practice was commissioned for Esso's five motorway 'Tavernas'. Bridge restaurants were too costly to develop and alter, so new service stations were based on square or rectangular boxes, with hard slick exteriors of brick or cement block and few fixed internal walls. Where possible, landscaping and tree planting created a barrier between the motorway and restaurants.

Washington-Birtley Tavern, A1(M) (fig. 123), was referred to as the country's 'first robot transport café' (*Gateshead Post*, 11 September 1970) because its catering was facilitated through the use of vending machines and some of the first

123 Washington Birtley, AI(M), 1970. Collection: David Lawrence.

microwave ovens available to the public anywhere in Britain. Northbound
motorists found the main restaurant on the far side of the motorway, reached by
a footbridge that connected with a gallery within the building. Air travel once
again provided a model for egalitarian design: architect Frederick Steyn remembers that the interior layout was 'deliberately like an airport concourse, which
was felt appropriate to handle people, let them mill around, decide what they
wanted to do, and not be compartmentalised. The free movement was also to
encourage impulse buying.'[11] Discussing the exterior, which was originally to
have been finished in pink bricks, Steyn comments that the design had 'no relation to the local area—the motorway made its own architecture'.[12] Challen
Floyd Slaski Todd produced entirely different buildings for Woolley Edge and
Birch, responding to the exposed site and agricultural context by using roofs that
swept down on outrigger beams over the walls. This feature seems to originate in
buildings designed for heavy snowfall and can be seen in the Howard Johnson
chain of motels in North America dating from the 1960s. Leigh Delamere and
Southwaite (fig. 124), by Castle Park Dean Hook, were deliberate attempts to

124   Southwaite, M6, 1972. Photograph: Hook Whitehead Associates.

minimise the impact of buildings in the country but still provide all the necessary facilities. Plain walls and large windows seem to confirm the temporary
nature of this roadside architecture: changes would be cheap and easy to make
without spoiling the visual appearance. Leigh Delamere, originally the only rest
stop on M4 between London and the Severn crossing, was made distinctive by its
roof of twelve asymmetrical pyramids, likened to tents in the woods.[13] Esso
wanted to concentrate on selling fuel, and reportedly could not make their sites
pay. The five service areas passed to Granada in 1973.

   A move towards more landscaped sites is seen in two projects by Howard V.
Lobb and Partners for Ross Group. Ross would have preferred to build a bridge
restaurant at Membury (M4, 1972) but could not countenance the cost of traffic
diversions.[14] As an alternative, both Membury and Hartshead Moor (M62,
opened 1973) were positioned so that diners in the fully integrated catering spaces
could contemplate grassy banks through large picture windows. Picking up on
the theme of strong roof designs, Membury's two identical, south facing amenity
buildings were set under canopies designed like rolling waves. But the design
proved too grand: customers did not want to climb a ramp up to the dining areas,
and space beneath the roof required extensive heating in the winter.

125 Corley, M6, 1972.
Photograph: David Lawrence.

Fortes added three new sites in the early 1970s. Garnett Cloughley Blakemore and Associates worked on the Corley (M6, 1972) project (fig. 125), developing prefabricated fibreglass wall units for the footbridge and parts of the main
building, so that they could be delivered by lorry and craned into place. Besides
making large areas of uninterrupted colour possible (yellow and beige predomi-
nated), the fibreglass moulding process produced easy contours. Fortes felt the
high specification of this project was excessive for a motorway service area and
decided they would appoint other architects for future work. Thus Building
Design Associates were brought in for Fleet (M3, fig. 126) — the final service area
to be double-sided with an integral bridge — and the single-sided site at Gordano
(M5), both opened in 1973. These buildings were based on four adjoining blocks
below slated roofs with glass top lights like maltings or oasthouses.[15] When
asked to reflect on his approach to the styling of these buildings, architect Issy
Spektor commented that 'the early service areas were very mechanical things
made of metal and glass. I thought that when people got out of their car — which

126   Fleet, M3, see in 1999. Photograph: David Lawrence.

was a metal and glass mechanical enclosure—they should go into something completely different ... using softer, familiar materials—wood and quarry tiles, earthy things.'[16]

Fortes' last service area of the early 1970s was Burtonwood (M62, 1974), designed by Patrick Gwynne working as a sole practitioner. Gwynne had made good use of polygonal plans in his designs for two restaurants built for Fortes in Hyde Park, London, during 1963–71.[17] A bird flying over the Burtonwood site would pass two perfectly octagonal buildings. Behind full-height glass walls, every bit of space was put to use for kitchen, dining spaces and offices. On each building a steeple-like form rose up from the low-set roof. The steeples hid chimneys and water tanks – there was no direct water supply available for miles around—and were floodlit at night to act as a beacon. With the buildings surrounded by grass, Gwynne wanted to paint the roofs a conspicuous bright red, but the Royal Fine Art Commission who vetted the design objected to this and copper sheeting was used, which has now weathered to a green patina. Burtonwood proved to be an economic disappointment, because the opening of this portion of M62 coincided with a national recession which impacted heavily on

Liverpool, the ultimate western destination of this route. In 1975, the year after Burtonwood opened, Gwynne designed a service area for Fortes at Chigwell on M11. The building plan was a development of the Burtonwood theme, comprising clustered circular buildings. Fortes won the tender competition but withdrew, as projected income did not justify the estimated building costs.

Changes in the industry

The oil crisis beginning in 1973 and financial difficulties inherited by the incoming Labour Government of 1974 contributed to a national recession. New service area development was suspended pending the results of an inquiry into the state of their operation. By 1974 there were thirty-three motorway service areas in England, with a further twenty-two proposed for opening in the period to 1980. Bev Nutt, who had undertaken research on motorway service areas for the government, wrote an article for *Design* magazine that reviewed changes in the industry after the publication of the University College Report in 1967. Seeing little change to operating conditions or standards of service, Nutt restated his view that financial requirements imposed on caterers restricted competition and therefore the potential for improvement. The brief for buildings did little to encourage good design. Nutt speculated on the role of motorway services, in the light of his forecast that their future use would increasingly be for rest and relaxation, and suggested that they would need to diversify in order to survive. Operators began to recognise that to attract increased custom, it was better to improve the environment of the service area. Companies looked to developments in the United States and began to import fast food techniques. Grill rooms were removed, free-flow cafeterias installed, and the interior landscape of amenity buildings became more open plan, gradually drifting towards the model of food court adopted by large indoor shopping centres. After the regimented rows of seats installed during the 1960 and 1970s for cost and security reasons, individual booths were reinstated to divide up dining areas. Fortes began to transfer catering methods and themes from the relatively easy-going environment of their department store cafés, coffee shops and park restaurants to the motorway services.

Despite the national financial predicament, RoadChef grew in size rapidly in the mid-1970s, contributing some cheap and strangely appropriate service buildings from Kinnair Associates. Jack Kinnair and his assistant Tony Cooper in fact shared office space with the London management of RoadChef, so the working relationship was close and less dogged by disagreement that might be the case when an external practice was used. Rownhams (M27) was planned in 1970-71, but not opened until 1977. Kinnair envisioned the scheme as a glass block (for the food and shopping court) 'rising out of the ground', anchored at each end by polygonal brick pods. At a meeting held before construction began, the local planning officer expressed his desire for the tree-filled vista to be preserved, requesting that the service station roof be planted with grass, shrubs and trees.[18] This hanging garden proved too expensive to implement, but rather than obscure the view with a footbridge, a tunnel was provided to link the two sides. Just south of Glasgow, Hamilton (M74 northbound) and Bothwell (M74 southbound) were both completed in 1975. Design here was for rapid construction: brick and wood buildings decorated with mock colonnades of white fibreglass 'tee' pieces that seems to mimic the style of Scratchwood. Free-standing water towers acted as advertisements carrying the RoadChef brand name. Increases in traffic soon made the addition of Portakabins necessary, unwittingly creating essays in portable architecture that might be envied now, but in the end Hamilton and Bothwell almost fell apart and were replaced by solid, safe, neo-vernacular farmsteads which still serve motorists today.

RoadChef's biggest site at Sandbach (M6, 1976) picked up on the formal theme of Rownhams. On either side of the motorway, square blocks enclosed almost entirely in bronzed glass were set between lower level brick service buildings, which wrapped around the blocks in the form of 'y' shapes.[19] Exterior details were minimal, and the interior was a clear space with few columns, decorated in a colour scheme of brown and orange.

After a second government inquiry was published in 1978,[20] central control of service area operation began to relax. Motivated by the prospect of better profits, operators transformed their services. The Inquiry took a comprehensive look at aspects of activity and use at motorway services and reported on both their poor public perception and how this might be improved by future government policy. Competition between operators accelerated, forcing companies to increase investment and work harder at innovating ideas. Focusing on the appearance of interiors, in-house designers worked with consultants to create higher quality environments where investment was directed at a sense of comfort and relaxation, rather than resistance to abuse.

127 Tebay East, M6, 1993. Photograph: David Lawrence.

Countrified

From the mid-1980s, subject to pressure from local authority planners and environmental groups, design of new buildings for service areas began to follow the trend of the out-of-town supermarket shed. Large structural shells with clear internal spaces like warehouses were styled to imitate the idealised image of rural vernacular architecture: brick walls, tiled roofs and rustic details (fig. 127). Examples of this building type can be found on M25 and at several other motorway and trunk road sites added as infills between established service areas or on extensions of existing motorways. In a shed-like structure, it is a simple matter to reconfigure the whole interior rapidly without extensive disruption to business. In openly imitating agricultural buildings, this aesthetic hides behind the suggestion that the service area is part of the pre-motorway environment, that progress has come full circle and gone back to the land. I would also suggest that it is as anonymous as the less distinguished products of 1960s modernist architecture – with the brick box simply made bigger and decorated with the past, rather than the future, in mind. Through the 1980s, the particular nature of the service area that had been modelled on the roadside cafeteria began to evaporate in favour of a more universal experience of consumption. RoadChef's Clacket Lane service area between Junctions 5 and 6 of M25, commenced full operation in July 1993. Clacket Lane exemplifies the retrospective approach to architecture set in a rural landscape. The architecture could be compared to a modern interpretation of the country manor, in carefully planned areas of tree planting to imitate the surrounding woodland and screen parking areas. In the entrance foyer of the amenity buildings, bay windows were arranged to suggest individual shop fronts.

Deregulation of service area provision into the private sector took place in August 1992, relieving the government of responsibility for obtaining planning consents on new sites. Site freeholds were sold off in 1996. New on-line (on motorway) service areas are likely to meet opposition from local residents and amenity groups. A potential monopoly situation can arise because very few organisations have the expertise to complete the process. This has had the effect of promoting service area construction on A-class trunk roads and, coupled with the near saturation of the industry, this seems to be where most operators favour future developments. Modern vehicle comfort and performance has significantly reduced the need for a series of journey stops. To maintain and increase the facilities and profits, operators have widened the available range of services, including a range of food choices, business centres and mini shopping malls. In this way the service area once again parallels the airport: it is a place of transient occupation for the motorist, who has the opportunity for rest, and is also distracted from the process of travel by food and shopping.

Granada (now Moto) has identified the positive image that airports have in the travel experience. It is pursuing the development of mini shopping malls which maximise use of the permissible retail floor area by creating shops like fairground side-shows, equipped with rapidly changing goods, a till and credit card terminal. The biggest part of the outlet is the brand name sign over the space. In combining food court refreshment areas with several shopping spaces (and of course toilets) Granada claimed it was creating service areas of the future that will be like 'a little town beside the road'. I would compare this approach with the example of decentralised retail centres developed over the last half-century in North America, to serve commuters and out-of-town shoppers.[21] Donington Park (fig. 128), opened on 8 July 1999 at Junction 23a on M1, is the first full example of this approach. Development of service areas as destinations — places that people drive to, rather than through — is still opposed by the government on the safety grounds that it would increase traffic overcrowding at junctions and slip roads. Asserting that Donington Park is aimed at convenient express shopping for

128   Donington Park, M1, 1999. Photograph: David Lawrence.

the commuter motorist, Granada is pushing against the government definition of
a destination. How this plays out remains to be seen. The scale of facilities may
also change. Like the more sophisticated of their counterparts on other roads, fuel
forecourt shops at the newer service areas can provide a full off-peak catering service. Commuters can now have their photographs processed or dry cleaning done
during the day and collect it on the way home. Fuel sales have become a smaller
proportion of the total possible income from the forecourt.

On taking over the former Fortes service stations, Welcome Break has
invested some £150 millions (at 1999) in refurbishing service area facilities.
Extended foyer spaces, new toilet, restaurant and shopping areas have given

somewhat run-down sites such as Newport Pagnell, Charnock Richard and Woodall much needed improvements. Architects for the new works are J. Ward Associates. Based on the style of its brand logo, Welcome Break chose a wave-form canopy roof for entrances. In designing this latest essay in roadside build-ing at Oxford Wheatley (M40), the architects looked to Stansted Airport and the Waterloo Eurostar Terminal. The result is something in between the two. An aluminium sheet roof spans the thirty-metre uninterrupted space of the con-course and food court, and carries on over the perimeter wall and water channel as a sunscreen. This lightweight roof is made of the same material as Sir Norman Foster's transport interchange for North Greenwich Jubilee Line station and the Millennium dome. Road Chef's super-shed service area opened at Winchester (M3) during 2000 and comprises a food court, with several different catering options, and a large retail space, all under a roof not dissimilar to the Welcome Break Oxford project. Road Chef has recently opened Britain's first service area on a toll road, north of Birmingham at Norton Canes (M6 Toll).

On the road again— a conclusion

Out there on the motorways, dispersed according to government-determined interval rather than geography or topography, is a genre of buildings which has borrowed from several other genres rather than develop its own. Born out of functionalism and cheap building construction methods, the basic standards of the earliest examples were initially overlooked because of their novelty. Several of the earlier service station buildings were experiments in how far mass concrete and prefabricated walling could be taken in the expression of modern transport architecture and design, right in the middle of a new faster Britain. Using expres-sive forms and adventurous engineering, the designers of Forton and Hilton Park produced buildings equal to their dynamic situations, buildings that seem particularly appropriate for situations that have no other locating element than the regular and apparently infinite strip of the motorway.

Stifled by Government, abused by some of the customers and much of the media, they deteriorated into places that might relieve urgent need, but were unlikely to do much else. The caterers that provided the full English breakfasts, and the people designing the buildings to serve them in, tried to evolve facilities in which they could trade efficiently and profitably. Buildings became simple boxes for the necessary services, sometimes distinguished by an unusual roof, but otherwise doing their best not to be noticed at all. In the late 1970s, after the worst of the football hooligans had vanished in the distance, and restrictive practices had been partially lifted, the service area became a relatively sophisticated enterprise. When finally freed from tight government control, operators invested further in the quality and range of services. Conversely the design of buildings began to retreat into a nostalgic revivalism. Recent motorway service area schemes have suggested a renewed energy in design, with buildings aimed at comprehensive retail and catering activities. Many of the eccentricities that gave service stations a particular character have now been edited out, but the new places promise another kind of travel environment.

When I look for an image of pleasurable travel in Britain, the Canterbury Tales still come to mind. The comradeship and ritual journey breaks make travel a pleasure as well as a necessity. We are still people on a journey, travelling hopefully and often together. Of course we can achieve in a few hours the distances that took Chaucer's pilgrims some days, but as a model for the function of motorway service areas, the inn can still provide a useful and pertinent example, albeit hampered by the fact that service stations have been ruled as alcohol-free places. Motorists and their vehicles have basic requirements: relief, food and fuel. Overnight accommodation on a long haul is a bonus if reasonably priced. Anything else is a convenience only, available at a premium price to avoid having to leave the motorway. We have become bound into the modern conception of hermetic journey-making which avoids deviation from route or any unnecessary encounters with other travellers – service stations can, and do, seat a few hundred people at a time but very few of them talk to each other. Without this social interaction, and the environment to engender it, the evolution of the service area into another out of town shopping outlet seems assured.

1   For a description of the American bridge restaurants, see Daniel J. Boorstin, *The Image: Or What Happened to the American Dream* (Harmondsworth: Penguin Books, 1962), p. 121.

2   W. R. Thomson, 'Institute of Highway Engineers: Motorways in Worcestershire', *Traffic Engineering and Control*, 1963, vol. 5 (2) p. 101.

3   Anon., 'A model service station on M1', *Architectural Review*, 1960, vol. 128 (766) pp. 417-19.

4   Howard V. Lobb and Partners had completed a headquarters building for Ross Group at Grimsby in 1963.

5   James A. Roberts worked on several large reconstruction projects, including the redevelopment of Birmingham's Bull Ring area and Liverpool's St. John Centre.

6   See *Granada Grapevine* (in-house newspaper), Autumn/Winter 1977.

7   Besides Aust, which had particular location circumstances as a result of the special site, Scratchwood was probably the first built example of a change in planning approach for service stations. Its situation away from the main road would become a standard pattern for developments during the late 1970s and after.

8   Anon. 'Keeping the Motorway Away', *Architects' Journal*, 1969, 149 (25), p. 1614.

9   Ian Breach, 'Design on the Motorway', *Design*, December 1972, vol. 288, p. 45.

10   Bev Nutt, 'Research report on motorway service areas,' *Traffic Engineering and Control*, 1967, 19(2), pp.84-88, 92.

11   Frederick Steyn to David Lawrence, 25 November 1998.

12   Frederick Steyn to David Lawrence, 25 November 1998.

13   Architect Christopher Dean proposed the pyramids, and they were engineered by Tony Hunt.

14   Michael Boyle, former managing director, Ross Motorway Services, to David Lawrence, 29 August 1999.

15   The design of both these sites seems to owe much both formally and materially to Louis Kahn's main building and bath house for the Trenton Jewish Community Center built in 1955-56.

16   Issy Spektor of BDA Design (formerly Building Design Associates) to David Lawrence, 23 November 1998.

17   The park restaurants Patrick Gwynne designed for Fortes were 'The Serpentine' (1963-4, extended 1965 and 1971, now demolished) and 'The Dell' (1965). The use of complex polygonal shapes seems particularly appropriate in settings designed for leisure and fantasy and recurred in projects by Gwynne.

18   As recalled by Tony Cooper, development director for Road Chef, in an interview with David Lawrence 29 April 1999.

19   Y-shaped plans had been the basis for so-called 'butterfly' houses of the Edwardian period. Dutch architect Jan Duiker made use of the pattern in the 1920s, and in the context of motorway services, the form was present in the design of Hilton Park (M6, 1966-70) by T. P. Bennett and Partners.

20   Peter J. Prior et al., *Report of the Committee of Inquiry into Motorway Service Areas* (London: HMSO, 1978).

21   For a detailed discussion of out of town retail centres see Richard Longstreth, *City Center to Regional Mall* (first paperback edition, Cambridge, Mass.: The MIT Press, 1998).

Contributors

Susie Barson is Head of the London Architectural Investigators' Team at English Heritage. One of her earliest projects was to assess the architectural and historic interest of every station on the London Underground network, an exercise which introduced her to the philosophy, sophistication and quality of the collaborative work of Frank Pick and Charles Holden. She has contributed to a number of publications including *A Farewell to Fleet Street* (1988), *London Suburbs* (2000), *The Peabody Estates: Guidelines to Conservation* (2001), *The Grammar of Architecture* (2002), and *Scene/Unseen: London's West End Theatres* (2003).

Neil Bingham, BA (Hons), PhD, architecture and design historian, was for nearly twenty years a curator of architectural drawings at the Royal Institute of British Architects. His latest book, with Andrew Weaving, is *Modern Retro: Living with Mid-Century Modern Style* (translated into nine languages). His next book will be *The New Boutique: Fashion and Design*. Neil's first flight was on an Air Canada Douglas DC8-63 'stretched-eight' to visit Expo '67, Montreal.

Colin Davies is a professor of architecture at London Metropolitan University, where he teaches design, architectural history and building technology. A former editor of *The Architects' Journal* and a regular contributor to architectural magazines worldwide, his books include *High Tech Architecture, Hopkins, Hopkins 2*, and various monographs on the work of architects such as Norman Foster and Nicholas Grimshaw.

Brian Edwards is Professor of Architecture at Edinburgh College of Art and author of *The Modern Station* (1997) and *The Airport Terminal* (2000).

Elain Harwood is the Inspector of Historic Buildings at English Heritage primarily responsible for its post-war research and listing programme. She is currently writing a book on British architecture in the years between 1945 and 1975, and is studying for a PhD at Bristol University.

Julian Holder is Director of the Scottish Centre for Conservation Studies, Edinburgh College of Art. He writes regularly in the architectural press and was a contributor to the Pevsner *Architectural Guide to Manchester* (2002).

David Jeremiah is Research Professor at Plymouth University and a Research Fellow at the London Institute. He has published *Architecture and Design for the Family in Britain 1900-70* (2000) and is currently researching a book *Graphic Images and the Ideas of British Motoring*.

David Lawrence is an architect and historian of design and transportation. He teaches at the universities of Westminster and Brighton, and is a Research Fellow in the department of architecture at the University of Westminster. His books include *Underground Architecture* (1994), a study of building design for London's subway system, *Always a Welcome: the glove compartment history of the motoway service area* (1999), and *A Logo for London* (2000), a history of London Transport corporate design. He is presently working on a history of Charles Holden's London stations, and a celebration of the Little Chef–Happy Eater roadside dining phenomenon.

Steven Parissien is Dean of Arts at the University of Plymouth and formerly assistant director of the Paul Mellon Centre for Studies in British Art. He is the author of books, among others, on Robert Adam and on George IV.

Gavin Stamp, MA, PhD, Hon FRIAS, Hon FRIBA, was born three months after the nationalisation of the railways and brought up at the end of the Southern Electric line to Hayes. Having taught at the Mackintosh School of Architecture, Glasgow School of Art, he is a Mellon Senior Fellow for 2003-04. He is chairman of the Twentieth Century Society.